THE DISCOURSE OF RACE
IN MODERN CHINA

近代中國之種族觀念

白者寒瘦如蟯炭黑土醜惡如雲煤

梁啟超

FRANK DIKÖTTER

The Discourse
of Race
in Modern China

STANFORD UNIVERSITY PRESS
STANFORD, CALIFORNIA

Stanford University Press
Stanford, California
© 1992 Frank Dikötter
Originating publisher: C. Hurst & Co., London
First published in the U.S.A. by
  Stanford University Press, 1992
Printed in Hong Kong
Cloth ISBN 0–8047–1994–2
Paper ISBN 0–8047–2334–6
Original printing 1992
Last figure below indicates year of this printing:
03 02 01 00 99 98 97 96 95 94
This book is printed on acid-free paper.

CONTENTS

PREFACE

'Race' is a growing area of interest in the social sciences. In history, considerable research has laid bare the extent of racial prejudice in Western countries. Racism, it is well known, was not peculiar to a bigoted and ignorant minority in Europe: it was an attitude shared by many highly respected people until the 1930s at least. In the United States, racial discrimination did not disappear with the abolition of slavery, but officially persisted until a few decades ago and continues to affect many aspects of social life. Racial discourse was upheld by popular bodies of opinion, political groups, and scientific institutions until the end of the Second World War.

It is less well known, however, that racial discourse also thrived in societies outside Europe and North America. It is generally assumed that racial prejudice can only be a 'white' phenomenon under which other people, lumped together under the heading 'coloured', have to suffer. The narrow focus of such historical research, which may partly be explained by a sense of guilt in post-colonial Western societies and by a still dominant feeling of euro-centrism, has distorted our comprehension of racial problems in non-Western countries.[1] In China, a discourse of 'race' appeared at the end of the nineteenth century. The use of racial categories of analysis influenced many thinkers in China in the twentieth century. Although the importance of this discourse has been recognized by several historians, no systematic study of it has ever been undertaken.

The first chapter of this book presents the historical background

---

1 Some notable exceptions include J. Blackburn, *The white men: The first response of aboriginal peoples to the white man*, London: Orbis, 1979; G. Jahoda, *White man: A study of the attitudes of Africans to Europeans in Ghana before independence*, London: Oxford University Press, 1961, an anthropological inquiry based on interviews; V. Görög, *Noirs et blancs. Leur image dans la littérature orale africaine*, Paris: SELAF, 1976, based on the textual analysis of 161 documents of oral literature.

to Chinese assumptions about 'race'. It introduces a broad spectrum of material on traditional attitudes towards skin colour, the social perception of physical differences, the concept of 'barbarians', ideas of environmental determinism, and ethnocentric theories. The second chapter considers the formation and composition of racial stereotypes during the nineteenth century. Chapter 3 discusses the emergence of a racial discourse among the reformers at the turn of the century. The latter integrated the construct of race into a new vision of time and space. Racial discourse was perpetuated by the revolutionaries, and this is analyzed in chapter 4. It was central to the formation of the concept of nation and dominated nationalist ideology during the first decades of the twentieth century. Chapter 5 focuses on the institutionalization and habitualization of racial categories by the academic community in Republican China (1911–49). The last chapter is devoted to eugenics, the pseudo-science of race improvement. 'Race' remained an alternative form of discourse after the communist takeover in 1949; this is briefly discussed in the epilogue.

'Race', of course, is a cultural construct with no relationship to objective reality. Phenotypical variations like hair texture or skin colour are subjectively perceived and culturally constructed by social groups: some may focus on skin colour, others on eye colour. These biological differences do not of themselves induce cultural differences, but are utilized to legitimize role expectations: physical features are given social meaning. Classifications based on physical appearance have no scientific foundation. Races do not exist, they are imagined. The assignment of racial categories varies according to the sociocultural environment. Race as an identifying construct evolves according to changes in the symbolic universe in which the group operates. Alterations in the symbolic universe will lead to a displacement of identifying constructs. From this perspective, a history of racial discourse can only adopt a nominalist approach: it describes how 'race' has been defined, and how these definitions have changed historically. The word 'race' should always be enclosed in quotation marks, were there no practical or stylistic drawbacks. I translate by 'race' (*zu, zhong, zulei, minzu, zhongzu, renzhong*, in Chinese) terms that appear to stress the biological rather than the sociocultural aspects of different peoples. 'Racial' is used here as the adjectival form of 'race'.

The analytical framework of this study is centred around the concept of group definition. Groups are socially constructed entities that fulfil a purpose of identification and organization. The forms which groups assume are largely of an impermanent and transitory nature. Changes in the ingroup's perceptions and valuations of outgroups will lead to changes in its membership definition. Group membership is a notion that can only exist in a relational context, with reference to other groups. The network of intergroup relations can cause a group to ascribe to itself several definitions, which will have varying degrees of overlap. This study is confined to group definitions based on the construct of race.

My analysis of racial discourse in modern China is based on a wide range of source material. It incorporates the writings of leading intellectuals, influential political texts, scientific journals, popular periodicals, travel accounts, textbooks and translations, as well as scientific literature and popular texts on evolution, biology, medicine, anthropology, genetics, eugenics, racial hygiene and human geography. Most of these sources are the product of the educated stratum of the population. If it is possible to distinguish between different cultural levels, then this study clearly represents an élitist history: it is concerned with the educated fringe of society. Popular culture has not been considered for practical reasons. The illiteracy of the subordinate classes, the scarcity of reliable information, but above all the restricted contact peasants and workers had with outgroups suggest that the place to begin is with élite culture. Although the nature of the relationship between 'élite' and 'popular' culture is still an important point of debate, it might be hypothesized that a high degree of reciprocal influence existed between the two. A careful study of popular discourse would probably reveal many parallels to the views held by the educated élite.

Similarly, this study assumes that in their confrontation with and interpretation of the outside world, the majority of scholar-officials interacted with the dominant symbolic universe in a manner that transcended their individual ethnic background. Although the focus is on the Han Chinese, I believe there were no pervasive differences between them and the Manchus with respect to racial perceptions of outgroups. Nor is it in the nature or scope of this work to examine Han perceptions of ethnic minorities.[2] The phenotype of most minorities was not significantly at variance with that of the Han Chinese: there was a physical continuity that precluded the elaboration of racial theories. Despite many disparaging comments on the supposedly bestial origins of the minorities, the Han perception of minority Chinese remained embedded in an ethnocentric framework that stressed sociocultural differences. This study investigates how the élite constructed a discourse about physically discontinuous peoples, mainly Westerners and Africans, or the *waiyi*, 'outside barbarians', in opposition to the *neiyi*, 'inside barbarians'.

Finally, it should be emphasized that the study of racial discourse in non-Western societies is still in its incipient stage. This book does not pretend to be final: it is open to radical criticism. If it is able to generate a fruitful discussion, it will have achieved its main purpose.

ACKNOWLEDGEMENTS

This book is largely based on a doctoral dissertation written under the supervision of Timothy H. Barrett of the School of Oriental and African Studies (SOAS), University of London, and I would like to express my gratitude for his constant support and enthusiasm. I also thank R.G. Tiedemann, of the same institution, who was very generous with his time and knowledge. Particular

2 Han perceptions of national minorities have already been extensively treated. For an introduction, see T. Heberer, *China and its national minorities*, Armonk, N.Y.: M.E. Sharpe, 1989; J.T. Dreyer, *China's forty millions: Minority nationalities and national integration in the People's Republic of China*, Cambridge, Mass.: Harvard University Press, 1976, and J.N. Lipman, 'Ethnicity and politics in Republican China', *Modern China*, 10, no. 3 (July 1984), pp. 285–316.

mention must be made of Ladislas Mysyrowicz, University of
Geneva: without his help, the book would not have been possible.

I acknowledge with gratitude a two-year scholarship of the
Fonds National Suisse de la Recherche Scientifique, generously
granted by the Commission de Recherche of the University of
Geneva: it allowed me to carry out most of the research and to
complete the dissertation. The Ministerie van Onderwijs en
Wetenschappen of the Netherlands liberally supported fieldwork
in China. A grant from the British Council Central Research
Fund enabled me to conduct fieldwork in Hong Kong and Taiwan
during the summer of 1988, and the School of Oriental and
African Studies made a small contribution towards travel expenses.
The thesis was revised with the help of a Postdoctoral Research
Fellowship of the British Academy.

I wish to express my gratitude to Jerome Ch'en of the York
University, Toronto, Frederic Wakeman of the University of
California, Berkeley, Erik Zürcher of the University of Leiden,
and Erik Maeder for their encouraging and helpful responses to an
early research plan. Professor Ch'en, whose incisive *China and the
West* (Hutchinson, 1979) remains a model in the historiography of
modern China, kindly commented on subsequent research out-
lines. Michael Banton was also very supportive. The structure of
this book was inspired by his *Racial theories* (Cambridge, 1987),
a classic in the field of race studies. I also acknowledge the influence of two books on constructivism: Peter Berger and Thomas
Luckmann's *The social construction of reality* (New York, 1966) and
Siegfried J. Schmidt (ed.), *Der Diskurs des radikalen Konstruktivismus* (Frankfurt, 1990). Pamela Kyle Crossley, of Dartmouth
College, was very generous in sharing the results of her unpub-
lished research with me. Her work on the ideology of Manchu
rule and on ethnicity in modern China has been most useful. Many
thanks are due to the constructive comments of William T. Rowe
of The Johns Hopkins University. I would like to convey further
my appreciation to Robert F. Ash, Contemporary China Institute
at SOAS; Peter Bowler, The Queen's University of Belfast; Jean-
Claude Favez, University of Geneva; Alfred H.Y. Lin, University
of Hong Kong; Herman Mast III, University of Connecticut;

Werner Meissner, Freie Universität Berlin; Frank Pieke, University of Leiden; Roy Porter, The Wellcome Institute for the History of Medicine; Kaoru Sugihara, Japan Research Centre at SOAS; Hans van de Ven, University of Cambridge; and Paul Weindling, University of Oxford. Many thanks also to Lillian Chia, who was very kind in guiding me with the Chinese character processing. I appreciate the help I received from Charles d'Orban, Assistant Librarian at the School of Oriental and African Studies.

I take pleasure in thanking many of the friends who helped to advance the writing of this book. Patrick McGinn critically followed the progress of the work from its inception; Christian von Somm brought new developments in radical constructivism to my attention and Lars Laamann and Frank Pöhlmann read and commented upon the thesis. Apart from her interest in the progress of my work, Gillian Macrae was a most hospitable friend, especially when I first arrived in London. I owe a special debt of gratitude to Uschi Zürcher. I also wish to thank Fethi Ayache, Claude Bouguet, Colin Clark, Martin Jelenic, Martin Lau, and Xiong Mei.

Responsibility for the views expressed in this book, as for errors and omissions, is mine alone.

Have you heard about the origin of the world's human races? This is a story unique to us Hakka people. Before, when there was no trace of man on earth, Tai Bai decided to create mankind. He used clay, just as we make pottery or porcelain, and after having moulded it into a human figure, he put it into the kiln. The first one was fired too long, and was badly burnt: it was all black! This was not so good, and Tai Bai threw it away, using all his strength, throwing it a long way. He threw it to Africa; hence afterwards everyone in Africa was black. As a result of this first failure, the second one was fired more carefully. It was allowed to bake only for a little while and then taken out of the kiln. Look: too white! This wasn't very good either, and Tai Bai again threw it away. This time, he did not throw it so far. He threw it to Europe, hence afterwards everyone in Europe was white. Experience now allowed the third one to be baked to perfection: not too long, not too short. Pretty good! Neither black nor white, but all yellow. Tai Bai was very satisfied, and put it down on the ground. Hence afterwards everyone in Asia was yellow. (*Taiwan Kejia suwenxue* [Folk literature of the Hakka in Taiwan], retold by Zhou Qinghua, Taipei: Dongfang wenhua shuju, 1971, pp. 149–50)

1

RACE AS CULTURE:
HISTORICAL BACKGROUND

SECTION ONE

In an article on the role of skin colour and physical characteristics in non-Western countries published in the 1960s, Harold Isaacs argued that racial prejudice among non-Europeans existed long before their exposure to the ideas of the conquering white Europeans, and that the charge of Western responsibility for the racial attitudes of ex-colonies was only partly valid. 'Where responses to Westerners took place in racial terms, they were superimposed upon strongly-rooted attitudes about race and skin color that long antedated this encounter.'[1] The purpose of this introductory chapter is threefold. It attempts to show, first, how attitudes about skin colour and physical characteristics are of great antiquity in China; secondly, that significant parts of the Confucian universe predisposed the Chinese to perceive the new world order created by Western expansion in terms of race; and, thirdly, that successive periods of contact with frontier peoples fostered proto-nationalist feelings and generated a strong consciousness of biological continuity. Ethnic groups that conquered and ruled China include the Jin (1115–1234), the Mongols (1280–1368) and the Manchus (1644–1911). It should be emphasized that in the absence of substantial studies concerning the construct of race or the social perception of physical features in traditional China, this introduction can only be tentative. It is by no means intended to discuss the traditional Chinese world view in a systematic way.[2]

1 H.R. Isaacs, 'Group identity and political change: The role of color and physical characteristics', *Daedalus*, Spring 1967, p. 367.
2 For a general introduction to the traditional Chinese world view and the tributary system upon which relations with foreign countries were often based, see J.K. Fairbank (ed.), *The Chinese world order: Traditional China's foreign relations*, Cambridge, Mass.: Harvard University Press, 1968.

1

For our purposes, it will suffice to point out that a racial consciousness existed in an embryonic form well before the arrival of Europeans in the nineteenth century.

THE BARBARIAN IN THE CLASSICS

Social groups are in a constant process of redefinition and reorien-
tation, thereby changing themselves and the symbolic universe to
which they relate. But the symbolic universe sets the context and
gives meaning to change. The symbolically constructed network
of meanings, rules, conventions, signs and values form a struc-
tured system in which the group operates. In traditional China,
the classics of Confucianism formed the core of this symbolic
system. The Five Classics are the ancient books which comprised
the syllabus for the disciples of Confucius, namely the *Shujing*
(Book of History), the *Shijing* (Book of Odes), the *Yijing* (Book of
Changes), the *Liji* (Book of Rites), and the *Chunqiu* (Spring and
Autumn Annals).

The classics are generally believed to have been oriented towards
the world, or *tianxia*, 'all under heaven'. The world was perceived
as one homogeneous unity named 'great community' (*datong*).
The absence of any kind of cultural pluralism implicit in this
symbolic universe has been called a 'political solipsism':[3] the ruling
élite, dominated by the assumption of its cultural superiority,
measured alien groups according to a yardstick by which those
who did not follow 'Chinese ways' were considered 'barbarians'.
It is assumed that this world view, originating mainly from
the *Gongyang* school (commentaries on Confucius' *Chunqiu*),
generated at least one valuable tendency: it obliterated racial distinctions to emphasize cultural continuity. A theory of 'using the
Chinese ways to transform the barbarians' (*yongxiabianyi*) was
strongly advocated. It was believed that the barbarian could be culturally absorbed – *laihua*, 'come and be transformed', or *hanhua*,
'become Chinese'. The *Chunqiu*, a chronological history of the
Spring and Autumn period (722–481 BC), traditionally attributed

---

3 Hsiao Kung-chuan, *A history of Chinese political thought*, Princeton University Press, 1979, p. 24.

to Confucius, hinged on the idea of cultural assimilation. In his commentary on the *Gongyang*, He Xiu (129–182 AD) later distinguished between the *zhuxia*, the 'various people of Xia [the first Chinese empire]', and the Yi and Di barbarians, living outside the scope of the Chinese cultural sphere. In the Age of Great Peace, an allegorical concept similar to the Golden Age in the West, the barbarians would flow in and be transformed: the world would be one.

The delusive myth of a Chinese antiquity that abandoned racial standards in favour of a concept of cultural universalism in which all barbarians could ultimately participate has understandably attracted some modern scholars. Living in an unequal and often hostile world, it is tempting to project the utopian image of a racially harmonious world into a distant and obscure past. To counterbalance this highly idealized vision of the Chinese past, some researchers have drawn attention to passages from the classics which are apparently incompatible with the concept of cultural universalism. Most quoted is the *Zuozhuan* (fourth century BC), a feudal chronicle : 'If he is not of our race, he is sure to have a different mind' (*fei wo zulei, qi xin bi yi*).[4] This sentence seems to support the allegation that at least some degree of 'racial discrimination' existed during the early stage of Chinese civilization.

The culturalistic and the racialist perspectives have in common the adoption of a Western conceptual framework that distinguishes sharply between culture and race, corresponding respectively to ethnocentrism and racism when used as a yardstick to diminish alien groups. The dichotomy between culture and race, which has proved to be a viable conceptual tool in analyzing modern attitudes towards outsiders, should be abandoned in our case. It introduces an opposition so far not supported by historical evidence, and tends to project a modern perception into a remote phase of history.

Physical composition and cultural disposition were confused in Chinese antiquity. The border between man and animal was

---

4 J. Legge, *The Chinese classics*, London: Henry Frowde, 1860–72, vol. 5, part 1, pp. 354–5.

blurred. 'The Rong are birds and beasts.'[5] This was not simply a derogatory description: it was part of a mentality that integrated the concept of civilization with the idea of humanity, picturing the alien groups living outside the pale of Chinese society as distant savages hovering on the edge of bestiality. The names of the outgroups were written in characters with an animal radical, a habit that persisted until the 1930s: the Di, a northern tribe, were thus assimilated with the dog, whereas the Man and the Min, people from the south, shared the attributes of the reptiles. The Qiang had a sheep radical.

The *Liji*, or Book of Rites (third century BC), underlined that 'the Chinese, the Rong, the Yi and [the other] peoples of the five quarters all have [their own] nature, which cannot be moved or altered.'[6] The 'five quarters' referred to a cosmographical plan which first appeared in the *Tribute of Yu*, a part of the *Shujing*, or Book of History (fifth century BC). This plan divided the world into five concentric configurations. Around the imperial centre (*didu*), the hub of civilization, came the royal domain (*dianfu*) and the lands of the feudal princes (*houfu*). Beyond these two areas lay a zone of pacification (*suifu*) that separated civilization from the last two zones, inhabited by steppe people and savages.[7] As noted by Ruth Meserve, the very name of the last zone, called the 'submissive wastes' (*huangfu*), evoked a dreadful imagery of drought and famine, of barrenness and desolation.[8]

Throughout history, the ruling élite viewed the people of the northern steppes with an almost traumatic apprehension. The sea, on the other hand, gave a feeling of natural protection. The spherical concept of the world inherent in most of China's

5 Yang Lien-sheng, 'Historical notes on the Chinese world order' in Fairbank, *The Chinese world order*, p. 24. This quotation from the *Zuozhuan* has not been translated by James Legge.
6 See Lionello Lanciotti, ' "Barbaren" in altchinesischer Sicht', *Antaios*, 6 (March 1968), p. 573.
7 See C. Waltham, *Shu ching, book of history: A modernized edition of the translation of James Legge*, London: Geo. Allen and Unwin, 1971, pp. 39–54.
8 Ruth I. Meserve, 'The inhospitable land of the barbarian', *Journal of Asian History*, 16 (1982), p. 54.

cosmological representations was conveniently completed by surrounding all habitable ground by four seas (*sihai*). China was placed at the centre of the world. Exogenous groups were relegated to the peripheries: they were referred to as the 'barbarians of the four quarters' (*siyi*).

Every barbarian tribe's name could be combined with a particular colour. The ancient texts repeatedly mentioned the red or black Di, the white or black Man, the pitch-dark Lang.[9] These colours were symbolic. They indicated either the dominant tint of the minorities' clothes or the five directions of the compass: white for the West, black for the North, red for the East, blue-green for the South. Yellow represented the Centre.

Every civilization has an ethnocentric world image in which outsiders are reduced to manageable spatial units. Ancient India opposed the pure land of the Aryans to the territories of the *mleccha*, or 'barbarians'.[10] The Europeans, from the Greeks onwards, viewed the world as composed of three continental parts: Asia, Europe and Africa. During the Middle Ages, this tripartite division of the earth was associated with the three sons of Noah. Europe, however, occupied only a quarter of this universe, as was noted by Isidore of Seville, a seventh-century bishop and author of a representative geographical compilation:

> The ancients did not divide these three parts of the world equally, for Asia stretches right from the south, through the east to the north, but Europe stretches from the north to the west and thence Africa from the west to the south. From this it is quite evident that the two parts Europe and Africa occupy half the world and that Asia alone occupies the other half.[11]

The eurocentric vision of the West was tempered by a threefold

9 See C.C. Müller, 'Die Herausbildung der Gegensätze: Chinesen und Barbaren in der frühen Zeit' in W. Bauer (ed.), *China und die Fremden. 3000 Jahre Auseinandersetzung in Krieg und Frieden*, Munich: C.H. Beck, 1980, p. 62.
10 R. Thapar, 'The image of the barbarian in early India', *Comparative Studies in Society and History*, 13 (1971), p. 411.
11 G.H.T. Kimble, *Geography in the Middle Ages*, London: Methuen, 1938, p. 24.

representation of the earth. It was also marked by the fact that the centre of civilization was outside Europe in Jerusalem. As a result of a complex combination of factors, the discussion of which exceeds the framework of present considerations (one could mention geographical isolation and cultural seclusion), China's imagination was trapped by a narrow dichotomy that opposed the civilized centre to the barbarian periphery.

THE BARBARIAN IN MYTHOLOGY

The degree of remoteness from the imperial centre corresponded to levels of cultural savagery and physical coarseness. In the *Shanhaijing* (fourth century BC), a work of geographical mythology, spirits and monstrous beasts roamed the edges of the world beyond the Great Wilderness (*dahuang*): they were half-man half-animal – the spirit Yingzhao had a human face and the body of a horse.[12] Barbarians living beyond the realm of Chinese civilization were dehumanized. The mythological function of the *Shanhaijing* clearly supplanted its ethnographical purpose: there was a tribe of one-eyed people (*Yimuguo*), as well as a country of three-headed barbarians (*Sanshouguo*). One-armed barbarians with three eyes also appeared. Cultural intolerance towards the outsider in China was associated with a feeling of physical discontinuity.

Skin colour branded the barbarian with the indelible stigma of animality. A mythical country in the west was inhabited by white people whose long hair covered their shoulders. Barbarians from another tribe had a human face, 'but their eyes, hands and feet are entirely black.' Only the Chinese were described as *ren*, 'man', or 'human being', thus implicitly degrading alien groups to bestiality.

The *Huainanzi* (a Daoist work of the second century BC) also associated cultural inferiority with physical oddity. 'In the West is the high land where streams and valleys come out, where the sun

---

12 The following examples are taken from Rémi Mathieu, *Etude sur la mythologie et l'ethnologie de la Chine ancienne. Traduction annotée du Shanhai jing*, Paris: Institut des Hautes Etudes Chinoises, 1983, pp. 89, 414, 389, 397, 445, 451–2.

and moon enter. There its men have mean faces, are deformed, have long necks, walk upright, and have a hole going through the nose. The skin is like leather. The white color governs the lungs. They are intrepid, but not virtuous.'[13] The north was 'gloomy and dark, not bright and fresh. That [i.e. the light] is obstructed, and there is only wintry ice. Therefore even insects hibernate. Whosoever is there hides and its people contract the appearance of short necks, large shoulders, and a cavity going down to the end of the spine, cold bones. Black governs the kidneys. Its people are simple and stupid, like beasts, and are long-lived.'[14]

Cultural intolerance associated with a feeling of physical discontinuity in ancient China has only a partial equivalent in the ancient Western world. When Ethiopians first appeared in Homeric poems as the most remote people on earth, their image was essentially favourable. Greek theories of the influence of environment upon people explained man's diversity: black Ethiopians exemplified the broad scale of human faculties and potentialities. In the early Roman Empire, Pliny the Elder reported that the less-known regions of the distant north and south were inhabited by imaginary creatures. Skin colour, however, did not play a significant role in antiquity's imagery. Frank Snowden believes that the familiarity with Ethiopian realities as well as the general pattern of white-black encounters in antiquity hindered the emergence of the idea of skin colour as an outward manifestation of cultural inferiority.[15]

ENVIRONMENTAL DETERMINISM

Yin and Yang Confucianism is perhaps at the origin of a belief in environmental determinism that contributed to the dehumanization of the alien. Yin and yang, the two primogenial forces of nature, produced all living organisms. Yin was the negative fluid, associated with the earth; it was female, dark, cold, moist and quiescent. Yang was the positive fluid, related to heaven; it was

13 Meserve, 'The inhospitable land', p. 55.
14 Ibid., p. 56.
15 Frank M. Snowden, *Before color prejudice: The ancient view of Blacks*, Cambridge, Mass.: Harvard University Press, 1983, pp. 46 ff. and 63.

male, active, warm and light. The yin pole was situated in the north, where it produced cold and darkness. The yang pole was in the south and generated heat and light. Only man was the result of a perfect harmony of both fluids. The furred and feathered creatures were dominated by the yang fluid, whereas the scaly and shell-covered ones owed their existence to the yin fluid.[16]

The five colours of the points of the compass also described the differences in the nature of China's soils, which were supposed to exert a decisive influence on nature and man: 'It is yellow, red, or black, of superior, average, or inferior quality.'[17] The Liji stressed how 'the bodily capacities of the people are sure to be according to the sky and earthly influences'.[18] In his commentaries on the Liji, Zheng Xuan (127–200 AD) explained that differences in the natural constitution of the barbarian were caused by the local 'earth fluid' (diqi).[19] Such environmental theories were developed under the Tang (618–907). Du You (735–812) believed that the barbarians of his time were backward partly because they were less favoured in terms of climate and environment than the Han. They lacked the spiritual guidance of the sages whom China's environment had produced, nurtured by the pure ethers of Heaven and Earth.[20]

'RAW' AND 'COOKED' BARBARIANS

'The people of those five regions [. . .] had all their several natures, which they could not be made to alter. The tribes on the east were called Yi. They had their hair unbound, and tattooed their bodies.

16 On the Yin-Yang school, see A. Forke, *The world conception of the Chinese: Their astronomical, cosmological and physico-philosophical speculations*, London: Arthur Probsthain, 1925.

17 Wang Chong, *Lun-heng*, transl. A. Forke, New York: Paragon Book Gallery, 1962, vol. 1, p. 390.

18 James Legge, *The Li Chi*, Hong Kong University Press, 1967, p. 228.

19 E. Zürcher, *The Buddhist conquest of China: The spread and adaptation of Buddhism in early medieval China*, Leiden: E.J. Brill, 1959, p. 265.

20 D. McMullen, 'Views of the state in Du You and Liu Zongyuan' in S. Schram (ed.), *Foundations and limits of state power in China*, London: School of Oriental and African Studies, 1987, p. 64.

Some of them ate their food without its being cooked.'[21] Food was a social signifier. It contributed to the symbolic differentiation between social groups and circumscribed cultural identity. Table habits expressed degrees of cultural alienation. In most civilizations, the main distinction was between raw and cooked food.[22] The transforming power of fire was a symbol of culture.

Two categories of barbarians lived within the Middle Kingdom. The *shengfan*, literally 'raw barbarians', were considered savage and resisting. The *shufan*, or 'cooked barbarians', were tame and submissive. The consumption of raw food was regarded as an infallible sign of savagery that affected the physiological state of the barbarian. Nature and nurture were closely associated in the Chinese mind. Official rhetoric often separated the Li of Hainan into 'raw' and 'cooked' barbarians. The tame Li lived on the coast of the island, enjoying all the benefits of Chinese civilization. The wild Li populated the dark forests of the centre, far from the humanizing influence of the Han Chinese.

Black slaves from Africa were treated similarly in élite culture. The *Pingzhou ketan*, written by Zhu Yu at the beginning of the twelfth century, noted that rich people in Canton used to keep African 'devil slaves' (*guinu*):

> Their colour is black as ink, their lips are red and their teeth white, their hair is curly and yellow. There are males and females . . . They live in the mountains (or islands) beyond the seas. They eat raw things. If, in captivity, they are fed on cooked food, after several days they get diarrhoea. This is called "changing the bowels" [*huanchang*]. For this reason they sometimes fall ill and die; if they do not die one can keep them, and after having been kept a long time they begin to understand human speech [i.e. Chinese], although they themselves cannot speak it.[23]

21 Legge, *Li Chi*, p. 229.
22 See Claude Lévi-Strauss's classic *Mythologiques: Le cru et le cuit*, Paris: Plon, 1964.
23 J.J.L. Duyvendak, *China's discovery of Africa*, London: Arthur Probsthain, 1949, p. 24; I have replaced Duyvendak's translation of 'people's language' (*renyan*) by 'human speech'.

Whereas popular Daoism held that a human had to change bones (*huangu*) to become immortal, the black had to change bowels (*huanchang*) to become half-human. Physical change enhanced intellectual capacity, although the black would never reach the level of inter-human communication. Although further research would be necessary to evaluate how representative this example was, it clearly corroborates the hypothesis of a mental link between the physical constitution and the cultural level of the barbarian in the Chinese mind.

SKIN COLOUR

It was not only in mythology that skin colour played a significant role: the élite developed a white-black polarity at a very early stage. Henri Maspero underlined that the Chinese called their own complexion 'white' from the most ancient times.[24] A white complexion was highly valued, as Chinese poetry has shown in many instances. This is how the *Shijing*, the earliest collection of poems, extols the whiteness of a famous princess:

> *Her fingers were like the blades of the young white grass;*
> *Her skin was like congealed ointment;*
> *Her neck was like the tree-grub;*
> *Her teeth were like melon-seeds;*
> *Her head cicada-like,*
> *Her eyebrows the silkworm moth.*[25]

White jade was used as a metaphor for a light complexion. Although it was mainly a canon of feminine beauty, it could also apply to men. Wang Yan, the last prime minister of the Western Jin dynasty (265–316 AD), was famed for his grace, in particular

24 H. Maspero, *La Chine antique*, Paris: Imprimerie Nationale, 1955, p. 13; see also R. Wilhelm, 'Chinesische Frauenschönheit', *Chinesisch-Deutscher Almanach*, 1931, p. 23.
25 J. Legge, *The Chinese classics*, 4:i, *The She king*, London: Henry Frowde, 1860–72, p. 95; see also p. 77.

for the 'jade-like' whiteness of his hands.[26] At court, male nobles even used powder to whiten their faces.[27]

As a result of the increase in maritime activities and contacts with foreigners, the Southern Song (1127–1279) witnessed a heightening of colour-consciousness. The Buddhist pantheon was sinicized, including the transformation of the Bodhisattva image from a 'swart half-naked Indian to a more decently clad divinity with a properly light complexion.'[28] Colour consciousness was sustained by encounters with people from neighbouring countries, who were generally of a darker complexion. When Albuquerque first arrived in Malacca in 1511, the natives drew his attention to the existence of 'white' people in the region: he found Chinese emigrants.[29] A Chinese geography of the early Ming corroborates this anecdote by reporting that 'people in Malacca have a black skin, but some are white: these are Chinese.'[30]

Not all Chinese had the privilege of a light complexion. Labourers were called 'black-headed people': the label established a symbolic distance between the peasants and the landlord class. Though this term changed in meaning as a result of an official decree issued in 221 BC, it was associated with a negatively valued dark complexion. According to the *Shuowen* (first century AD), the common people were called black-headed because of their pigmentation. The *Chunqiu* emphasized the black complexion of the peasant, burned swarthy by the sun. Under the Zhou, slaves were called *renli*. *Li* referred to a large cooking utensil stained by smoke and blackened by fire. It was a metaphor for the black faces

26 A. Waley, 'The fall of Loyang', *History Today*, 4 (1951), p. 8, quoted in A.F. Wright, *Buddhism in Chinese history*, Stanford University Press, 1959, p. 31.
27 B. Hinsch, *Passions of the cut sleeve: The male homosexual tradition in China*, Berkeley: University of California Press, 1990, pp. 65–6.
28 A. Soper, 'Hsiang-kuo-ssu, an imperial temple of Northern Sung', quoted in Wright, *Buddhism*, p. 98.
29 P. Huard, 'Depuis quand avons-nous la notion d'une race jaune?', *Institut Indochinois pour l'Etude de l'Homme*, 4 (1942), p. 40.
30 Zhang Xie, *Dong Xi yang kao* (Geography of south-east Asia), Beijing: Zhonghua shuju, 1981, p. 67.

of the slaves who tilled the fields under the burning sun. It implied contempt and disdain.[31]

The polarity between white and black, derived from a differentiation of social classes and a particular aesthetic value system, was projected upon the outside world when the Chinese came into contact with alien groups. Black symbolized the most remote part of the geographically known world. Chinese texts up to the Tang dynasty presented the distant peoples of the Nam-Viet Cham empire as black, wavy-haired barbarians of the mountains and the jungles. They were seen as 'devils' or 'ghosts' (*gui*).[32] The Khmers were also called kunlun people, by reference to a mythical mountain appearing in the *Shanhaijing*. The Kunlun mountain delimitated the western edge of the world. As geographical knowledge progressed, the location of the kunlun people shifted. In the eighth century, the term was applied to Malaysians. In 750, Jianzhen (688–765) noticed the presence of many 'Brahmans, Persians and Kunluns [Malays]'[33] in Canton. The *Book of the Tang* reported that 'every year, Kunlun merchants come in [their] ships with valuable goods to trade with the Chinese.'[34] Madagascar, discovered during the Song, was called *Kunluncengqi*, *cengqi* transcribing the generic Arabic word for blacks, *Zang*. The island was believed to have 'many savages with bodies as black as lacquer and with curly hair'.[35]

Between white, the centre of the civilized world, and black, the negative pole of humanity, relegated to the edge of the known

31 See Shih Lun, 'The black-headed people' in Li Yu-ning (ed.), *First emperor of China: The politics of historiography*, New York: International Arts and Sciences Press, 1975, pp. 242–58.
32 E.H. Schafer, *The vermilion bird: T'ang images of the south*, Berkeley: University of California Press, 1967, p. 16; see also p. 73.
33 J. Takakusu, 'Le voyage de Kanshin en Orient (742–754)', *Bulletin de l'Ecole Française d'Extrême-Orient*, 28 (1928), p. 466.
34 Wang Gungwu, 'The Nanhai trade: A study of the early history of Chinese trade in the South China Sea', *Journal of the Malayan Branch of the Royal Asiatic Society*, 31, no. 182 (1958), p. 75.
35 A. Netolitzky, *Das Ling-wai tai-ta von Chou Ch'ü-fei. Eine Landeskunde Südchinas aus dem 12. Jahrhundert*, Wiesbaden: Franz Steiner Verlag, 1977, p. 49.

world, lay a whole range of nuances. Shades of colour became more precise as the Chinese grew familiar with aliens. Under the Tang, observes Jane Mahler, 'the darker skin of India seems to have interested some of the Chinese image makers; one supposes at times that they were confused by the dark-skinned people, for they did not distinguish clearly between Hindus, Negroes and Malays.'[36] During the Song, which saw an increase in the social perception of skin colour, distinctions become more common. Zhao Rugua's work notes that people in Ceylon were 'very black' (*jifu shenhei*). In Malabar, people were of a 'purple complexion' (*zise*). The savages of the Andaman islands, who were feared to be cannibals, were described as 'resembling black lacquer' (*shen ru heiqi*).[37]

During the early Ming, several expeditions to distant countries were organized by Zheng He as part of the expansionist policy of the Yongle emperor (*r.* 1403–24). Ma Huan accompanied Zheng He on three expeditions and in 1451 published an account entitled *Yingya shenglan*. The bodies of the people in Malacca were 'slightly black' (*shenti weihei*), whereas the faces of Bengalis were 'completely black' (*ren zhi rong jiehei*). Natives of Ormuz had a 'clear white' complexion (*qingbai*); the inhabitants of Mecca had a 'purple-chest colour' (*zitangse*).[38]

WHITE ASH

Westerners, despite their white pigmentation, were as weird as Africans.[39] An early mention by Yan Shigu (eighth century AD), a

36 J.G. Mahler, *The Westerners among the figurines of the T'ang dynasty of China*, Rome: Istituto Italiano per il Medio ed Estremo Oriente, 1959, p. 84.
37 Zhao Rugua, *Zhufanzhi* (Records on the various barbarians), Beijing: Zhonghua shuju, 1956, *juan* 2, pp. 10b, 16a and 34a.
38 Ma Huan, *Yingya shenglan jiaozhu* (Annotated overall survey of the ocean shores), edited, with notes, by Feng Chengjun, Beijing: Zhonghua shuju, 1955, pp. 23, 59, 63, 69.
39 The Chinese discovered Europeans in the sixteenth and seventeenth centuries with the same apprehension with which the European encountered blacks during their exploration of Africa. Jan Nieuhof, who accompanied Peter

commentator of the *Qianhanshu*, noted that they had 'blue eyes and red beards; they look like macaques [*mihou*].'[40] In Chinese eyes, Europeans were just another variety of physically defective creatures, comparable to albinos in the Western mind: they provoked curiosity mingled with a feeling of repulsion and pity. Their complexion was not merely white, it was 'ash-white'(*huibai*), the exteriorization of the demonological forces that drove the foreign devils to undertake their expansion overseas. Zhang Xie, who also mentioned the presence of 'white' Chinese in Malacca, described the Portuguese as follows: 'They are seven feet tall, have eyes like a cat, a mouth like an oriole, an ash-white face, thick and curly beards like black gauze, and almost red hair.'[41] These hairy goblins were naturally associated with their black counterparts from beyond the Kunlun mountains, as the verses of a nineteenth-century poem on the British and Indian troops reveal: 'The white ones are cold and dull as the ashes of frogs, the black ones are ugly and dirty as coal.'[42] Social status distinguished them: the black was a slave.

BLACK COAL

Zhang Xinglang has argued that African slaves were imported into China as early as the Tang dynasty.[43] According to Duyvendak,

---

de Goyer and Jacob de Keyser on the first European mission to the Qing in 1655, was struck by this inversion of roles. When a crowd of officials and courtiers loitered nearby in Beijing, he remarked that they stared at them 'as if some new monster from Africa had arrived'; J. Nieuhof, *Het gezantschap der Neerlandtsche Oost-Indische Compagnie aan den Grooten Tartarischen Cham den tegenwoordigen Keizer van China*, Amsterdam: Jacob van Meurs, 1665, p. 173.

40 Zhang Xinglang, 'Zhongguo renzhong Yindu-Riermanzhong fenzi' (Indo-Germanic elements in the Chinese race), *Furen xuezhi*, 1, 1928, p. 180.

41 Zhang Xie, *Dong Xi yang kao*, p. 93.

42 Jin He, 'Shuo gui' (About ghosts) in A Ying (comp.), *Yapian zhanzheng wenxue ji* (Collection of literary writings on the Opium War), Beijing: Guji chubanshe, 1957, p. 44.

43 Zhang Xinglang, 'Tangshi Feizhou heinu shuru Zhongguo kao' (The importation of African black slaves into China during the Tang), *Furen xuezhi*, 1, 1928, pp. 101–19.

the first definite reference to the African continent appears in the *Youyang zazu*, written by Duan Chengshi (?–863) at the end of the Tang dynasty. It is significant that this early reference already integrates the African with the lowest scale in the social hierarchy, namely slavery:

The country of Po-pa-li [Berbera] is in the south-western sea. [The people] do not eat any of the five grains but eat only meat. They often stick a needle into the veins of cattle and draw blood which they drink raw, mixed with milk. They wear no clothes except that they cover [the parts] below the loins with sheep-skins. Their women are clean and of proper behaviour. The inhabitants themselves kidnap them, and if they sell them to foreign merchants, they fetch several times their price.[44]

During the same period, black slaves became a popular topic in literature. The *Taiping guangji* (981) contains many tales about the kunlun slaves, believed to be simple-minded but courageous in obeying orders regardless of the possible danger.[45]

Under the Song, reports on the Arab slave trade became more common. Zhou Qufei wrote that Madagascar had many savages, who were 'enticed by food and then caught and carried off; thousands are sold as slaves.'[46] Zhao Rugua made the same remark and added that 'they are used for gate-keepers [lit., to look after the gate-bolts]. It is said that they do not long for their kinsfolk.'[47] Black slaves, carried to Asia by Persian and Arab merchants, could fetch three taels of gold or its equivalent in scented woods per head on the Chinese market.[48] Zhu Yu called the black door-keepers *yeren*, 'wild man', or *guinu*, 'devil slave'. He also mentioned

---

44 Duyvendak, *China's discovery*, p. 13.
45 See E. Wang, 'The k'un-lun slave: A legend', *Asia*, 41 (1941), pp. 134–5.
46 Netolitsky, *Ling-wai tai-ta*, p. 49.
47 F. Hirth and W.W. Rockhill, *Chau Ju-kua: His work on the Chinese and Arab trade in the 12th and 13th centuries, entitled Chu-fan-chi*, St. Petersburg: Printing Office of the Imperial Academy of Sciences, 1911, p. 149.
48 See P. Wheatley, 'Geographical notes on some commodities involved in Sung maritime trade', *Journal of the Malayan Branch of the Royal Asiatic Society*, 32, no. 186 (1959), p. 54.

'kunlun slaves', a variety of black creatures from near the sea 'that can enter the water without blinking the eyes': these slaves worked on ships and were forced to repair seams that had sprung leaks below the water-line.[49] African stewards also served on Chinese ships during the Song.[50] As late as the nineteenth century, crews on Chinese-owned ships were Manila men and 'seedies', natives from Africa.[51] They were despised by the Chinese as 'black devils', according to a missionary's report.[52]

During the Song period, medieval Europe had little interest in Africa as such, despite its geographical proximity.[53] Information about Africa was obtained mainly through the Moors in Spain, who had been exploring parts of the continent since the seventh century. From the twelfth century onward, Christians had a growing number of slaves, mainly Muslims from the Maghreb but also some blacks. This trade steadily increased during the fourteenth and fifteenth centuries, chiefly in the hands of European merchants.[54] Contempt for and aloofness from black slaves seems to have been common among certain social classes in southern Europe, an attitude not shared by the north at that period.[55] The equation of 'black' with 'slave', an important factor in the development of racial discrimination,[56] was thus realized at a relatively

49 Zhu Yu, *Pingzhou ketan* (Anecdotes and stories), Changsha: Shangwu yinshuguan, 1935–6, *juan* 2, p. 2b.

50 Lo Jung-p'ang, 'The emergence of China as a sea power during the late Sung and early Yüan periods', *Far Eastern Quarterly*, 14, no. 4 (1955), p. 500.

51 W.C. Hunter, *The 'fan kwae' at Canton before the treaty days, 1825–1844*, Shanghai: Kelly and Walsh, 1911, p. 148.

52 *Wanguo gongbao* (The Globe Magazine), 15, 2 Dec. 1882, pp. 146a–7.

53 See F. de Médeiros, 'Recherches sur l'image des noirs dans l'Occident médiéval, 13e–15e siècles', unpubl. doctoral thesis, University of Paris, 1973.

54 See C. Verlinden, 'Esclavage noir en France méridionale et courants de traite en Afrique', *Annales du Midi*, 128 (1966), pp. 335–443.

55 J. Devisse and S. Labib, 'Africa in inter-continental relations' in D.T. Niane (ed.), *Unesco general history of Africa*, Berkeley: University of California Press, 1984, vol. 4, p. 652.

56 The Académie Française equated the term *nègre* with slave in the eighteenth century. *Noir* partly supplanted *nègre* during the latter half of the eighteenth century, as is attested by the title of a French abolitionist society founded in

early stage in China. It existed well before Westerners established themselves at the frontiers of the Empire.

When the Portuguese settled in Macao during the second half of the sixteenth century, they imported many slaves from their colonies in Africa, India and Malacca. Black African women and numerous female Timorese slaves were brought to Macao after 1555.[57] Antonio Bocarra, writing in 1635, reported that each Portuguese household in Macao had an average of six slaves, 'amongst whom the majority and the best are negroes and such like.'[58] These African slaves sometimes ran away into China, and eventually constituted a community of their own in a district of Canton. Chinese merchants who engaged in foreign trade occasionally used them as interpreters.[59] Matteo Ricci (1552–1610) now and then intervened by returning runaway slaves to the Portuguese. He himself had black interpreters in his years of apprenticeship, but gradually switched to native servants, presumably because the 'blacks frightened the Chinese'.[60]

Blackness had always been a symbolic expression for slavery. In the Confucian universe, the Portuguese merely followed the native tradition of keeping kunlun slaves. In this respect at least, it seemed that the barbarians faithfully adopted 'Chinese ways'.

1788, La Société des Amis des Noirs. See W.B. Cohen, *The French encounter with Africans: White response to blacks, 1530–1880*, Bloomington: Indiana University Press, 1980, p. 132.

57 C.R. Boxer, *Portuguese society in the tropics: The municipal councils of Goa, Macao, Bahia and Luanda, 1510–1800*, Madison: University of Wisconsin Press, 1965, p. 65.

58 C.R. Boxer, 'Macao as a religious and commercial entrepot in the 16th and 17th centuries', *Acta Asiatica*, 26 (1974), p. 65.

59 A. Coates, *A Macao narrative*, Hong Kong: Heinemann, 1978, p. 35.

60 J.D. Spence, *The memory palace of Matteo Ricci*, London: Faber and Faber, 1985, p. 209.

SECTION TWO

The first section of this chapter focused on the social perception of physical features. This section will briefly examine the political theories that rejected the dominant rhetoric of cultural universalism. It should be remembered that even if the exclusionist approach remained limited in effect, it did create theoretical precedents that may have nurtured defensive reactions during the last two centuries.

The most salient aspect of the exclusionist approach is a belief in the incompatibility between the respective natures of the Chinese and the barbarian. The origin of this belief is usually traced back to the classics, particularly to a passage in the works of Mencius (372–289 BC?). In this passage, Mencius reproached Chen Xiang for having abandoned the learning of China, saying: 'I have heard of men using the doctrines of our great land to change barbarians, but I have never heard of any being changed by barbarians.'[61] The nature of the Chinese was regarded as impermeable to the evil influences of the barbarian; no retrogression was possible. Only the barbarian might eventually change by adopting Chinese ways.

Mencius' remark was first expounded during the Six Dynasties (221–589 AD), when the efflorescence of Buddhism threatened the sense of cultural superiority which had buttressed the social status of the ruling class since antiquity. Anti-Buddhist arguments were based mainly on the words of Mencius quoted above, but their meaning was expanded into a position of mutual exclusiveness.

ANTI-BUDDHISM

Buddhism was a curiosity which was confined to the court under the Han dynasty. Only after the fall of the Han empire in 221 AD and the partition of the empire into rival kingdoms did it begin to expand rapidly. By the fifth century it had flourished to such an extent that it provoked Daoist opposition.

Gu Huan (390–453) was a prominent enemy of Buddhism. In a

61 Legge, *Classics*, 2, pp. 253–4.

treatise entitled *Yixialun* (About Chinese and barbarians), he argued that Buddhism was inferior to Chinese systems because of its foreign origin:

> Buddhism originated in the land of the barbarians; is that not because the customs of the barbarians were originally evil? The Tao originated in China; is that not because the habits of the Chinese were originally good? . . . Buddhism is not the way for China, Taoism is not the teaching of the western barbarians. Fishes and birds are of different origins, and never have anything in common. How can we have Buddhism and Taoism intermingle to spread to the extremities of the empire?[62]

The comparison of Buddhism and Daoism to fishes and birds underlined a basic discontinuity between the two religions. The idea of a fundamental difference between the natures of Chinese and Indians had also been put forward by He Chengtian (370–447):

> The inborn nature of Chinese is pure and harmonious, in accordance with altruism and holding to righteousness – that is why the Duke of Chou and Confucius explained to them the doctrine of (original unity of) nature and (differentiation by) practice. Those people of foreign countries are endowed with a hard and obstinate nature, full of evil desires, hatred and violence – that is why Sakyamuni severely restrained them with the five prohibitive rules (for laymen).'[63]

The Daoist work *Sanpolun* attacked Buddhism even more violently. It contained an unabashed appeal to the extermination of the barbarians:

> The barbarians are without benevolence, unyielding, violent and without manners, and are not different from birds and beasts . . . They are also coarse and uncivilized. Desiring to exterminate their evil progeny, Lao-tzu ordered the males not

---

62 K. Ch'en, 'Anti-Buddhist propaganda during the Nan-Ch'ao', *Harvard Journal of Asiatic Studies*, 15 (1952), p. 172.
63 Zürcher, *Buddhist conquest*, p. 265.

to take wives, and the females not to take husbands. When the entire country submits to the teaching of Lao-tzu, they will be exterminated as a matter of course.[64]

These criticisms were formulated during a period of disunity marked by widespread violence and massacres between Chinese and alien intruders following the latter's conquest of the north of China in 317. Most anti-Buddhist arguments were articulated in the south, where a large number of people had taken refuge, escaping from the barbarian invasions. Migrations beyond the Yangzi moved the cultural centre south to the newly-acquired territories.

Although this train of thought was limited in its appeal, it reappeared occasionally throughout Chinese history, particularly when the élite's position was menaced by a foreign creed or alien conquerors. The political threat posed by alien invasion or foreign religions challenged the traditional ideal of cultural universalism. Such a threat could generate a defensive reaction leading to the adoption of beliefs clustered around the negative pole of the dominant value-system, as was to reoccur during the Song dynasty.

SONG LOYALISM

The Jurchen empire of the Jin, originally based in Manchuria, invaded the north of China in 1126. The Song were unable to resist the nomad cavalry and had to retreat south of the Yangzi: this was the second partition of the empire between an alien conqueror and the Chinese. The Song retained the Yangzi valley and everything south of it.

The philosophical controversies of the Southern Song (1127–1279) were concerned mainly with the self-preservation of the dynasty by means of adopting conciliatory policies towards the Jin. Discarding the traditional tribute system, officials from the tenth to the thirteenth centuries pursued a realistic and pragmatic foreign

64 K. Ch'en, *Buddhism in China: A historical survey*, Princeton University Press, 1964, pp. 137–8.

policy: neighbouring states were accepted as equals. The realistic appraisal of powerful states, however, did not prevent officials from continuing to despise foreigners as 'barbarians'. According to Herbert Franke, 'the principle of reciprocity in diplomatic relations with these states was nothing more than an enforced concession, which was but grudgingly granted because of the Sung's military weakness.'[65] Internal official records and private correspondence remained full of xenophobic sentiments: foreigners were referred to as inferior peoples, 'barbarians', 'caitiffs' or simply 'animals'.[66] Although equality with neighbouring states was recognized, Tao Jing-shen has noticed the appearance of a nationalistic imagery which was critical, for instance, of intermarriage with the Khitan (an ethnic group from Manchuria), a practice normally favoured by the Chinese.[67]

Despite the official rhetoric of equality, some uncompromising scholars based their arguments in favour of recovering the lost territories on 'anti-barbarian' grounds. Chen Liang (1143–94), a utilitarian theorist who argued against the philosophical speculations of Neo-Confucianists, wanted to restore the north to the control of the Song by driving out the Jin. Chen, like other pragmatic renovators of the Southern Song, searched for practical elements in the symbolic universe that could lead to a stronger state and a better society. According to Hoyt Tillman, Chen's denigration of foreigners was closely related to anti-Buddhist literature.[68] His call to expel the foreigner also rested on a belief in environmental determinism. Different environments had different spatial energies (qi), and only China possessed the central and most beneficial one in the cosmos. Foreigners had an inferior energy

65 H. Franke, 'Sung embassies: Some general observations' in M. Rossabi (ed.), *China among equals: The Middle Kingdom and its neighbors, 10th–14th centuries*, Berkeley: University of California Press, 1983, p. 121.
66 Tao Jing-shen, 'Barbarians or Northerners: Northern Sung images of the Khitans' in Rossabi (ed.), *China among equals*, pp. 71–6.
67 Tao Jing-shen, *Two sons of heaven: Studies in Sung-Liao relations*, Tucson: University of Arizona Press, 1988.
68 H.C. Tillman, 'Proto-nationalism in twelfth-century China?', *Harvard Journal of Asiatic Studies*, 39, no. 2 (Dec. 1979), p. 404.

that perverted the spatial energy of the Central Plain. Chen Liang expounded his ideas to the emperor in a memorial:

> Your obedient servant ventures to suggest that only China (*Zhongguo*) -the standard energy (*zhengqi*) of heaven and earth- is that which the heavenly mandate to rule (*tianming*) endows, where the hearts of the people gather, where the rituals of civilization cluster, and that which kings and emperors have inherited for a hundred generations. Is it at all conceivable that [such a country] could be violated by the perverse energy (*xieqi*) of the barbarians? . . . The pure air of heaven and earth has been restricted and enveloped by the offensive odor of sheep and goats [of nomadic barbarians] and for long has not attained release; it surely must and will vent itself. The hearts of the people and the mandate to rule are certainly not long confinable to a peripheral area of the world.[69]

Ye Shi (1150–1223), a friend of Chen Liang and author of several utilitarian studies, was even more outspoken about the Jin.[70] Ye, like Chen, was attracted by a strand of learning called *jingshi*, 'practical statecraft'. This was characterized by a pre-occupation with concrete results in statecraft at the expense of philosophical contemplation. His 'Postscript', written shortly before his death, contained several programs of action against the Jurchen. Ye urged the emperor to issue a proclamation inciting the Northerners to abandon the enemy armies. The Song government should also pay a bounty of five hundred strings of cash for each head of a dead 'barbarian' (*huren*). Decapitation of the enemy would force its withdrawal to the northern steppes. Ye Shi abandoned the traditional notion of barbarians versus Chinese and attempted to see Song-Jin relations in more realistic terms. 'Within the microcosm of Ye Shih's mind, Confucian cultural universalism had to be dethroned before militant nationalism could hold sway,'[71] writes his biographer Winston Wan Lo.

69 Ibid., p. 408.
70 The following is based on Winston Wan Lo, *The life and thought of Yeh Shih*, Hong Kong: Chinese University Press, 1974.
71 Ibid., p. 141.

China was finally united in 1279, but not quite in the way the Southern Song had anticipated: the Mongols, whose invasions had started in 1235, reunified the country by conquest and ruled it until 1368 as the Yuan dynasty. The Mongols divided the population of the empire into four official categories: the Mongols, the *semu* ('coloured eyes', Western and Central Asians), the *Hanren* ('Han people' or Northern Chinese, Khitans, Jurchens and Koreans), and the *Nanren* ('Southerners'). Scholars have not been able to agree on the exact meaning of these terms. Whereas some believe that the Mongol hierarchy denotes ethnic differences, others describe it as a reflection of geopolitical divisions.[72] In any case, it seems reasonable to suggest that racial consciousness among the Chinese élite was raised during the Yuan dynasty as a result of foreign rule.

Chinese officials were summoned to serve the Mongol administration. Many Confucian literati participated actively in public service, but some Song loyalists (*yimin*) withdrew from public life. They sought refuge in Daoist monasteries in south China and refused to serve an alien conqueror. Deng Mu and Ye Lin died in 1305 after starving themselves for two months in response to an imperial edict to serve the government.[73] Although Song loyalism was motivated largely by political and moral considerations, Frederick Mote has noticed that 'an incipient racism made brief appearance, contradicting in its spirit the traditional patronizing Chinese attitude toward "barbarian" neighbours.'[74] Hu Han (1307–91), a scholar concerned with the reappraisal of Chinese relations towards foreigners, invoked the traditional criteria of the *Chunqiu*, based on a strict dichotomy between Han and non-Han

72 See E. Endicott-West, *Mongolian rule in China: Local administration in the Yuan dynasty*, Cambridge, Mass.: Harvard University Press, 1989, p. 142, n. 51.
73 Fu Lo-shu, 'Teng Mu, a forgotten Chinese philosopher', *T'oung Pao*, 52 (1965), p. 43.
74 F.W. Mote, 'Confucian eremitism in the Yüan period' in A.F. Wright (ed.), *The Confucian persuasion*, Stanford University Press, 1960, p. 202.

rule.[75] Though he was far from renouncing the myth of the barbarian, his repudiation of the Mongols was close to that of Ye Shi. Hu also insisted on the institution of the lineage (*zu*) as a system of social regulation within the state.[76] Most remarkable was a bitter denunciation by Zheng Sixiao (1239–1316), whose work was found buried in an iron box near Suzhou during the late Ming period. It described the Mongols as 'of a non-human origin' (*fei renlei*) and compared them to 'dogs and goats'.[77] The authenticity of this work has been disputed, but it should be remembered that most of the proponents of anti-foreign theories had to write in secret for fear of persecution. The works of these authors have often been lost, if not voluntarily destroyed. The result is a certain imbalance in the literary heritage of Chinese history.[78]

Fang Xiaoru wrote after the fall of the Mongol Yuan dynasty and the foundation of the Ming dynasty in 1368. Under the influence of Hu Han, he also made a categorical distinction between Chinese and barbarians: 'To elevate them to a position above the Chinese people would be to lead the world to animaldom. If a dog or a horse were to occupy a human's seat, even small boys would be angry and take a club to them . . . why? Because the general order would be confused.'[79] John Fincher believes that a ' "racist" strain dominates Fang's metaphors though culturalism retains a hold on his logic.'[80]

Fang Xiaoru insisted that the emperor could not be a barbarian.

---

75 Chan Hok-lam, *Legitimation in imperial China: Discussions under the Jurchen-Chin dynasty, 1115–1234*, Seattle: University of Washington Press, 1984, p. 129.
76 J.W. Dardess, *Confucianism and autocracy: Professional elites in the foundation of the Ming dynasty*, Berkeley: University of California Press, 1983.
77 J.D. Langlois, 'Introduction' in J.D. Langlois (ed.), *China under Mongol rule*, Princeton University Press, 1981, p. 17.
78 On censorship, self-censorship and the editing of Song loyalism, see J.W. Jay, 'Memoirs and official accounts: The historiography of the Song loyalists', *Harvard Journal of Asiatic Studies*, 50, no. 2 (Dec. 1990), pp. 589–612.
79 J. Fincher, 'China as a race, culture and nation: Notes on Fang Hsiao-ju's discussion of dynastic legitimacy' in D.C. Buxbaum and F.W. Mote (eds), *Transition and permanence: Chinese history and culture. A festschrift in honour of Dr Hsiao Kung-ch'üan*, Hong Kong: Cathay Press, 1972, p. 59.
80 Ibid., p. 60.

But he also considered Chinese usurpers, of which Wang Mang (first century AD) was a prototype, as 'barbarians'. His anti-foreign sentiment was still much embedded in a cultural tradition. It was only under the Qing that the racial factor became a significant argument in the delineation of the barbarian, bringing about a major departure from the cultural norms which traditionally prevailed.

ANTI-MANCHUISM

In 1644, a Manchu emperor ascended the throne in Beijing and founded the Qing dynasty, which was to last until its collapse in 1911. The conquest of China by this frontier people met with a wide range of responses from the Chinese. The north was occupied without marked opposition. Hard-pressed by peasant revolts and banditry, officials were quick to surrender, some even welcoming the Manchus as the restorers of law and order. These officials were placed in leading positions in an administration that retained most of its Chinese characteristics. In the south, however, resistance against the alien invader was actively organized by a rebellious gentry: it took the new dynasty several decades to achieve the conquest of the regions beyond the Yangzi. Yunnan was captured only in 1682. Thousands of loyal Chinese were massacred, and many retired from official life after the failure of the rebellion. Among these retired scholars, some developed loyalist ideas characterized by racial hostility to the new dynasty. Gu Yanwu (1613–82), for instance, refused to serve the new dynasty. He refuted the idea that barbarians could be morally transformed and emphasized the sense of shame in serving a barbarian ruler.[81] The strict separation of barbarians and Chinese into distinct spheres, where each could live in accordance with his inborn character, was unavoidable.[82] Lü Liuliang (1629–83), a scholar

81 Mi Chu Wiens, 'Anti-Manchu thought during the early Ch'ing', *Papers on China*, 22A (1969), p. 8.
82 Paolo Santangelo, ' "Chinese and barbarians" in Gu Yanwu's thought' in *Collected papers of the XXXIXth Congress of Chinese Studies*, Tübingen, 1988, pp. 183–99.

from Zhejiang province, entered the Buddhist monkhood after the Manchu conquest. Most of his anti-Manchu ideas were elaborated in commentaries on the Confucian classics. From 1728 to 1732 he became the focus of an official campaign which attempted to suppress literati who continued to insist on ethnic differences between the Manchus and the Han Chinese.[83] Lü was accused of having distorted the classics in order to propagate anti-Manchu views based on racial grounds.[84] His corpse was disinterred and decapitated by imperial edict in 1733.

The most virulent critic of alien rule was Wang Fuzhi (1619–92). Wang retired into seclusion after the failure of an uprising against the Manchus which he had led in Hunan, and devoted most of his energies to writing. He recast traditional ideas concerning environmental determinism and the difference in nature of the barbarian in a theory about the isolated development of groups. Most of his philosophical system was based on the concept of ether. This was the creative force of the universe, which agglomerated to assume different forms and images, strictly differentiated by the concept of category (lei):

> They accept what is similar and oppose what is different, and thus all things flourish in profusion and form their various categories. Each of these categories has its own organization. So it is that dew, thunder, frost, and snow all occur at their proper times, and animals, plants, birds, and fish all keep to their own species . . . Nor can there be between man and beast, plant and tree, any indiscriminate confusion of their respective principles.[85]

Universal order was based on clear distinctions between cate-

83 On this campaign, see the biography of Zeng Jing in A.W. Hummel (ed.), *Eminent Chinese of the Ch'ing period (1644–1912)*, Washington, DC: US Govt. Printing Office, 1944, pp. 747–9.

84 See T.S. Fisher, 'Accommodation and loyalism: The life of Lü Liu-liang (1629–1683)', *Papers on Far Eastern History*, 15 (March 1977), p. 102.

85 I. McMorran, 'Wang Fu-chih and the Neo-Confucian tradition' in W.T. De Bary, *The unfolding of Neo-Confucianism*, New York: Columbia University Press, 1975, p. 438.

gories. This philosophical system had important political implications. If the Chinese did not mark themselves off from the
barbarians, the principle of ether would be violated, since they and
the barbarians both belonged to different categories. Chinese were
the 'ether of Heaven' (*tianqi*), whereas the barbarians were 'impure
ether' (*jianqi*).[86] The vital distinction between purity and impurity
was implicit in the title of Wang's central work, entitled the
Yellow Book (Huangshu) (1656): the last chapter placed the colour
yellow (*huangse*), one of the five pure colours, in opposition to
mixed colours (*jianse*).[87] China was named the 'yellow centre'
(*huangzhong*). Distinctions between Chinese and barbarians could
not be blurred. Everything distinguished them:

> Chinese and barbarians are born in different places, which
> brings about the differences in their atmospheres, which in turn
> are responsible for the differences in their customs. When their
> customs are different, their understanding and behaviour are all
> different.[88]

The purity of categories (*qinglei*) had to be preserved by strict
boundaries (*juezhen*) and a specific *Lebensraum* (*dingwei*). The territory of the Chinese race was the 'middle region' (*zhongqu*) or
'divine region' (*shenqu*): 'North of the deserts, west of the Yellow
River, south of Annam, east of the sea, the ether is different,
people have a different essence, nature produces different things.'[89]
The first duty of the emperor was to keep the boundaries between
races clear:

> Now even the ants have rulers who preside over the territory of
> their nests and, when red ants or flying white ants penetrate
> their gates, the ruler organises all his own kind into troops to
> bite and kill the intruders, drive them far away from the anthill
> and prevent foreign interference.[90]

86 E. Vierheller, *Nation und Elite im Denken von Wang Fu-chih (1619–1692)*,
Hamburg: Gesellschaft für Natur- und Völkerkunde Ostasiens, 1968, p. 30.
87 Ibid., p. 124, n. 5.
88 Mi Chu Wiens, 'Anti-Manchu thought', p. 11.
89 Vierheller, *Wang Fu-chih*, p. 34.
90 I. McMorran, 'The patriot and the partisans: Wang Fu-chih's involvement

This famous metaphor seems to be unique[91] and should not be placed outside of the global perspective of Wang's work. The idea of racial purity, however, pervaded most of his political thought. Its logical consequence was the rejection of the notion of cultural universalism and the exclusion of the other races from the divine soil of the Middle Kingdom.[92] Both biological inheritance and environmental determinism erected boundaries between Chinese and barbarians that should not be crossed. Wang claimed that the Mongols had exploited the emperorship in order to enforce artificially a proximity of alien peoples with the Chinese. On this point, his historical analysis converged with the discussions of Song Lian and Fang Xiaoru. In fact, ethnological discourse about the barbarians was officially encouraged by the Ming at the dawn of the seventeenth century. In order to understand the moral character of contemporary tribal peoples, their ancestors were studied in the *Zuozhuan* and the *Chunqiu*. The repository for such knowledge was the *siyiguan* (four barbarians' bureaux) and the dynastic histories.[93] The majority of anti-Manchu works were banned by the *siku quanshu* (Four Treasuries) project under the Qing, but were revived by the reformers and the revolutionaries at the end of the dynasty. At the beginning of the twentieth century, Ming loyalists came to be highly regarded by a growing number of young intellectuals: Mao Zedong eventually joined a Wang Fuzhi study society in Hunan, his home province.

The idea of group was expressed in categorical terms such as *qun*, 'herd', 'group' or 'flock', and *lei*, 'type', 'sort', 'class', and in terms of fictive ancestry like *zu*, 'lineage'. Originally, *zu* had two distinct meanings: a small descent group tied by a blood-

---

in the politics of the Yung-li court' in J.D. Spence and J.E. Wills (eds), *From Ming to Ch'ing: Conquest, region, and continuity in seventeenth-century China*, New Haven: Yale University Press, 1979, p. 157.

91 V.G. Burov, *Mirovozzrenie Kitaiskogo myslitelya XVII veka Van Chuan'-shanya*, Moscow: Izdatel'stvo Nauka, 1976, p. 197, n. 20.

92 Vierheller, *Wang Fu-chih*, pp. 29 and 37.

93 See P.K. Crossley, 'Ming ethnology' (article in prep.); I am indebted for information on late Ming ethnology to P.K. Crossley (personal communication, 16 Dec. 1990).

relationship like the family or the clan; and a larger group of people inhabiting the same territory.[94] Later, the term came to express the idea of lineage. *Zu*, with a strong connotation of horizontal continuity maintained by ancestor worship, was particularly emphasized by Wang. The term could be translated into English as 'race', a term similarly dominated by the idea of lineage in sixteenth- and seventeenth-century Europe. As Europe emerged from the Middle Ages, it continued to be dominated by a Church that regulated every aspect of life. The Bible was read regularly; Adam was considered the ancestor of humankind. The book of *Genesis* explained that Shem, Ham and Japheth had founded separate nations after the flood. God's curse on Ham accounted for his black skin. Foxe, in his *Book of Martyrs* (1570), wrote that men were of 'the race and stocke of Abraham'.[95] In the context of the seventeenth century, 'race' and *zu* are etymologically and semantically similar enough to be compared with each other. Adam's race, however, had spread and populated the three known continents of the world, whereas the Chinese *zu* was confined to the Middle Kingdom.

Chinese attitudes towards outsiders were fraught with ambivalence. On the one hand, a claim to cultural universalism led the élite to assert that the barbarian could be 'sinicized', or transformed by the beneficial influence of culture and climate. On the other hand, when their sense of cultural superiority was threatened, the élite appealed to categorical differences in nature to expel the barbarian and seal the country off from the perverting influences of the outside world. In both cases, the foreigner was never faced: the myth of his inferiority could be preserved. Absorbed or expelled, he remained a nonentity.

The defensive reaction, however, remained exceptional. Physically, the relative similarity of the Mongols and Manchus to the

94 Peng Yingming, 'Guanyu woguo minzu gainian lishi de chubu kaocha' (Preliminary investigation with respect to the history of the concept of nation in our country), *Minzu yanjiu*, 1985, no. 2, pp. 5–7.
95 M. Banton, *Racial theories*, Cambridge University Press, 1987, p. 2.

Han impeded the development of theories based on categorical differences. Culturally, apart from Buddhism, which had spread through China during a period of disorder, no serious challenge had ever affected the élite's symbolic universe. It was only in the nineteenth century that the Confucian universe would gradually disintegrate in the face of a complex combination of endogenous and exogenous factors.

2

RACE AS TYPE (1793–1895)

During the nineteenth century, a new social environment was shaped by internal and external developments. Population growth, social dislocation, peasant rebellions, administrative fragmentation and political crises were the most important aspects of internal change. Western intrusions from the Opium War (1839–42) onwards were superimposed upon this established pattern of internal decline.

The arrival of Westerners by the middle of the nineteenth century also impinged upon pre-existing tensions between various trends of Confucianism. In the eighteenth century, discontent with imperial orthodoxy among Qing literati led to the flourishing of an alternative trend of thought that emphasized evidential research (*kaozhengxue*) at the expense of philosophical speculation.[1] It attacked the dominant Neo-Confucian ideology and hoped to reconstruct original Confucianism as formulated by the sage-kings of antiquity. Encouraged by the Jesuits' introduction of aspects of Western exact sciences during the late Ming and early Qing, the evidential research movement was also characterized by a concern with precise scholarship and practical matters. It was interested in linguistics, astronomy, mathematics, geography and epigraphy. The assault of evidential research on Neo-Confucian orthodoxy would lead to the theoretical rejection of the entire Confucian legacy during the New Culture Movement at the beginning of the twentieth century. The evidential research movement also set the stage for the social and political conclusions drawn by the New Text movement.[2] The revival of former Han

1 On the development of the evidential research movement, see B.A. Elman, *From philosophy to philology: Intellectual and social aspects of change in late imperial China*, Cambridge, Mass: Harvard University Press, 1984.
2 B.A. Elman, *Classicism, politics, and kinship: The Ch'ang-chou school of New Text Confucianism in late imperial China*, Berkeley: University of California Press, 1990.

31

New Text Confucianism in the eighteenth century led to the forging of an ideological framework for statecraft reform at the beginning of the nineteenth century. Well before the first Opium War, New Text scholars were seeking pragmatic solutions to organizational breakdown in the empire.

Seen from an internal perspective, the eighteenth and nineteenth centuries were an age of profound transition for the Confucian world. The intrusion of the West increased existing tensions between different schools of thought and accelerated the deliquescence of the Confucian symbolic universe as a whole. A symbolic universe, as was underlined in the preceding chapter, is a set of beliefs that integrates different provinces of meaning and encompasses the institutional order in a symbolic totality. It can be seen as a collective delusional system that legitimizes the structure and values of a society; it provides people with an all-encompassing frame of reference which defines reality and bestows meaning to life. The presence of Europeans, supported by military strength, economic power and organizational ability, confronted the Confucian élite with a divergent symbolic universe. By its very existence, Western social cosmology demonstrated that the Confucian world view was purely relative. Chinese intellectuals increasingly discovered that the Confucian universe in which they operated was neither total nor absolute. The social construction of reality, it appeared, was precarious and needed to be defended. Reform-minded scholars from Wei Yuan (1794–1856) to Kang Youwei (1858–1927) responded both to developments of particular schools of thought within the Confucian universe and to the confrontation of this universe as a whole with the Western world.

It would be arbitrary to assign a date to the confrontation of an imperial cosmology to a Christian universe. There was never a 'clash' between China and the West, only a gradual phenomenon of interaction. As a concession to periodization, one could tentatively consider the Macartney mission to the Qianlong court in 1793 as a point of departure. The failure of the British mission was partly due to divergent visions of court ritual. Imperial cosmology, for instance, gave a privileged position to differentiation, whereas the European vision emphasized homogeneity.[3] Naitō Konan, a leading sinologist at the beginning of the twentieth century, also began his analysis of the racial issue in late imperial China with the Macartney mission.[4]

The threat posed by Western military and economic power during the nineteenth century was not insignificant, but it may have been exaggerated. The military threat comprised a series of short campaigns that resulted in two treaties. At the end of the first 'Opium War', the treaty of Nanjing ceded a barren island called Hong Kong to Britain and opened five ports to British residence and trade. The concessions granted to the coastal trading powers in this treaty (mainly extraterritoriality, an indemnity, taxation rights, and most-favoured-nation treatment) were based on concessions made to the Khan of Kokand in Xinjiang between 1831 and 1835.[5] The Nanjing agreement was more part of a general change in frontier policy initiated by the Qing than an 'unequal treaty' exacted by foreign imperialism. The Anglo-French invasion and the second treaty settlement (1857–60) enlarged the scope and nature of foreign activities in China and opened most of the empire to Western contact. Two decades later, the French took Vietnam, China's principal tributary in the south. Foreign military threats, however, never matched the intensity, scope and duration of China's internal military challenges, such as the Taiping war (1850–64), described as the most destructive war in the nineteenth century, with casualties of at least twenty million. Moreover the economic impact of the West was so insignificant that it has been aptly described as 'a flea in the elephant's ear'.[6] In fact, Chinese merchants benefitted from the transport and

3 See James L. Hevia, 'A multitude of lords: Qing court ritual and the Macartney embassy of 1793', *Late Imperial China*, 10, no. 2 (Dec. 1989), pp. 72–105.
4 J.A. Fogel, *Politics and sinology: The case of Naito Konan (1866–1934)*, Cambridge, Mass.: Harvard University Press, 1984, p. 135.
5 See Joseph Fletcher, 'The heyday of the Ch'ing order in Mongolia, Sinkiang and Tibet' in D. Twitchett and J.K. Fairbank (eds), *The Cambridge history of China*, Cambridge University Press, 1978, vol. 10, part 1, pp. 375–85.
6 P.A. Cohen, *Discovering history in China: American historical writing on the recent Chinese past*, New York: Columbia University Press, 1984, p. 125.

banking facilities provided by foreign companies and developed their enterprises in symbiosis with European partners.

The development of a racial consciousness during the nineteenth century, however, was due largely to internal developments. Pamela Kyle Crossley has convincingly demonstrated that the sense of identity through racial descent became important to the Qing court in the eighteenth century. By the Qianlong period (1736–95), the Manchu court was progressively turning towards a rigid taxonomy of culturally-distinct races (*zu*) within China. The reasons for this increasingly racialist orientation are complex, as Crossley's article on the Chinese-martial banners demonstrates.[7] For the purpose of this study, however, it will suffice to observe that racial taxonomies were being formed well before the intrusion of Europeans in China.

Besides the official Qing construction of race, it has also been noted that ethnic prejudice permeated different levels of society during the first half of the nineteenth century. According to Mark Elliott,[8] whose work focuses on ethnic conflicts in nineteenth-century Jiangnan, ethnic rivalry and prejudice existed well before the Opium War. The threshold for the articulation of ethnic hostilities was the Taiping war, which was derived partly from Hakka-Punti hostility. The anti-Manchu arguments that had been developed by Ming loyalists during the seventeenth century struck a popular chord with the Taiping.[9] They were also influenced by heterodox religions, mainly millenarian Buddhism and Protestant Christianity. The Old Testament, translated by Taiping rebels,

7 Pamela Kyle Crossley, 'The Qianlong retrospect on the Chinese-martial (*hanjun*) banners', *Late Imperial China*, 10, no. 1 (June 1989), pp. 63–107; see also her 'Thinking about ethnicity in early modern China', *Late Imperial China*, 11, no. 1 (June 1990), p. 20, and *Orphan warriors: Three Manchu generations and the end of the Qing world*, Princeton University Press, 1990.
8 Mark Elliott, 'Bannerman and townsman: Ethnic tension in nineteenth century Jiangnan', *Late Imperial China*, 11, no. 1 (June 1990), pp. 36–74.
9 Y. Muramatsu, 'Some themes in Chinese rebel ideologies' in A.F. Wright (ed.), *The Confucian persuasion*, Stanford University Press, 1960, p. 253; see also V.Y.C. Shih, 'Some Chinese rebel ideologies', *T'oung Pao*, 44 (1956), pp. 150–226, and V.Y.C. Shih, 'The ideology of the T'ai-p'ing t'ien-kuo', *Sinologica*, 3 (1953), pp. 1–15.

supported the idea that 'races can be classified according to their colour' (*yi se lie zu*).[10]

Until the 1890s the Chinese discourse of race can best be understood as a process of defensive stereotyping, comparable to European racial thought of the first half of the nineteenth century. Before Darwin, European typology divided mankind into several permanent racial types, each of which was believed to have existed without change since its creation on earth.[11] Although such typology can be found in an embryonic form in nineteenth-century China, it never achieved a significant level of theorization. The word 'type' is used here rather as a synonym for stereotype, or the simplified image which a given group has about an outgroup.

It should be underlined that, as in nineteenth-century Europe, only a section of the educated élite felt compelled to reduce outgroups to manageable stereotypes. Although the racial imagery described below is by no means representative of the whole of Chinese society, it did appeal to an authoritative fraction of the scholar-gentry. How the subordinate classes reacted or participated in the formulation of a racial imagery is an important question which still remains to be investigated. Generally, the population remained relatively unaffected by the theories elaborated at élite level. It may be hypothesized, however, that a certain degree of reciprocal influence existed between élite and popular culture. Whereas the scholar-gentry could transcribe ideas formulated at a popular level into the official rhetoric, it is equally plausible that the racial imagery used at élite level filtered down to the subordinate classes. It would be more fruitful to describe relations between dominant culture and popular culture as a phenomenon of circularity,[12] or constant interaction, rather than as one of strict autarky. Furthermore, as Berger and Luckmann have emphasized, the coexistence of a more or less naive mythology at a popular level

10 Peng, 'Guanyu woguo minzu gainian', pp. 5–7.
11 See Banton, *Racial theories*, ch. 2.
12 The idea of circularity between different cultural levels was first formulated by Mikhail Bakhtin in *Rabelais and his world*, Cambridge, Mass.: Harvard University Press, 1968.

with a more sophisticated cosmology among the élite often serves to maintain the *same* symbolic universe.[13]

DEMONOLOGY

A common historical response to serious threats directed towards a symbolic universe is 'nihilation', or the conceptual liquidation of everything inconsistent with official doctrine. Foreigners were labelled 'barbarians' or 'devils' to be conceptually eliminated. The official rhetoric reduced the Westerner to a devil, a ghost, an evil and unreal goblin hovering on the border of humanity. Many texts of the first half of the nineteenth century referred to the English as 'foreign devils' (*yangguizi*), 'devil slaves' (*guinu*), 'barbarian devils' (*fangui*), 'island barbarians' (*daoyi*), 'blue-eyed barbarian slaves' (*biyan yinu*), or 'red-haired barbarians' (*hongmaofan*). Officials in Canton wrote that 'even though the people have had social intercourse with the barbarians, they still call them *fan-kuei*. They do not even consider them to be human beings.'[14] The only English textbook available in the bookshops near the factories in Canton was simply called *Devils' Talk*.[15] On a more sophisticated level, Wang Kaiyun (1833–1916), a celebrated scholar from Hunan province, compared foreigners to matter (*wu*), an entity without life.[16] The perception of foreigners as devils, which permeated official rhetoric until the beginning of the 1860s, was important enough to incite missionaries to contribute articles in Chinese on the correct distinction between humans and devils.[17]

---

13 P.L. Berger and T. Luckmann, *The social construction of reality: A treatise in the sociology of knowledge*, New York: Doubleday, 1966, p. 129.
14 F. Wakeman, *Strangers at the gate: Social disorder in south China, 1839–1861*, Berkeley: University of California Press, 1966, p. 79.
15 Hunter, *The 'fan kwae'*, p. 63.
16 Hao Yen-p'ing and Wang Erh-min, 'Changing Chinese views of Western relations, 1840–1895' in D. Twitchett and J.K. Fairbank (eds), *The Cambridge history of China*, Cambridge University Press, 1980, vol. 11, part 2, p. 186.
17 The *Wanguo gongbao*, in 1882–3 alone, published several articles on humans and devils: 'Renguibian' (Distinguishing men from devils), 8 July 1882, pp. 421b–22; 'Bianzheng rengui lun' (About properly distinguishing men

Dehumanization of the enemy is a process common to all societies. During religious violence in early modern France, for instance, the state's enemies were transformed into 'vermin' or 'devils' before being dragged through the streets and having their genitalia mutilated and their limbs chopped off.[18] Diabolization of the enemy not only sanctioned violence, it also enhanced group identity. In the face of foreign threats, group cohesion was promoted by dichotomizing the world into subhuman aliens and human Chinese. It is legitimate to wonder to what extent the use of a derogatory terminology in China reflected genuine feelings of superiority or merely a passive compliance with an established discourse. As with most historical texts of this sort, it is difficult to distinguish personal feelings from official rhetoric. Did Joseph Goebbels, for example, genuinely subscribe to the idea of Jewish inferiority or was he consciously exploiting an official Nazi theme for propaganda purposes? The historian will never know, and Goebbels might not have known himself. The whole question of the 'reality' of a belief, however, seems a somewhat empty one: the existence of a textual discourse, whether imposed by circumstances or freely chosen, reflects a certain consciousness. It is this consciousness which is of interest to the anthropological historian, not the personal state of mind of an author. Even if certain officials did not 'really' believe in the barbarian nature of foreigners, they did actively participate in the maintenance of a hierarchical consciousness by accepting a discourse based on the notion of foreign inferiority.

In fact, invaders were perceived as demons as early as the Song dynasty. Japanese scholarship even traces the foreign-demon in Daoism to the late fourth century AD. Timothy Barrett emphasizes that, although there is no clear evidence for the existence of an indigenous tradition of fundamentalist religious racism, the equation of invaders with demons by the populace in

---

from devils), 2 Dec. 1882, pp. 146–7; 'Lun rengui yi bian' (About distinguishing between humans and devils), 26 Aug. 1883, and others.
18 N.Z. Davis, *Society and culture in early modern France*, Stanford University Press, 1975, p. 181.

seventeenth-century China is to be taken seriously.[19] There is nothing to suggest that this perception was much altered during the nineteenth century. Both popular religion and élite rhetoric demonized the foreigner in an attempt to maintain a common symbolic universe.

TERATOLOGY

Skin colour performed an important function of social differentiation in demonological terminology. 'The Chinese call the barbarians "devils", and differentiate them according to their skin colour,' wrote Xu Shidong (1814–73) in the 1840s.[20] There were 'white devils' (*baigui*) and 'black devils' (*heigui*), presumably the Indian Sepoy troops in the service of the British. 'The white ones are cold and dull as the ashes of frogs, the black ones are ugly and dirty as coal,' explained Jin He (1819–85).[21] White ash and black coal, both were the teratological products of death, two facets of the same unreality: the foreign demon.

Social position distinguished whites from blacks: 'Black devils are slaves, white devils are rulers,' commented one perceptive author.[22] The origin of the black devil was not always clear, as one report on the British troops in Ningbo testifies: 'They carry off young men, shave their heads, paint their bodies with black lacquer, give them a drug which makes them dumb, and so turn them into black devils, using them to carry heavy loads.'[23] Others believed that the blacks were recruited merely because of their

19 For a discussion of this religious demonology and references to the relevant literature, see T.H. Barrett, 'History writing and spirit writing in seventeenth-century China', *Modern Asian Studies*, 23, no. 3 (1989), pp. 606–7.
20 Xu Shidong, *Toutouji* (Notes on stealing a head) in A Ying, comp., *Yapian zhanzheng wenxue ji* (Collection of literary writings on the Opium War), Beijing: Guji chubanshe, 1957, p. 836.
21 Jin He, 'Shuo gui' (About ghosts) in A Ying, *Yapian zhanzheng*, p. 44.
22 Quoted in A Ying, *Yapian zhanzheng*, p. 967.
23 Arthur Waley, *The Opium War through Chinese eyes*, London: Geo. Allen and Unwin, 1958, pp. 163–4.

stupidity: idiots were easier to handle.[24] Such stereotypes abound in the literature of the first half of the nineteenth century, after which they started to filter down to the lower levels of popular culture. The ease with which the élite image of the black slave was accommodated by the popular lore of the kunlun slave, the black deities of the Buddhist hell and traditional barbarian imagery remains to be assessed, however.

Within higher culture, a well-established aesthetic value system contributed to the rise of racial typification. Prose and poetry derided the physical appearance of the foreigner. For example:

> When the foreign devil entered China, he heaved a first sigh: he saw the elegantly chiselled features of the Chinese, embodiment of human feelings, neatly dressed and capped. The foreigner and the Chinese are greatly different! The foreign devil heaved a second sigh when he looked in the mirror: [. . .] yellow hair on the head, curly hair on the body, green pupils. Disconsolately sitting head in hand, he looks like a monkey goblin![25]

In official documents as well as in poetic literature, descriptions of foreigners were highly stereotyped, often merely repeating the age-old clichés traditionally reserved for frontier peoples. Many characterizations were conveniently encapsulated in the formula 'blue eyes black beard' (*biyanwuxu*), in which both colours could vary. Wang Zhongyang, for instance, pictured the English as having 'the beak of an eagle, the eyes of a cat, red beards and hair'.[26] His portrayal of the foreigner was simply plagiarized from the *Mingshi* (History of the Ming). Wang shared the common belief that the green 'cat' eyes of the foreigner could not stand the

24 Cui Guoyin, *Chushi Mei Ri Bi riji* (Mission to America, Japan and Peru), Beijing: Huangshan shushe, 1988, p. 105.
25 Author unknown, 'Waiguo yangren tan shi sheng' (The foreigner sighs ten times) in A Ying, *Yapian zhanzheng*, p. 253; the original text has been lost, and some parts of the poem remain obscure.
26 Wang Zhongyang, 'Gengzi liuyue wenzhou shanjing' (Alarm at hearing the foreign ships beyond the mountains in the sixth month of 1840) in A Ying, *Yapian zhanzheng*, p. 191.

sunlight, and had to remain shut at noon. Another poet, writing during the Opium War, found that the eyes of the foreign ghost were 'blue and dizzy'.[27] For one observer, 'the white ones are really ghosts; the sounds of their speech are similar to birds, their shins and chest are covered with hair, their green eyes suffer when they look in the distance.'[28] Demonology and popular lore converged in the ascription of a negative ontological status to the white man. A popular text entitled *Short study of the English red-haired barbarians* expressed the belief that foreign soldiers 'cannot run, as their legs and feet are bandaged, and are difficult to bend or to stretch; if they fall forward, they cannot rise again: this is why they often suffer from a bleeding nose [in other words, are often defeated in battle].'[29] This cliché was repeatedly used at the highest levels,[30] for instance by Yuqian (1793–1841), the governor-general of Liang-Jiang who had tortured several British captives to death during the Opium War. Statecraft scholars like Bao Shichen (1775–1855) questioned such a belief,[31] but it was still being put forward by some high-ranking officials at the end of the nineteenth century.[32] It was also adopted by the subordinate classes. In 1949, for example, an Anglo-Chinese girl returned to China to join the revolution. Her room-mates in the army assailed her with questions: 'Is it true English people only have one straight bone in the leg and can't bend their knees?'[33] This example clearly illustrates how ideas could shift from one cultural level to another.

27 Zhu Kuizhi, *Miao jixiangshi shichao* (Collected poems from the wonderfully propitious room) in A Ying, *Yapian zhanzheng*, p. 171.
28 Lu Song, 'Jiangzhou shugan' (Relating impressions from Jiangzhou) in A Ying, *Yapian zhanzheng*, p. 143.
29 Wang Wentai and Huang Pengnian, *Hongmaofan Yingjili kaolüe* (A short study of the English red-haired barbarians) in A Ying, *Yapian zhanzheng*, p. 757.
30 Hao and Wang, 'Changing Chinese views', p. 153.
31 Qi Sihe *et al.* (eds), *Yapian zhanzheng* (The Opium War), Shanghai: Shenzhou guoguangshe, 1954, vol. 4, p. 466.
32 For instance the prominent Manchu bannerman, Gangyi; see Tang Zhijun, *Wuxu bianfa renwu zhuangao* (Draft biographies of leading figures of the reform movement), Beijing: Zhonghua shuju, 1982, p. 530.
33 Esther Ying Cheo, *Black Country girl in red China*, London: Hutchinson, 1980, p. 32.

ANATOMY

Speculations about the physiology of the alien confirmed his congenital inadequacy. Some upheld the belief that the foreigner's digestive system was dependent on tea and rhubarb. Without these two fundamental ingredients, the barbarian would become blind or would suffer from serious diseases of the intestines.[34] This misconception prevailed among a substantial number of scholar-officials after the Opium War.

The Chinese popular imagination was stimulated by the relative lack of familiarity with anatomical knowledge until the middle of the nineteenth century.[35] The human body was considered a gift from the ancestors that should be preserved intact; mutilation or dissection of a corpse was perceived as disrespectful to the whole lineage. Traditional medicine merely hinted at human organs in their relation to cosmological elements.[36] Only by the end of the

---

34 Hao and Wang, 'Changing Chinese views', p. 154.

35 See M. Porkert, *Die chinesische Medizin*, Düsseldorf: ECON Verlag, 1982, p. 41.

36 The last recorded dissection dated from the Song dynasty. It described the vivisection of fifty-six political prisoners (Sugimoto Masayoshi and D.L. Swain, *Science and culture in traditional Japan, A.D. 600–1854*, Cambridge, Mass.: MIT Press, 1978, p. 379). Basic elements of anatomy introduced by the missionaries in the seventeenth century remained virtually unnoticed. Adam Schall (1591–1666), a German Jesuit, had presented a treatise on anatomy to an inquiring scholar from Shandong named Bi Gongchen. It was translated by Jean Terrenz as *Renshenshuo* (On the human body) and published at the instigation of Bi in 1635, entitled *Taixi renshen shuogai* (Elements of the Westerner's body) (see A.W. Hummel, 'Pi Kung-ch'en' in *Eminent Chinese*, pp. 621–2). A second source was provided by the Jesuit Dominique Parennin (1665–1741). The emperor Kang Xi (1662–1722), after having been relieved of a malignant fever by French Jesuits in 1692, showed a genuine interest in Western medicine. Responding to an imperial edict, Parennin compiled a text on anatomy in the Manchu language, complete with ninety drawings of human organs (see F.R. Lee and J.B. Saunders, *The Manchu anatomy and its historical origin*, Taipei: Li Ming Cultural Enterprise Co., 1981).

Nathan Sivin denies that anatomy was underdeveloped, and underlines the importance of forensic medicine in China. The two sources he refers to, however, indicate that forensic medicine did not undergo any significant developments after the thirteenth century. To downplay differences between China

eighteenth century did a Chinese doctor begin to record human dissections scientifically. Wang Qingren (1768–1831)[37] dissected a number of corpses which he had obtained after an epidemic of measles and dysentery in his home province in 1798: 'I thus saw about thirty perfect bodies and in this way I came to know and compare the various parts with the ancient drawings and found they did not agree.'[38] When he finally published a small volume on

---

and the West further, Sivin asserts that anatomical knowledge in Europe was developed only for reasons of academic prestige and had no clinical utility until the mid-eighteenth century (N. Sivin, 'Science and medicine in imperial China – the state of the field', *Journal of Asian Studies*, 47, no. 1 (Feb. 1988), p. 59). This may be a misleading claim. The immediate effect of new anatomical knowledge in the sixteenth century was an improvement in surgery. Military practitioners like Ambroise Paré adopted anatomy to meet the concrete needs of surgery in the imperial armies; the anatomist Girolamo Fabrizio developed mechanics of muscular motion which also found practical application; even plastic surgery was developed by Gaspare Tagliacozzi on the basis of anatomical knowledge. Anatomy and dissection were popular with artists, the best known example being of course Leonardo da Vinci. As Philippe Ariès has brilliantly demonstrated, anatomy was also a highly fashionable science with the educated public as early as the sixteenth and seventeenth centuries, a phenomenon linked to the emergence of a morbid eroticism, the illegitimate union of Eros and Thanatos; P. Ariès, *Essais sur l'histoire de la mort en Occident*, Paris: Seuil, 1975, p. 114. Anatomical knowledge may have been fairly sophisticated in the Qing within certain professional circles, but it was certainly not common among the wider public.

37 On Wang, see Ma Kanwen, 'Zuguo Qingdai jiechu de yixuejia Wang Qingren' (Wang Qingren, outstanding medical scientist of the Qing dynasty), *Kexueshi jikan*, 6 (1963), pp. 66–74.

38 K. Chimin Wong and Wu Lien-teh, *History of Chinese medicine*, Tianjin: The Tientsin Press, 1932, p. 223. The Japanese had reached the same conclusion half a century earlier. Some physicians discovered by the mid-eighteenth century that traditional Chinese medical texts were at variance with what they had actually seen. It was concluded that there had to be some physiological differences between Chinese and Japanese. Dr Sugita Gempaku (1733–1817) witnessed a post-mortem dissection of an old woman in 1771, and found out that his observations agreed with a Dutch textbook of anatomy, which he subsequently undertook to translate; see D. Keene, *The Japanese discovery of Europe, 1720–1830*, rev. edn, Stanford University Press, 1969, pp. 21–2.

his work in 1830, he was condemned by colleagues as inhuman, sadistic and mad.[39]

The absence of common anatomical knowledge lent itself to speculation about barbarian physiology. A pornographic novel of the eighteenth century, for instance, wondered whether the European body functioned in the same way as that of the Chinese.[40] Yu Zhengxie (1775–1840), a major scholar noted for his strong interest in research and his liberal ideas, observed the following differences between the foreigner and the Chinese:

– Foreign devils had four lobes in the lungs, Chinese had six.
– Foreign devils had only four chambers in the heart, Chinese had seven.
– The liver of the foreign devil was located at the right side of the heart, the Chinese liver was situated at the left.
– The foreign devil had four testicles, Chinese had two.[41]

Such misunderstandings were clearly replicated by popular culture in Europe. It was not an uncommon belief, for instance, that Chinese women had horizontal vaginas, somehow matching their slant eyes. Until the 1860s, Chinese females were displayed in zoos and exhibitions. A Chinese lady ('with small lotus feet, only 2½ inches in length!') was exhibited in Hyde Park from 1843 to 1851.[42] European perceptions of race, however, are clearly beyond the considerations of this study.

Driven by the vigour of his four testicles, the satyr-like foreigner was relentless in the pursuit of sensual pleasures. Anti-Christian leaflets spread the idea that Christians practised sodomy with their fathers and brothers and fornicated with their mothers and sisters. 'During the first three months of life the anuses of all

39 Yen Chung-nien, 'A Chinese anatomist of the nineteenth century', *Eastern Horizon*, 15, no. 5 (1976), p. 50.
40 K. McMahon, 'A case for Confucian sexuality: The eighteenth-century novel, *Yesou puyan*', *Late Imperial China*, 9, no. 2 (Dec. 1988), p. 38, n. 22.
41 Li Ao, *Dubai xiade chuantong* (Tradition descended as a monologue), Taipei: Wenxing shudian, 1988, p. 4.
42 J. Ch'en, *China and the West: Society and culture, 1815–1937*, London: Hutchinson, 1979, plate between pp. 224–5.

[Christian] infants – male and female – are plugged up with a small hollow tube, which is taken out at night. They call this "retention of the vital essence". It causes the anus to dilate so that upon growing up sodomy will be facilitated'. Celestials became the objects of the devils' licentiousness. Chinese ladies were ravished in the confessional. Young Chinese boys were abducted by missionaries to be sodomized, claimed another anti-Christian pamphlet.[43] Projection certainly plays a role in the formation of group types. People often tend to attribute to outsiders unacceptable impulses within themselves. Stereotypes of the outgroup are fantasies derived from unconscious needs of the ingroup. In the presence of the foreigner, strait-laced Confucian ethics were thrown overboard and imagination was allowed to run amok. A feeling of sexual inadequacy also lurked behind the amplification of the barbarian's reproductive organs: it was believed that Christians gave Chinese female converts aphrodisiacs and initiated them in the pleasures of sex; they would then despise their husbands.[44] Xenophobia found an easy ally in sexual fear, especially among the common people.

The foreign threat was further circumscribed by stigmatization. Many Chinese were struck by the hairy appearance of foreigners. Centuries before, the bearded missionaries had already made a durable impression. Giulio Aleni, for instance, had been described as a 'man with blue eyes and the beard of a dragon' during his first visit to Fujian province between 1625 and 1639.[45] As cultural clichés about the barbarians gradually turned into racial stereotypes after the Opium War, hair became a central element when the foreigner was being described. The New Text adherent Lin Zexu (1785–1850), the Imperial Commissioner appointed to

43 P.A. Cohen, 'Christian missions and their impact to 1900' in D. Twitchett and J.K. Fairbank (eds), *The Cambridge history of China*, Cambridge University Press, 1978, vol. 10, part 1, p. 569.

44 P.A. Cohen, *China and Christianity: The missionary movement and the growth of Chinese antiforeignism, 1860–1870*, Cambridge, Mass.: Harvard University Press, 1963, p. 91.

45 Jacques Gernet, *China and the Christian impact: A conflict of cultures*, Cambridge University Press, 1985, p. 250, n. 12.

suppress the Canton opium trade, focused on beards in his diary:
'They have heavy beards, much of which they shave, leaving one
curly tuft, which at first sight creates a surprising effect. Indeed,
they do really look like devils; and when the people of these parts
call them "devils" it is no mere empty term of abuse.'[46] Zhigang,
head of the first diplomatic mission to the West from 1866 to
1870, confided to his journal that he was shocked by the natives of
Ceylon, whose 'black hair, about four centimetres long, covers
their chest and all of their back.'[47]

Fixation on hair transcended the private realm of the diary. In
1848, Xu Jiyu (1795–1873), governor of Fujian province, published an influential work on world geography, in which Europeans were described as follows:

Europeans are tall and fair-skinned. They have high noses,
recessed sockets and yellow eyes (some have black eyes). Their
hair is often left on the temples or coiled around the cheeks.
Some have it straight like Chinese, some have curly whiskers,
some are entirely shaven, some leave it long, some separate the
whiskers and the moustache like the Chinese. Young and old
alike, the hair is worn about a decimetre long; it is cut when it is
longer. Hair and beards are often yellow or red (during the
Ming, the Dutch were called 'red-haired', and recently the
English too have been called 'red-haired', both because their
hair is yellowish-reddish. However, all Europeans are like this,
not only people from these two countries). Some of them have
black hair (those with black hair also have black eyes). This is
also true for the hair and eyes of girls.[48]

During the second half of the nineteenth century, there were
further detailed descriptions of barbarian hair-growth to satisfy
the curious reader. Zhang Deyi (1847–1919) reported from Europe
that 'when about twenty years old, the moustache and beard of

46 Waley, *The Opium War*, pp. 68–9.
47 Zhigang, *Chushi Taixiji* (Notes on the first mission to the West), Beijing:
Yuelu shushe, 1985, p. 374.
48 Xu Jiyu, *Yinghuan zhilüe* (A brief survey of the maritime circuit), Osaka:
Kanbun edn, 1861, *juan* 4, p. 7b.

foreign men start to grow. As a rule, they do not cut or shave them, allowing them to develop. At the age of fifty or sixty, either they start to trim the moustache, or they cut both moustache and beard, as it is said that when men become older and weaker, there is no further need to wear them, as they hinder whilst drinking or eating.'[49] Even Western females were thought to be hairy beings.[50] In France, noticed Zhang, 'many women have long beards and moustaches.'[51]

The pictorial world of late imperial China, situated at the privileged juncture of high culture and folk beliefs, also teemed with furry bogeymen. Picture-story books for popular consumption, called *lianhuan tuhua*, started representing foreigners from the Ming onwards.[52] A booklet on Macao, popular in the south during the eighteenth century, included ten drawings of the 'various barbarians'.[53] Bearded, moustached and whiskered, tall like a vision, with a conch-like nose and squinting eyes, the Westerner loomed regularly in the Chinese iconography of exotic countries during the late Qing.[54] From the xenophobic drawings of the Empire

---

49 Zhang Deyi, *Suishi Faguo ji* (Notes on following the mission to France), Beijing: Yuelu shushe, 1985, p. 450.

50 One foreigner travelling in the interior of China during the 1870s reported how his abundantly bearded but exceedingly short companion was consistently taken to be his wife. He overheard one observer explain to bystanders that 'in their country the women have beards exactly the same as the men'; C. Holcombe, *The real Chinaman*, New York: Dodd and Mead, 1895, p. 173. Misconceptions were of course rife on both sides: Zhang Deyi complained that in Russia many people mistook him for a woman because of his queue (pigtail) and his gown; Zhang Deyi, *Hanghai shuqi* (Travels abroad), Beijing: Yuelu shushe, 1985, p. 553. Chinese diplomats used to ride ladies' bicycles because of their long gowns, thereby reinforcing their female appearance to Westerners; see W.W. Yen, *East-West kaleidoscope 1877–1946: An autobiography*, New York: St John's University, 1974, p. 21.

51 Zhang Deyi, *Suishi Faguo ji*, p. 395; see also p. 424.

52 See A Ying, *Zhongguo lianhuan tuhua shihua* (History of the picture-story book), Beijing: Renmin meishu chubanshe, 1984.

53 Yin Guangren and Zhang Rulin, *Aomen jilüe* (Notes on Macao), 1751 edn, *juan* 2, ten plates.

54 See for instance the *Dianshizhai huabao*, a pictorial published by the highly popular *Shenbao* in Shanghai from 1884 to 1898.

to the anti-imperialist cartoons of the People's Republic, the
negatively accented vision of the foreigner would be dominated
by the stigma of hair. This early fixation on hair was due also to a
difference in customs, as can be seen from a missionary's description of a barber in the Middle Kingdom at the end of the eighteen-
eighties:

> The streets of every town abound in barbers, who find plenty of
> work shaving the heads and faces of the natives. It is not con-
> sidered good form to grow a moustache till a man is about forty
> years of age, and even then probably only half-a-dozen strag-
> gling hairs will appear on each side, while only old men wear a
> beard. The Chinese barber shaves every nook and cranny of the
> face with great care, even to the eyelid, nose, and ear, both
> inside and out.[55]

Odour was another characteristic of the foreigner. To be sure,
the nausea induced by sea travel and lax standards of hygiene
among many Europeans certainly did nothing to lessen the initial
shock of encounter. In texts concerning the Opium War, the
arrival of foreign troops was usually announced by an 'atmosphere
of demons' (*yaofen*) and a 'wind carrying the smell of rotten fish'
(*xingfeng*). At a lower level, the influential anti-Christian tract
Bixie jishi (1861) spread the idea that Westerners used to drink the
menstrual flow of women, which they regarded as a precious gift
conferred by God: this explained their unbearable stench.[56] Such
imagery rested upon genuine sensitivities, as foreign reports tes-
tify. One European was warned not to be shocked if a Chinese
lady held a handkerchief to her nose, 'for you as a foreigner are
credited with a nasty smell.'[57] John Hardy commented that 'what
they call our European odour is quite as nauseous to them as their

55 J.A. Turner, *Kwang Tung, or five years in south China*, Hong Kong: Oxford
University Press, 1988 (1st edn 1894), p. 136.
56 Cohen, *China and Christianity*, p. 50.
57 G.G. Barnes, *Enter China! A study in race contacts*, London: Edinburgh
House Press, 1928, p. 104.

yellow smell [*sic*] is to us',[58] revealing how easily natural perceptions could be polarized into reciprocal antagonism.

GEOGRAPHY

Interest in more pragmatic scholarship had been revived by the evidential research movement in the eighteenth century. Notions of world geography, however, remained minimal until the middle of the nineteenth century. Before the skirmishes with the English in Canton in the early 1840s, the Chinese public was dependent upon a small number of works for elementary notions of world geography. They were Chen Lunjiong's *Record of things seen and heard about the maritime countries* (*Haiguo wenjian lu*, 1730), Wang Dahai's *Annals of the barbarian maritime islands* (*Haidao yizhi*, 1760), and Xie Qinggao's *Maritime record* (*Hailu*, 1820). All three were based on the traditional barbarian imagery that had been passed down for hundreds of years. The widely used work of Chen Lunjiong, for instance, still referred to red-haired barbarians and the black devils of the dark continent. Ethnocentric aesthetic criteria were projected upon outsiders such as the Japanese, whose 'features and skin texture cannot be compared to the Chinese'.[59] These books were based on distorted information copied from previous compilations. Widespread plagiarism compounded the confusion and superficiality. For example, was England another name for Holland or was it a dependency of Holland? Portugal was near Malacca. France was originally Buddhist, later turned Catholic, and was finally believed to be the same as Portugal.[60]

During the 1840s, scholar officials directly involved in foreign affairs became increasingly aware of the need for a more adaptive

---

58 E.J. Hardy, *John Chinaman at home*, London: T. Fisher Unwin, 1907, p. 325.
59 Chen Lunjiong, *Haiguo wenjian lu* (Record of things seen and heard about the maritime countries), Zhengzhou: Zhongzhou guji chubanshe, 1985, p. 36.
60 These examples are taken from the new edition of the Guangdong provincial gazetteer edited under Ruan Yuan in 1819–22; see J.K. Fairbank, E.O. Reischauer and A.M. Craig, *East Asia: The modern transformation*, Boston: Houghton Mifflin, 1965, pp. 126–7.

perspective. Officials like Lin Zexu and New Text Confucianists such as Xu Jiyu or Wei Yuan compiled geographies concerned with more practical evaluations of the outside world. Their works, however, were fraught with ambivalence. On the one hand, they actively contributed to the dissolution of sinocentrism by relativizing their own universe's position: they revealed that China was only one nation among many others. On the other hand, their view of outsiders was deeply influenced by stereotypes. The *Yinghuan zhilüe*, for instance, was a geographical account compiled from various Western and Chinese sources by Xu Jiyu in 1848. Despite his personal contacts with foreigners in Xiamen, the author still believed that 'the hair and eyes of some [foreigners] gradually turn black when they come to China and stay for a long time. The features of such men and women half-resemble the Chinese.'[61] It was perhaps reassuring to know that residence in the Celestial Empire could half-humanize the foreigner.

Compensation characterized these early attempts at the construction of a different world view. 'In his discussion of the continents, he [Xu Jiyu] attempted to compensate for China's occupation of only a corner, and control of less than a half, of Asia by observing that Asia was the largest of the world's continents. He also felt compelled to deliver an opening statement on China's magnificence.'[62] Wei Yuan's treatise adopted a traditional vocabulary and categorized the world in ocean-regions that were in conformity with the classical image of China as a centred maritime world.[63]

Manipulation of spatial structures was combined with negative typification of outgroups. Xu Jiyu's account presented Africa as a desperately chaotic continent, inhabited by retrograde black barbarians. 'It is scorching, miasmic and pestilential. Its climate and its people are the worst of the four continents.' Ethiopians were described as animals 'living in holes and catching insects for food.'

61 Xu, *Yinghuan zhilüe, juan* 4, p. 7b.
62 F.W. Drake, *China charts the world: Hsu Chi-yü and his geography of 1848*, Cambridge, Mass.: Harvard University Press, 1975, p. 66.
63 J.K. Leonard, *Wei Yuan and China's rediscovery of the maritime world*, Cambridge, Mass.: Harvard University Press, 1984, p. 109.

In West Africa, the blacks 'go half-naked, not covering their genitals', freely coupling 'without distinguishing races' (*zhongzu wu bie*); enslaved, they 'never complain and never try to escape',[64] a remark that echoed the legends on the kunlun slave. Others compared Africa to the *hundun*, or Chaos, the primeval state of the universe according to Chinese folklore.[65] Tan Sitong (1865–98), a brilliant philosopher who would become one of the most radical reformers during the 1890s, also resorted to traditional concepts to divide the world into three regions in his 'Views on the management of world affairs' (1889). China, Korea, Tibet, Vietnam and Burma formed the core of the universe, called *huaxia zhi guo*, or Chinese states; Japan, Russia, Europe and North America constituted the *yidi zhi guo*, or States of the Barbarians; and Africa, South America and Australia were relegated to the lowest category, the *qinshou zhi guo*, or States of the Beasts.[66] The graphic portrayal of foreign countries in the popular Chinese press of the treaty ports was also replete with contempt for 'barbarian' continents like India and Africa, indicating that prejudice was not confined to sectors of the élite.[67] Popular encyclopedias, called *riyong leishu* (encyclopedias for daily use), channelled élite prejudice down to the lower levels of popular culture. Similar to Western almanacs, they dealt with household affairs, elementary education, sample contract forms for the ordinary citizen and clan regulations, and provided information on a range of topics that included food, clothes and travel routes.[68] Sakai Tadao, who has investigated these popular encyclopedias in detail, noted that sections on foreign barbarians were common even under the Ming.[69]

64 Xu, *Yinghuan zhilüe, juan* 8, pp. 1a, 5b, 17a.
65 Cui, *Chushi*, pp. 154, 179, 225, 294.
66 Tan Sitong, *Tan Sitong quanji* (Collected writings of Tan Sitong), Beijing: Zhonghua shuju, 1981, vol. 1, pp. 231–6.
67 J.S. Schmotzer, 'The graphic portrayal of "all under heaven" (*t'ien-hsia*): A short study of Chinese world views through pictorial representations', unpubl. doctoral thesis, Washington, DC: Georgetown University, 1973.
68 E.S. Rawski, *Education and popular literacy in Ch'ing China*, Ann Arbor: University of Michigan Press, 1979, pp. 114–15.
69 Sakai Tadai, 'Mindai no nichiyō ruishu to shomin kyōiku' (Ming popular

The reshapening of cultural representations, the remodelling of classificatory frames and an alteration of spatial organization were partial responses to shifting perceptions of the social environment during the middle of the nineteenth century. Just as the Midi – the South of France – was invented by revolutionary France to explode a regionalist discourse which impeded the conceptualization of vaster geographical frames,[70] so the formulation of a racial cosmology in China was part of a new identifying construct. As in France or anywhere else in nineteenth-century Europe, it was precisely those who attempted to forge new collective identities who were most eager to assign a negative status to outsiders. The relativization of the ingroup required the conceptual debasement of specific outgroups.

Negative typification, moreover, clearly acted as a kind of surrogate for emotional stability. When one looks at prejudices from a perspective that takes biological factors into account, they can be regarded as some sort of compensation. The need for emotional stability correlates with the formation of stereotypes, especially in times of anxiety.[71]

TYPOLOGY

Hereditary patterns of perception determine the mental representation with which the human species approaches the world. Our modes of perception can only be described as rough approximations. Exactly how much these biological limitations contribute to the formation of a racial consciousness still remains to

encyclopedias and popular education) in Hayashi Tomoharu, *Kinsei Chūgoku kyōiku shi kenkyū* (History of modern Chinese education), Tokyo: Kokudosha, 1958, p. 119.

70 See Philippe Martel (ed.), *L'invention du Midi. Représentation du Sud pendant la période révolutionnaire*, Aix-en-Provence: Edisud, in the series *Amiras: Repères Occitans*, no. 15–16, 1987.

71 See Heiner Flohr, 'Biological bases of social prejudices' in V. Reynolds, V. Falgar and I. Vine (eds), *The sociobiology of ethnocentrism: Evolutionary dimensions of xenophobia, discrimination, racism and nationalism*, London: Croom Helm, 1987, pp. 190–207, esp. p. 203.

be determined. Fear of strangers is certainly a major input into the ethnocentric syndrome. This affective reaction appears during infancy, but gradually fades before the end of the first year. It is probable, however, that there remains a readiness to react in a xenophobic way towards persons who are substantially different from one's expectations, and that this can be actively encouraged within highly discriminatory cultures.[72]

Foreigners travelling in China during the years after the Opium War were generally met with alarm. 'Indeed it was painful to observe the undue timidity that men, women, and children of all classes evinced at the sight of the foreigner [. . .] At fifty yards off, my appearance was the signal for women to bolt into their houses with the screaming children and bar the doors [. . .] A crowd of gaping mouths and staring eyes would follow at a distance.'[73]

Those who finally discovered that the foreigners' legs were not so stiff that they would simply fall, that they were not stone-blind, and that their faces were not uniformly red still judged their appearance awesome and ugly. 'They vote his large nose ugly, dislike his pale complexion, criticise the color of his eyes, and object to the angle at which they are set.'[74] Foreigners had 'huge feet' and were 'mightily tall'; some had a head 'as large as a bucket'.[75] These emotional reactions, the product of a complex interplay between ignorance, fear and prejudice, are still rife today, especially in the more secluded hinterland, and are nourished by a vivid popular imagery and a strong sense of biological exclusiveness. Needless to say, the same type of reaction can easily be found in Europe.

The first encounters of Chinese envoys abroad with coloured people were equally dominated by fear. Zhang Deyi found that the Mexicans had 'fat features, flat noses and big bones; they are black

72 I. Vine, 'Inclusive fitness and the self-system: The roles of human nature and sociocultural processes in intergroup discrimination' in Reynolds, *Sociobiology*, p. 69.

73 W.C. Milne, *Life in China*, London: G. Routledge, 1857, pp. 113–14.

74 Holcombe, *The real Chinaman*, pp. 172–3.

75 E.H. Parker, *Chinese account of the Opium War*, Wilmington: Scholarly Resources, 1972, pp. 35 and 138; Wang Zhi, *Haike ritan* (Notebooks of a journey to England), Taipei: Wenhai chubanshe, 1969, p. 261.

or yellow. Males and females, old and young, they all look like devils; they are shocking and scaring.'[76] Representatives of three East African countries whom he encountered in London were 'frightening with their iron faces and silver teeth'.[77] The Manchu dignitary Binchun, travelling abroad for the first time in 1866 in the company of Robert Hart, was scared by the prostitutes of Ceylon. 'They have their hair coiled up in a bun, deep-red lips and faces coloured like pale ink. When they see passing travellers, their laughing dimples, their exposed teeth, and their bare feet frighten people.'[78] The black whore did not inspire the Celestial; her Caucasian companion also failed to allure the diffident mandarin. The big-breasted, azure-eyed prostitute exuded a sexuality that scared the prospective client away. In the 1890s, one of these noted that 'most of them have big teeth and tousled hair, as ugly as devils and as frightful as lionesses. They freeze the hearts of beholders.'[79]

Traditional imagery distorted the Chinese perception of the foreigner. Chinese attracted by ethnology found only tedious accounts that tirelessly repeated age-old clichés, some dating back to the *Shanhaijing*:

> The student interested in ethnology may find in the bookstores of Peking and other Chinese cities to-day volumes containing descriptive accounts of some of these outside barbarians, with carefully executed representations of them done in water-colors. One type has ears reaching to the earth, another has no legs worthy of mention. The representation of one tribe forces the student to the conclusion that the Chinese must have heard, and with some accuracy, of the gorilla. One race is pictured as having its face as a sort of boss in low relief upon the breast, while another carries its head conveniently located under the

76 Zhang Deyi, *Ou Mei huanyouji* (Notes on travelling around Europe and America), Beijing: Yuelu shushe, 1985, pp. 649–50.
77 Zhang Deyi, *Suishi Ying E ji* (Notes on following the mission to England and Russia), Beijing: Yuelu shushe, 1985, p. 570.
78 Binchun, *Chengcha biji* (Travels abroad), Beijing: Yuelu shushe, 1985, p. 101.
79 Ch'en, *China and the West*, p. 217.

left arm. Small wonder that China desired no close acquaintance
with people concerning whom she knew so little and imagined
so much.[80]

Once adjusted, the Chinese envoys remained puzzled by the
phenotypical variety of foreign populations. They rapidly proceeded to codify this bewildering medley, thereby reducing its
apparent complexity and directing perception into the more
habitual channels. Zhang Deyi sub-divided the population of the
United States into three groups: those of a black mother and a
white father, those of a black mother and a native father, and those
of a native mother and a white father.[81] One of the first students to
be sent abroad under Yung Wing's auspices in 1872 also divided
the American people into three groups: the aborigines, the descendants of the African slaves ('many of whom are slaves'), and the
descendants of the English.[82] Li Gui (1842–1903), the Chinese
delegate at the Philadelphia Exhibition of 1876, noted in his diary
that the Westerners called the Indians 'reds', the Africans
'blacks', and themselves 'whites'.[83] Through typification, newly-
discovered peoples were designated a rank and a location; order
and meaning were restored in an expanding universe.

Not all travellers abroad perceived Westerners as 'white'
people. In the north of Europe, wrote Binchun, 'men and women
have broad faces and full cheeks, their flesh is reddish purple; they
cover themselves with fur and feathers, and greatly resemble the
Mongols.'[84] Most observers, however, accepted the adjective
'white', which was sometimes explained in curious ways. Zhigang
believed that the European's white skin and red hair was due to
daily baths of cold water.[85] Xue Fucheng (1838–94) affirmed that

80 Holcombe, The real Chinaman, p. 5.
81 Zhang, Ou Mei huanyouji, pp. 654–5.
82 Qi Zhaoxi, You Meizhou riji (Diary on my travels in America), Beijing:
Yuelu shushe, 1985, p. 225.
83 Li Gui, Huanyou diqiu xinlu (New records on my travels around the world),
Beijing: Yuelu shushe, 1985, p. 333.
84 Binchun, Chengcha biji, p. 125.
85 Zhigang, Chushi, p. 325.

the consumption of milk was responsible for the white skin of European babies.[86]

Chinese abroad increasingly referred to their own people as 'yellows'. The exact origins of the notion of a 'yellow race' remain obscure. A Song encyclopaedia of the tenth century recorded a popular legend on the origins of mankind which divided people between noble and ignoble classes: the noble had been made of yellow mud, the ignoble of vulgar rope.[87] In Europe, the notion of a yellow race probably originated at the end of the seventeenth century as a reaction to reports of the Jesuits on the symbolic value of the colour yellow. The concept did not exist in the ancient world, and was not used by travellers of the Middle Ages such as Marco Polo, Pian del Carpini, Bento de Goes, or any of the Arab traders. In 1655, the first European mission to the Qing described the Chinese as having a white complexion, 'equal to the Europeans', except for some Southerners whose skin was 'slightly brown'.[88] When a young inhabitant of the Celestial Kingdom was presented at the court of Louis XIV in 1684, he was described as a 'young Indian'.[89] According to Huard, the first scientific work in which the notion of a 'yellow race' appeared was François Bernier's 'Etrennes adressées à Madame de la Sablière pour l'année 1688'. In this work, Bernier distinguished four races, including the 'yellows'.

The notion of a 'yellow race' was rapidly popularized in Western literature during the nineteenth century. It reached China through the missionaries. During the early 1890s, mission schools in China even taught their pupils how to recognize the 'characteristic colours of the various races of mankind' (when asked

---

86 Xue Fucheng, *Chushi siguo riji* (Diary in four countries), Changsha: Hunan renmin chubanshe, 1981, pp. 192–3.

87 *Taiping yulan* (Song encyclopaedia), quoting the Later Han work 'Fengsutong', Taipei: Xinxing shuju, 1959, p. 1693 (360: 5a). See also Zhou Jianren, 'Renzhong qiyuan shuo' (Legends about the origins of human races), *Dongfang zazhi*, 16, no. 11 (June 1919), pp. 93–100.

88 Nieuhof, *Het gezantschap*, p. 56.

89 The following is based on Huard, 'Depuis quand avons-nous la notion d'une race jaune?', pp. 40–1.

what the colour of the Chinese was, one boy answered 'human colour').[90] An article on the division of mankind according to skin colour was finally published in Chinese by Westerners in 1892.[91]

It would be an oversimplification, however, to suggest that the Chinese passively accepted a label invented by Western anthropology. Yellow, one of the five 'pure' colours in China, was regarded favourably, since it symbolized fame and progress. Yellow was coupled with the concept of the middle, probably because the annual deposit of loess from the Gobi desert turned the plains of north China yellow.[92] It also became the colour of the Emperor of the Middle Kingdom, ancestral home of the descendants of the Yellow Emperor. The Yellow River is still regarded in China as a symbol of the country.[93] White, on the other hand, was associated with the West. It symbolized death.

Besides the symbolic values of the colour yellow, it should be noted also that the coding of colours has a direct influence on their visual perception. The Zuni Indians, for instance, frequently confuse yellow and orange as they use the same name for both colours.[94] In China, yellow generally covers a much broader range in the spectrum of colours than in Europe and is perceived as including shades ranging from broken white to light brown. Hence, for instance, the description of blond or brown hair as 'yellow'.

90 R.H. Graves, *Forty years in China, or China in transition*, Wilmington: Scholarly Resources, 1972 (1st edn 1895), pp. 37–8.
91 'Ren fen wulei shuo' (The theory of dividing mankind into five races), *Gezhi huibian*, 7, no. 2 (1892). Later, missionaries would also publish on the racial differences of mankind; see for instance the *Wanguo gongbao*, 185 (June 1904).
92 W. Eberhard, *A dictionary of Chinese symbols: Hidden symbols in Chinese life and thought*, London: Routledge and Kegan Paul, 1986, p. 322.
93 An official history for foreigners still mentions that by the end of the 'primitive clan society', 'the Huanghe (Yellow River) valley was inhabited by many tribes, among which the one headed by Huangdi (the Yellow Emperor) was very powerful with its culture highly developed'; see *Chinese history*, Beijing: Foreign Languages Press, 1987, p. 2.
94 M.D. Vernon, *The psychology of perception*, Harmondsworth: Penguin Books, 1971, p. 70.

In their search for ingroup similarity the Chinese turned more and more to the idea of a yellow race. Familiarity with outgroups led to an increased relativization of the ingroup's cosmological position and to making the ingroup's identity increasingly specific. Heightened awareness of differences between groups led to a tendency to underestimate the differences within the group. During prolonged contact with an outgroup, the Chinese provincial consciousness was increasingly supplemented with a racial consciousness. Already in 1895, Li Hongzhang (1823–1901) upheld the idea of perpetual peace and harmony between China and Japan, 'so that our Asiatic yellow race will not be encroached upon by the white race of Europe.'[95]

MISCEGENATION

Concern with intermarriage was common among the Chinese élite, although it never became as intense as in certain Western societies. Traditional attitudes were ambivalent. On the one hand, political alliances were sometimes sought by marrying female members of the imperial clan to tribal chiefs. On the other hand, successive invasions by neighbouring peoples had heightened the importance of descent. Whereas sinicization of the barbarian by means of intermarriage was officially encouraged, the élite stressed the origins of descent groups. This concern was reflected in the compilation of massive genealogies, in.ended to prove the 'purity' of the lineage. With the rise of racial taxonomies in the eighteenth century, miscegenation was increasingly presented as a form of mongrelization. Generally, however, the lack of substantial phenotypical differences between the various peoples living in China was conducive to a relatively tolerant attitude towards intermarriage, particularly when practised below élite level.

Exclusive attitudes were greatly enhanced through contacts with physically discontinuous people. The first reactions towards

95 S.Y. Teng and J.K. Fairbank, *China's response to the West: A documentary survey, 1839–1923*, Cambridge, Mass.: Harvard University Press, 1954, p. 126.

miscegenation between foreign groups came from official envoys abroad. Early reports noted how the mixture of Caucasian yang and coloured yin engendered shades of yellow, black, red and purple.[96] Copulation between 'the white barbarians with the black faces engenders bastards, [. . .] a yellow-faced curly-haired type', Linzhen observed.[97] Intermarriage between a Chinese and a foreigner was inconceivable. It was considered shameful for the individual and for the country. As a result of excessive contact between students and white women abroad, in 1910 students were expressly commanded not to approach foreign women. Marriage with an alien female, it was claimed, would only lead to the abandonment of the course of study, to a waste of money, and to national subjugation.[98] Such attitudes were widespread among the upper classes, reflecting social prejudice and lineage pride. Official disgrace and public opprobrium were the rewards of those who betrayed the race. Lu Zhengxiang (1871–1949), a future Minister of Foreign Affairs, married a Belgian girl in 1899 despite the formal disapproval of his superiors. His wife was not allowed to attend any official function for almost a decade.[99] Foreign husbands, observed Jerome Ch'en, provoked an 'acid feeling' among some Chinese males, who sneered at Chinese girls married to foreigners and would even write threatening letters urging them to stay 'pure'.[100]

Fear of racial impurity did not only haunt the educated élite. In Texas, the Chinese community grew considerably at the beginning of the 1880s with the arrival of the railroad. Despite the notable absence of Chinese women, few Chinese would marry a local girl: 'Through ostracism of those who did marry outside the

---

96 Zhang, *Ou Mei huanyouji*, p. 655.

97 Linzhen, *Xihai jiyou cao* (Draft travel notes on the Western seas), Beijing: Yuelu shushe, 1985, p. 37; see also Zhang, *Ou Mei huanyouji*, pp. 649–50, on the South American 'bastards'.

98 Shu Xincheng, *Jindai Zhongguo liuxue shi* (A history of Chinese students abroad in recent times), Shanghai: Zhonghua shuju, 1933, p. 177.

99 Lou Tseng-Tsiang, *Souvenirs et pensées*, Bruges: Desclée de Brouwer, 1945, p. 44.

100 Ch'en, *China and the West*, p. 166.

race, the Chinese were able to keep intermarriage with Mexicans to a minimum.'[101] In general, however, it seems that élite prejudice against intermarriage was only partly shared by the subordinate classes. In most cases, access to native females was the determining factor in marriage patterns. In Hawaii, for instance, Chinese labourers did marry local women in the middle of the nineteenth century, but they ceased to do so as soon as Chinese women became available in the 1920s.[102]

Sexual fear combined with racial prejudice to maintain social distance between the Chinese and the foreigner. Carnal contact with the alien was taboo, even at the level of the brothel. Before the 1840s, flower-boat girls would allure foreigners, but their services were reserved exclusively for the Chinese; aliens were not allowed to enter.[103] Strict rules of segregation eased somewhat after the treaties, especially in Shanghai, but sexual distance remained the public norm, for both Chinese and Westerners.

Even without prior expectations concerning the characteristics of an outgroup, inaccurate impressions may develop as a result of the selective perception or memory of the ingroup. In China, however, an extensive barbarian imagery had been built on this purely cognitive basis of prejudice since the earliest times. The result was that the perception of outgroups was reduced to highly typified patterns. Racial typification of outgroups evolved from these traditional patterns during the nineteenth century in order to defend a threatened symbolic universe, promote group cohesion, and to

101 N.E. Farrar, *The Chinese in El Paso*, El Paso: Texas Western University Press, 1972, p. 35.
102 S.W. Kung, *Chinese in American life: Some aspects of their history, status, problems, and contributions*, Seattle: University of Washington Press, 1962, p. 216.
103 C.T. Downing, *The fan-qui in China in 1836–1837*, London: Henry Colburn, 1838, vol. 1, p. 242. As late as 1911, Jean Rodes reports that the prostitutes in Shanghai would flee at the sight of him, as if he were a 'devil'; see J. Rodes, *Scènes de la vie révolutionnaire en Chine (1911–1914)*, Paris: Plon, 1917, p. 63.

compensate for a lowered self-esteem. It also reinforced racial consciousness.

Absence of familiarity with physically discontinuous people facilitated the emergence of a racial consciousness in China. Indians, in comparison, reacted to Westerners in a very different way. They developed an awareness of racial distinctiveness only after 1860, mainly as a reaction to the rise of Western racial theories that accompanied the extension of foreign economic dominance on the subcontinent. 'But probably most important, the subcontinent had seen too many alien conquests, all of them by people whose foreignness had both racial and religious aspects, to regard the English as significantly different, at least for the first century or so.'[104] China had only been invaded by people that were subsequently culturally and physically assimilated.

Racial consciousness appears first among those who have extensive contact with the outgroup. The Canton area in particular and the coastal regions generally were the first to develop a sense of racial identity, one that was to spread gradually to the whole of the country. Intellectuals directly exposed to foreigners were also vital in the activation of a racial consciousness.

Stereotypes and misconceptions were the chief agents in the emergence of a racial identity so vital in the process of relativization and adaptation. Misconceptions, however, can also hinder adaptation when it is dependent on accurate prediction or understanding of the outgroup's behaviour and intentions. The tension between these two mutually exclusive goals – the need for a strong ingroup identity and the urge for adaptation to an outgroup – would have dramatic effects on the course of modern Chinese history.

104 R. Murphey, *The outsiders: The Western experience in India and China*, Ann Arbor: University of Michigan Press, 1977, p. 67.

3

RACE AS LINEAGE (1895–1903)

The last decades of the nineteenth century were a period of profound social transformation in China, characterized by the emergence of new social categories and the fragmentation of the ruling classes.

The compradors (*maiban*) were one of the more important groups which took shape in response to the new economic opportunities created through contacts with Western traders.[1] They acted as intermediaries between foreign firms and the domestic market, but they also invested as individual merchants in new sectors and sometimes managed official undertakings. The compradors performed an important function in the process of economic restructuring. During the decade following the Sino-French War of 1884–5, a number of them started writing on institutional and economic reform, the most notable being Zheng Guanying (1842–1922), He Qi (1859–1914) and Wang Tao (1828–97).[2] Alongside the compradors, a new class of native merchants and financiers were to build their fortunes by interacting with overseas trade; by the end of the nineteenth century they had become shareholders and administrators of foreign registered companies. They encouraged the pursuit of Western studies and sponsored schools with Western curricula.

The economic development of the treaty ports in particular and the coastal region in general led to the gradual appearance of new social classes.[3] In the urban centres the liberal professions expanded

1 On the comprador group, see Hao Yen-p'ing, *The comprador in nineteenth century China: Bridge between East and West*, Cambridge, Mass.: Harvard University Press, 1970.
2 L.E. Eastman, 'Political reformism in China before the Sino-Japanese War', *Journal of Asian Studies*, 27, no. 4 (Aug. 1968), pp. 695–710.
3 I have drawn freely on Marianne Bastid's 'Currents of social change' in D. Twitchett and J.K. Fairbank (eds), *The Cambridge history of China*, Cambridge University Press, 1980, vol. 11, part 2, pp. 535–602.

as people trained as lawyers, physicians or journalists. Scholars began to participate in economic activities, investing in shares, launching enterprises and managing businesses. The scholars united with the merchants in the development of capitalist enterprise, from which emerged a new social stratum, the *shenshang* (gentry-merchant).

The rise to prominence of the *shenshang* was one of the characteristics of the fragmentation of the traditional ruling élites. The growth of the official élite after the Taiping war had accentuated regional disparities, strained cohesion, affected the exercise of power and diluted the legitimacy of the existing social order. Within the élite, new groups were formed. The cleavage between traditional and new élites, between north and south, as well as between the rural hinterland and the urban centres took on dramatic proportions during the Sino-Japanese War of 1894–5.

Japan, contemptuously designated as a country of 'dwarf slaves' (*wonu*) and still considered as a vassal of the empire,[4] dealt a heavy blow to the élite's self-confidence by gaining an overwhelming victory in the war. The Japanese victory was unexpected, even by those who had been aware of China's deficiencies, and led to an outpouring of patriotic agitation. Memoranda advocating reforms reached the throne after the Shimonoseki peace settlement of 1895. Conservative sectors of the scholar-gentry class, shocked and angered by the course of events, advocated prolonged warfare and clamoured for the punishment of those responsible for China's defeat.

In this atmosphere of intellectual ferment, study societies (*xuehui*) founded by the new élites burgeoned in the urban centres and in the southern provinces. Similar to the *sociétés de pensée* in pre-revolutionary France, study societies published journals and newspapers (*bao* or *xuebao*) to spread reformist ideas. The main concern was national survival. Polemical essays, news translated from the foreign press and educational articles promoted insti-

---

4 See S.C. Chu, 'China's attitudes toward Japan at the time of the Sino-Japanese War' in A. Iriye, *The Chinese and the Japanese: Essays in political and cultural interactions*, Princeton University Press, 1980, pp. 74–95.

tutional reform and intellectual renewal. Another task of study societies was the education and mobilization of the new urban classes. This urban orientation was reflected in the contents of the journals: apart from politics, some papers focused on industry (*Gongshang xuebao*), general education (*Tongxuebao*), science (*Gezhi xinbao*), or general world news (*Cuibao*), but also on less high-minded topics such as children's literature (*Qiuwobao*), pornography (*Qingloubao*) and *demi-mondaine* gossip (*Youxibao*). The discourse of race as lineage was a product of the reform-oriented journals. The rise of the press, furthermore, was closely linked to the emergence of the concept of public space (*gong*), represented in opposition to private spheres of activity (*si*). *Gong* was a notion which traditionally referred to the personnel and property of the state bureaucracy (*gongsuo*, 'government office'),[5] but between the late sixteenth and early eighteenth century, *gong* was increasingly associated with the collective, the 'public'. During the late nineteenth century, public space emerged as a conceptual category specific to the new élites. It was associated with urbanization, the rise of a commercial press, the appearance of reform societies and the spread of literacy.

By addressing a social stratum of readers much broader than the traditional scholar-literati class, the reform press contributed to the growth of urban nationalism. Whereas the traditional élite had sought to maintain its monopolistic claim to power by restricting access to the esoteric body of Confucian knowledge, the rival élite had to convince the public of the necessity of reform by spreading its ideas as widely as possible. Their journals reached a large regional or nation-wide readership, due partly to the patronage of provincial and prefectural governments. The *Shiwubao*, for

5 On the emergence of the public sphere in modern China and a discussion of Jürgen Habermas' concept of *Öffentlichkeit*, see William T. Rowe's excellent 'The public sphere in modern China', *Modern China*, 3 (July 1990), pp. 309–29. For the link between the discourse of race, the rise of medicine and the emergence of a concept of public space, see Frank Dikötter, 'The discourse of race and the medicalization of public and private space in modern China (1895–1949)', *History of Science* (forthcoming).

instance, had a circulation of 10,000 in April 1898.[6] When the Empress Dowager seized control at the palace in Beijing, many contributors fled abroad or sought safety in foreign concessions in the treaty ports. Thereafter the reform press continued to operate mainly from Japan. Liang Qichao's *Xinmin congbao*, for instance, was circulated in China with minimal difficulties, in spite of an imperial ban. Reprints ran to over a dozen. The fact that the reformers were outlawed merely increased their popularity with the reading public.

Despite its popularity, the intellectual content of the reform movement was complex. The reformers sought to overthrow the leadership of the traditional élite. Orthodox Confucianism existed largely in isolation from the shifts in the social structure described above, giving rise to a socio-political vacuum which competing groups like the reformers wished to fill. The latter supported New Text Confucianism.[7] New Text ideas, which reemerged in the late eighteenth century after centuries of neglect, were used to promote political reform, to attack imperial orthodoxy, and to construct an image of Confucius as a politically oriented sage-king. The impact of New Text Confucianism in the second half of the nineteenth century was heightened by the resurgence of a practically-orientated scholarship (*shiyong*). The so-called statecraft school (*jingshi*) represented a reaction against certain strains of Confucianism; it emphasized self-improvement and utilitarian statesmanship. Furthermore, there was a revival of interest in the classical non-canonical philosophies (*zhuzixue*) of Xunzi and Mozi. Interest in non-canonical ancient texts tended to be more practical than theoretical, and was only one aspect of the growing moral and practical activism of late Qing scholars. The late nineteenth century also witnessed a revival of Mahayana Buddhism among lay intellectuals. Buddhist studies were characterized by a practical orientation towards personal salvation that

6 R.S. Britton, *The Chinese periodical press, 1800–1912*, Shanghai: Kelly and Walsh, 1933, p. 93.
7 See Hao Chang, *Chinese intellectuals in crisis: Search for order and meaning (1890–1911)*, Berkeley: University of California Press, 1987.

favoured syncretism with other indigenous belief-systems. Thus it is important to remember that the reform movement was to a large extent the product of complex interactions and fusions of different indigenous patterns of thought which had little to do with Western learning. However, the multiplication of sub-universes during this period increased the difficulty of maintaining a stable universe for the whole of society. The fragility of this Confucian universe made the penetration of foreign systems of thought easier. Chaos also intruded through the interstices of a symbolic universe in dislocation. People acquired a heightened consciousness of the frailty of meaning. The traditional universe which gave meaning to life was fading away. The de-ritualization of Confucian society, like the secularization of the Christian West, led to the feelings of frustration and alienation which are so characteristic of the modern age.

New Text Confucianism, statecraft scholarship, Mahayana Buddhism and other trends interacted with Western systems of thought and incorporated elements from them. The influence of the West on the reformers, however, remains difficult to assess. Knowledge is never the result of passive reception, but the product of an active subject's industry. Cultural borrowings, then, can never be explained as a passive 'exposure to foreign influence'; they can be viewed only as the active creations of a discerning cognitive organism. There is a decision before the borrowing takes place and a decision about what should be borrowed. Foreign ideas were assessed against, and integrated within, a pre-existing framework. From this perspective, any attempt at systematic differentiation between 'native thought' and 'Western influence' would seem to be in vain. At a more general level, however, it is clear that the rise of Western power and Western thought systems significantly impinged upon and altered the Chinese symbolic universe. Subjective cultural interaction, instead of Western influence, is the notion which underlies the discussion of Western thought in China that follows.

This chapter considers the discourse of race as lineage in China from 1895 to 1903. It is confined mainly to the works of the reformers, with special emphasis on Liang Qichao. The year 1903 was a turning-point marked by the gradual emergence of a virulent nationalism represented by Sun Yatsen and his revolutionary group. The nationalists will be analyzed in the next chapter, which focuses on the discourse of race as nation (*minzu*), along with the reformers' contribution to the nationalist discourse and the question of so-called 'social Darwinism'.

Liang Qichao (1873–1929) was a precocious student from a farmer-scholar family in the southern coastal province of Guangdong. He passed the provincial examinations at the age of sixteen, and later studied under Kang Youwei (1858–1927). In 1894, he failed to pass the metropolitan examination and turned to foreign studies as an alternative path to power. After the defeat of 1895, Liang devoted his energies to study societies and to reform-oriented journals. Most of his articles first appeared in his own periodicals. Liang created a new style of writing, foreshadowing the literary revolution of 1917: he loosened the rigid sentence structure of classical Chinese to reshape it into an elegant yet flexible means of communication. He became a brilliant journalist, and exerted a lasting influence on two generations of intellectuals.

Although this chapter is confined to the writings of a small number of reformers like Liang Qichao, it should be emphasized that this study does not subscribe to the determining influence of individual writers. The limitations of the symbolic universe in which a group operates channel individual differences into specific directions. Changes in the global environment will lead to adaptive changes in the configuration of the symbolic universe, but the scope and expression of these adaptive changes are constrained by the very nature of the universe itself. Certain individuals like Yan Fu or Liang Qichao clearly exerted more influence than others, but in essence they were the first to articulate the adaptive changes that were possible within their universe: they were the buds that grew quicker from a common soil. There was a relative discursive homogeneity within the sub-universe of the reformers. As one contemporary reader observed, 'It was not just that Liang Qichao's writing was good; it was also that what he said seemed to be just what we had stored in our hearts and wished to express ourselves.'[8]

RACIAL WAR

The racial typology discussed in the previous chapter only attained a higher level of theorization with the reformers. Yan Fu (1853– 1921) was the initiator of a discourse of race based on lineage. He came from a respectable scholar-gentry family from Fujian. The death of his father and a reversal of fortune cut off the path to office through the traditional examination system. Yan opted for a bleak alternative: Western studies. He joined the Fuzhou shipyard school and was sent to England for two years in the 1870s. Yan embarked on a series of translations of English works in the 1890s. He introduced Darwin and Spencer to a Chinese readership in four essays published in 1895 in the *Zhibao*, a newly founded periodical edited in Tianjin. In these essays, Yan rejected the traditional distinction between a civilized centre and a barbarian periphery. He disengaged man from an imperial cosmology to embed him into a new spatial structure. Culture was abandoned: race became the norm by which group membership was assigned.

There are four main races on the earth: the yellow, the white, the brown and the black. The yellow race's territory is contiguous with Siberia in the north, extending to the South China Sea, bordered by the Pacific and up to the Kunlun mountains in the west. They have prominent cheek-bones, a shallow nose, long eyes and straight hair. The white race dwells west of the salt lakes of the Urals, on the ancient territory conquered by *Daqin* [Rome]. They have blue eyes and curly hair, a prominent forehead and deep-set eye-sockets. On the many islands south of Vietnam, west of Luzon and east of India is the brown race.

8 Quoted in L.O. Lee and A.J. Nathan, 'The beginnings of mass culture: Journalism and fiction in the late Ch'ing and beyond' in D. Johnson, A.J. Nathan and E.S. Rawski (eds), *Popular culture in late imperial China*, Berkeley: University of California Press, 1985, p. 368.

The black race is the lowest.[9] They live in Africa and in the territories around the tropics. They are the so-called black slaves.[10]

The discourse of race as type was static. It divided mankind into several permanent racial types, each of which was thought to have existed unaltered since their appearance on earth. Starting with Yan Fu, the reformers constructed a world which was engaged in a perennial process of evolution. Within this new temporal structure, the 'yellow race' was in a perpetual state of war with other 'races'. Slogans of the survival of the fittest (*youshengliebai*, 'the superior win, the inferior lose') underpinned a violent vision of racial conflagration. For Liang Qichao, for instance, races had developed side by side until they eventually engaged in struggle: 'What is history? History is nothing but the account of the development and strife of human races.'[11] Races could be divided into two categories: the historical races (*you lishi de zhongzu*) and the un- or ahistorical races (*fei lishi de zhongzu*). The latter were unable to expand and were subjugated by the former, which were more cohesive and united. The red, brown and black races were eliminated from the stage, leaving the drama of history to the yellows and the whites. The reformers became prophets both of doom and of strength. The future would be white or yellow.

The notion of racial war (*zhongzhan*) was only partly a construction of the reformers. It had a conceptual precedent in the notion of commercial war (*shangzhan*), which was first pro-

9 The expression 'lowest' reflects the Chinese belief in environmental determinism, and thus had a geographical as well as an evolutionary connotation. The 1959 Beijing edition explains how this was part of the 'persistent vilification of the black race by the capitalist and imperialist countries'. Yan Fu, *Yan Fu shiwen xuan* (Selected poems and writings of Yan Fu), Beijing: Renmin wenxue chubanshe, 1959, p. 39, n. 78.
10 Ibid., p. 20.
11 Liang Qichao, 'Xin shixue' (New historiography) in *Yinbingshi wenji* (Collected writings of Liang Qichao), Shanghai: Zhonghua shuju, 1941 (hereafter *YBSWJ*), 4, 9: 11; see also another important article entitled 'Lun minzu jingzheng zhi dashi' (About the general trend of racial struggles) in *YBSWJ*, 4, 10: 10–35.

pounded in 1862 in the writings of the general and scholar Zeng Guofan (1811–72).[12] It soon won the support of high officials and patriotic merchants in the treaty ports as an alternative to building up military strength, which focused on preparing for an armed confrontation (*bingzhan*). Trade, it was believed, could be used as a weapon to resist foreign encroachment. Zheng Guanying, for instance, proposed the fostering of talent, the modernization of agriculture, the promotion of commerce, and the elevation of the merchant's status in order better to compete with Western trade. This strategy echoed the legalist thinker Shang Yang (*d.* 338 BC), who had developed a program of *gengzhan*, or 'agricultural war'. After the Japanese victory in 1895, however, these efforts to develop commerce and industry in order to compete with foreigners seemed unlikely to succeed. Instead the focus shifted from trade to race. Many reformers gradually came to adopt a vision of a world order dominated by the white race against which the yellow race had to fight in order to survive.

Being engaged in a struggle for survival was nothing new. The nineteenth century was one of the most competitive periods in Chinese history. Demographic pressure and an increasing shortage of resources had led to a decline in social mobility. Intense competition was the norm in both public and private sectors. Thus common lineage and regional bonds were increasingly used to achieve social advancement.

The lineage (*zu*), or common descent group, came into being in its modern form under the Song.[13] A model of social organization generally confined to a village or a neighbourhood, where it owned land, schools and an ancestral hall, it instilled a sense of solidarity among its members. Descent lines were recorded in genealogies (*zupu*), a task that might require the labour of many *zu* members. The last edition of the genealogy of the Zeng lineage

---

12 On *shangzhan*, see Wang Ermin, 'Shangzhan guannian yu zhongshang sixiang' (The idea of commercial warfare and the importance attached to commerce), *Zhongyang yanjiuyuan jindaishi yanjiusuo jikan*, 5 (June 1966), pp. 1–91.
13 The following is mainly based on Hu Hsien Chin, *The common descent group in China and its functions*, New York: Viking Fund Publications in Anthropology, 1948.

in Hunan, which traced its descent from a prince of the Xia
dynasty whose father had reigned in 2218–2168 BC, involved 106
participants. Attempts to establish an hereditary link with a
mythical ancestor were based on the need for social prestige; moreover, genealogies proved that the lineage was pure and that there
had not been intermarriage with any of the ethnic groups that had
invaded and ruled China.

Considerable friction could arise between *zu*, nurtured by a feeling of rivalry, suspicion and envy. Open hostilities were often the
consequence of local contention and competition. Harry Lamley,
who has analyzed such lineage feuds, contends that they were a
major type of disorder in late imperial China.[14] They prevailed
throughout the empire, but were more common in the south-east,
where the institution of the lineage had grown more powerful
than in the north. Battles between lineages could involve many
thousands of combatants. *Zu* leaders even subsidized paramilitary
operations. Terror and wanton destruction of crops and villages
were the usual outcome of such feuds, called *xiedou*, 'armed
battles'.

During the Qing, interethnic conflicts (*fenlei xiedou*), or
'armed battles to separate types (*lei*)', became common between
Han and Muslims, Hakka (a minority group of south-east China)
and Hoklo (Hokkien-speaking Chinese), and Hakka and Punti
(native Cantonese). Ethnic feuds strove to 'clear the boundaries'
(*qingjie*) by ejecting exogenous groups from their respective territories. Such ethnic clashes could be extremely violent: a major
conflict between the Hakka and Punti in 1856–67 took a toll of
100,000 victims.

The reformers' interpretation of racial war was based on lineage
feuds. This vision was sustained by the semantic similarity between
zu as lineage and *zu* as race. *Huangzu* meant both yellow lineage
and yellow race. *Yizu* meant 'exogenous lineage' or 'foreign race'.
Zu was often combined by the reformers with *zhong* as *zhongzu*,
'breed of lineage'. *Zhong* was the central element of a complex

14 See H.J. Lamley, 'Hsieh-tou: The pathology of violence in south-eastern
China', *Ch'ing-shih Wen-t'i*, 3, no. 7 (Nov. 1977), pp. 1–39.

terminology; it meant 'seed', 'breed', or 'biological species', and was used in association with *lei*, 'type', 'category', in *zhonglei* at the discursive level of race as type. *Zhong* could also be used in connection with a particular colour, like *huangzhong* or *heizhong*, 'yellow species' or 'black species'.

Commonalities are created as groups develop symbols of identification and distinguish between in- and outgroup members. 'Race' was a symbol of fictive biological cohesion capable of overarching regional allegiances and linking lineage loyalties in the face of foreign aggression. 'Race', as will be demonstrated in the next chapter, would create nationhood. On the basis of internal conflicts between lineages, the reformers constructed a representation of external conflicts between races. Members of the yellow lineage had to fight against the members of the white lineage. The Yellow Emperor became the common ancestor of all Chinese. The ancestral territories, the divine soil of the Middle Kingdom traditionally associated with the colour yellow, in opposition to the 'red' and 'black' soils of the barbarians, needed to be defended against the white lineage. The 'white peril' was indeed a remarkable Chinese counterpart of the 'yellow peril' fear then prevailing in the West.[15]

RACIAL CONTINUITY

Continuity of the *zu* was a perennial concern in Chinese civilization. Males were highly valued for their potential as procreators of the *zu*. At élite level, concubines could be taken when the principal wife was sterile. The reformer Kang Youwei, more in conformity with tradition than with his own principles of sexual equality, took a concubine when he was without a son at the age of thirty-nine.

The Western sense of continuity was articulated in a different direction. All the way from the humble creeping worm up to God there was thought to exist a Great Chain of Being. The connection between animal and man was yet to be revealed: anthropology,

15 See H. Gollwitzer, *Die gelbe Gefahr. Geschichte eines Schlagworts*, Göttingen: Vandenhoeck und Ruprecht, 1962.

craniology and comparative anatomy were all in search of the missing link. Charles White, for instance, examined the anatomical features of over fifty blacks, and concluded that the African was closer to the ape than to the European. His account, published in 1799, was entitled *An account of the regular gradation in man, and in different animals and vegetables; and from the former to the latter.*[16] In 1792, the Dutch anatomist Peter Camper compared the skulls of apes and blacks: he too discerned a correlation between the primate and the African.[17] As late as 1831, a work was published in which the orang-utan was classified as human in the Great Chain.[18] When the rise of the idea of progress finally disentangled European thought from the teleological belief in static creationism, the missing link was discovered: Darwin thought that there was a biological step from ape to man.

The perception of nature, either static or evolutionary, rested upon the assumption of a continuity between animal and man. In China, as was briefly indicated in chapter 1, the border between man and beast could also be blurred, especially with respect to the 'barbarians' living outside the scope of Chinese civilization. Generally, however, man and animal were considered of separate origins and of different categories. When foreigners were associated with animals, it was often to highlight their categorical difference, not to degrade them on a fictive scale of beings.

RACIAL ORIGINS

The perception of origins also diverged between China and the West. China believed in polygenism whereas the West was absorbed by the Judeo-Christian thesis of monogenism. The Bible depicted the sons of Noah as the ancestors of all the peoples of the three parts of the world: humanity descended from one (*mono*)

16 Banton, *Racial theories*, p. 14.
17 J.C. Greene, *The death of Adam: Evolution and its impact on Western thought*, Ames: Iowa State University Press, 1959, pp. 188–92.
18 P.D. Curtin, *The image of Africa: British ideas and action, 1780–1850*, Madison: University of Wisconsin Press, 1964, p. 368.

kind (*genus*). In the nineteenth century, European thought had to eliminate Adam in order to reject the unity of mankind.[19]

The monogenist thesis was introduced to China by missionaries in the seventeenth century. The convert Li Zubai (*d.* 1665) wrote a history of the Christian church in Chinese in 1663, in which his people were presented as a branch of Judea that had migrated to China. It took Yang Guangxian (1597–1669), a prominent opponent of Christianity, only two years to publish a repudiation of Li's views:

> Schall's book says that one man and one woman were [created] as the first ancestors of mankind. He was not so bold as to state contemptuously that all the people of the world are the descendants of his religion. According to Li's book, however, our China is nothing but [an offshoot] of Judea; our ancient Chinese rulers, sages, and teachers were but the descendants of a heterodox sect; and our classics and sage teachings, propounded generation after generation, no more than the remnants of a heterodox religion. Are there no limits to foolishness?[20]

Within the context of race as culture, Yang Guangxian of course associated biological descent with a particular religion. At the end of the nineteenth century, however, the reformers opened up a new debate on origins at the discursive level of race as lineage. Liang Qichao mentioned the existence of both monogenist

19 The belief in the polygenist origins of mankind was shared by the Japanese, whose perception of racial matters had much in common with that of China. The first Japanese mission abroad stopped in Angola in 1860 on its way to the United States. The natives were thought to resemble the Buddhist images and it was concluded that 'the natives of India and Africa both belong to one and the same tribe, of whom that Buddha must have been a chieftain'. The diarist of the mission regretted that his country had worshipped such 'primitive people' for so long; see M.B. Jansen, *Japan and its world: Two centuries of change*, Princeton University Press, 1980, p. 47. For a study of the importance of skin colour in Japan, see Hiroshi Wagatsuma, 'The social perception of skin color in Japan', *Daedalus*, Spring 1967, pp. 407–43.
20 Cohen, *China and Christianity*, p. 25.

(*yiyuan*) and polygenist (*duoyuan*) theses in the West, but he never developed the monogenist version, upon which rested most European racial theory. Liang also typified the Hamites and the Semites as two branches of the 'historical white race' (as opposed to the 'historical yellow race').[21] Such misapprehensions were common: the reformers were only superficially acquainted with Western systems of thought. But it also indicated an ambivalent tendency to believe in 'bigenism' ('two kinds', or the belief that mankind descends from two origins): the yellow race was of one origin, the white and black races were of the other. Bigenism was further developed in the *Xinmin congbao* by Jiang Zhiyou, who collaborated with Liang Qichao. Jiang's inquiry into the origins of the Chinese race was dominated by the influence of Terrien de Lacouperie.[22] Jiang established a continuity between the Sumero-Akkadians, from whom the Yellow Emperor was descended, and the Finno-Tartar group, linguistically associated with the Mongolians, or the yellow race. The Semites, on the other hand, had overwhelmed the Sumero-Akkadians and engendered the Caucasians, or the white race. These speculations echoed Haeckel's theory, presented at the beginning of Jiang's study: Europeans and Africans descended from the African ape, whereas the Asians descended from the Asian apeman.[23] Bigenism achieved a higher theoretical level early in the twentieth century. Hu Bingxiong, for instance, developed a theory on the different origins of East and West. The Eastern monkey was big and had no tail, whereas the Western monkey was small and more 'animal-like'.[24] At the level of popular perceptions, belief in bigenism may also have been latent. Selby, for instance, reported at the end of the nineteenth century how some Chinese believed that foreigners were born entirely white or entirely black;[25] like a litter of puppies, they all came from the same stock.

21 Liang, 'Xin shixue' in *YBSWJ*, 4, 9: 12.
22 For a more detailed discussion of Lacouperie's thesis, see chapter 4, below.
23 Jiang Zhiyou, *Zhongguo renzhong kao* (Inquiry into the Chinese race), Shanghai: Huatong shuju, 1929 (1st edn 1910).
24 See Hu Bingxiong, 'Lun Zhongguo zhongzu' (About the Chinese race), *Dongfang zazhi*, 4, no. 8 (Aug. 1908), pp. 361–85.
25 Quoted in Hardy, *John Chinaman*, pp. 321–2.

The tension between monogenism and polygenism was resolved by a conceptual differentiation between *zhong* as species and *zu* as lineage: one original *zhong* had engendered several unequally endowed *zu*. This system encapsulated the belief in both a pure race and the existence of one human species, and became the standard interpretation of racial origins until 1949. The discourse of race as lineage depended on polygenism. The Yellow Emperor was the progenitor of the yellow race. Exogenous elements were of little interest.

RACIAL EXTINCTION

The emphasis on continuity led to fears of extinction. *Miezu*, the extinction of the lineage, became *miezhong*, the extinction of the race. Yan Fu was the first to raise the threat of racial extinction: 'They will enslave us and hinder the development of our spirit and body . . . The brown and black races constantly waver between life and death, why not the 400 million yellows?'[26] Coloured peoples performed a prophetic function in the discourse of race: darker breeds were harbingers of racial decline. They exemplified the fate that was in store for China if it did not catch up with the white lords of mankind. In America, the reformers argued, the ruthless law of evolution had already tracked down and killed off the 'red barbarians' (*hongyi*).[27] Liang Qichao pondered over the future of his country while touring the United States: was it not the destiny of the yellow Chinese to follow the red Indians, who would become museum-pieces within thirty years?[28] During a visit to Hawaii, he reported that the original inhabitants constituted only one-fifteenth of the total population. The aborigines, naive creatures sunk in ignorance, 'were not even aware of their extinction'.[29] The blacks in Africa and the browns in the Pacific

26 Yan, *Yan Fu shiwen xuan*, p. 22.
27 Liang Qichao, 'Shengjixue xueshuo yange xiaoshi' (Short history of the evolution of the science of livelihood) in *YBSWJ*, 5, 12: 4.
28 Liang Qichao, 'Xin dalu youji' (Travel notes on America) in Liang Qichao, *Yinbingshi zhuanji* (Writings of Liang Qichao), Shanghai: Zhonghua shuju, 1941 (hereafter *YBSZJ*), 5, 22: 99.
29 Liang Qichao, 'Xiaweiyi youji' (Travel notes on Hawaii) in *YBSZJ*, 5, 22: 196.

were all enslaved and would 'disappear from the face of the earth within several decades.'[30] Even cultural assimilation was unable to delete the stigma of race. American blacks, driven by a crude urge for sex, had reproduced themselves at a faster rate than the whites. But industrialization had outpaced them, leaving them on the fringes of society. Death was looming in the twilight of time: Liang quoted statistics that showed how the number of American blacks would fall by a third within a century.[31]

The spectre of racial extinction conveyed a sense of urgency to the message of reform. Repetition further sustained the power of words: race was hammered down the reader's throat. Appeals for the 'preservation of the race' (baozhong) were reiterated ad nauseam in the reformers' writings. It was even announced as a main goal in the Hunan periodical Xiangxue xinbao.[32] It is of course legitimate to question the extent to which the reformers genuinely believed in 'extinction'; they could be portrayed as a rival coterie of experts who merely constructed a Western threat in order to further their political interests. To ease access to power, the reformers tried to intimidate their opponents with images of racial doom and to persuade their audience of the benefits of their knowledge. Yan Fu, for instance, went to great lengths to counter potential sceptics vis-à-vis the idea of 'racial extinction'.[33] 'Western thought', moreover, could be no more than a competing source of knowledge that derived its legitimacy independently from the traditional examination system. It is a common historical phenomenon that the choice of a particular ideology by a group is not based on a genuine interest in its theoretical elements, but stems rather from chance encounter. 'Western thought' could have been harnessed by political interests with minimal reference to its contents. The 'West' would then be no more than a prestige symbol manipulated by the reformers.

30 Liang Qichao, 'Lun Hunan ying ban zhi shi' (About the affairs Hunan should handle) in YBSWJ, 2, 3: 41.
31 Liang, 'Xin dalu' in YBSZJ, 5, 22: 86.
32 Xiangxue xinbao (The Hunan news), 1, no. 1 (1897), reprinted, Taipei: Zhonghua shuju, 1966, p. 8.
33 Yan, Yan Fu shiwen xuan, pp. 20–2.

The 'white peril' could be an integral part of a rival definition of reality competing for power. Even in this case, power would be no more than the ability to determine reality; and for the reformers, reality was to a large extent defined in terms of race. The pervasiveness of racial discourse, moreover, indicates that the white peril was not merely a political weapon: racial extinction was a genuine concern shared by many Chinese who felt threatened by the West towards the end of the nineteenth century. Fear of extinction was deeply rooted in the social institution of the lineage. Any historical discussion which reduces a discursive practice to a power structure fails to acknowledge the essential complexity of human behaviour.

RACIAL CLASSIFICATION

An important function of racial discourse was categorization. Liang Qichao added the American Indians to Yan Fu's classification of races. Like most reformers, he divided mankind into five main races: yellow, white, red, brown and black. In Europe, Johann Blumenbach (1752–1840), a German anatomist considered to be one of the founders of modern anthropology, had also advanced a fivefold classification: Caucasian, Mongolian, Ethiopian, American and Malayan. Most Western scientists, however, propounded a white, yellow and black race when invoking the pigmentation criterion. This tripartite scheme corresponded to the three sons of Noah – Shem, Japheth and Ham – whose descendants had populated the three continents. The three continents elaborated by medieval geography were also correlated to the three orders, transformed into three estates in France during the later Middle Ages. The 'Third World' may be the modern counterpart of an ancient tripartite vision. Many Western scientists, however, were more interested in the search for biological continuities than in classifications. Samuel Stanhope Smith, an early American anthropologist, dismissed classifications as a 'useless labour' because it was impossible to draw a clear line between the various peoples of the world.[34] Doubts over the divisibility of mankind led

34 Greene, *The death of Adam*, p. 222.

to the multiplication of classificatory schemes within the West. The reformers were aware of Western classifications. Tang Caichang (1867–1900), a well-known reformer who died in an abortive uprising in Hankou in 1900, juxtaposed five continents to five skin colours (*Ya Ou Mei Fei Ao ye; huang bai hong hei zong*).[35] Zhang Zhidong (1837–1909), a highly influential scholar and governor-general of Hunan and Hubei, also correlated five races to five continents.[36] Tang Caichang's detailed study on races, published between November 1897 and February 1898 in the *Xiangxue xinbao*, mentioned the *Gezhi huibian* (The Chinese scientific magazine). The *Gezhi huibian* was an illustrated periodical edited by John Fryer, a translator who cooperated with the missionaries. Tang thus presented the Western view of mankind: 'Westerners divide mankind into five races: the Mongolian race, the Caucasian race, the African race, the Malaysian race and the American Indian race. Their skin colour differentiates them into yellow, white, black, brown and red peoples.'[37] In fact, Fryer had described the Mongolian race as 'reddish brown' (*zhe*) and the American Indians as 'bronze' (*tong*).[38] Liang Qichao also misrepresented Western systems of classification; he was aware of various schemes which ranged from one to sixty-three races, but nonetheless he adhered to a fivefold system.[39]

The reformers adopted a traditional pattern based on the symbolic number five; such wide-ranging elements as colours (*wucai*), sense organs (*wuguan*), flavours (*wuwei*), spices (*wuxiang*), metals (*wujin*) and natural elements (*wuxing*) were integrated into this numerical category. The *Liji* mentioned sixty-two different

35 Tang Caichang, *Juedianmingzhai neiyan* (Essays on political and historical matters), Taipei: Wenhai chubanshe, 1968, p. 141.
36 Zhang Zhidong, *Zhang Wenxiang gong quanji* (The complete papers of Zhang Zhidong), Beijing, 1937, *juan* 103, p. 16a.
37 Tang, *Juedianmingzhai*, p. 472.
38 See J. Fryer, *Gezhi congshu*, 1901, *ce* 1, *juan* 12, p. 2a. The compendium of Western science published in Hong Kong in 1897 also briefly mentioned the five races; see *Xixue gezhi daquan* (Compendium of Western science), Hong Kong: Xianggang shuju, 1897, *ce* 1, 'dili', p. 6a.
39 Liang, 'Xin shixue' in *YBSWJ*, 4, 9: 12.

groups of fivefold categories. Most aspects of the physical universe were manipulated to fit into a numerological set. The four seasons were meshed with the five phases.[40] During the period of Buddhist expansion in China, a system known as *geyi*, 'matching concepts', reconciled the Mahabhutas, or four elements, with the five Chinese elements.[41] Although this system was abandoned during the fifth century, it created an historical precedent that would influence subsequent attempts to incorporate foreign thought into indigenous patterns.

There were five directions: China was 'the Middle', surrounded by the barbarians of the four compass points. A cosmographic view of the world in the *Tribute of Yu* represented the Imperial Centre (*difu*) surrounded by five concentric configurations progressively approaching the waste lands (*huangfu*). Although it may not have directly influenced nineteenth-century intellectuals, the cosmological mapping which it expressed was an integral part of the Confucian symbolic universe. It would be wrong, however, to assume that the past influenced the reformers in a deterministic way. Tradition never affected the mental universe of the reformers to the same extent as the reformers determined what tradition should be. The past was manipulated in attempts to organize the present. The reformers subjectively made choices within Chinese tradition; they located events of the past to create a cohesive unity with the present. Order and meaning were reconstructed by subtle alterations to the collective memory.

Spatial representations were reformulated through the integration of fictive racial units with arbitrary geographical divisions: five races were correlated to five continents, just as in ancient China the barbarians of the four quarters (*siyi*) were associated with different symbolic colours.[42] This vision was supported by the character *zhou*, 'continent surrounded by water'. The semantic content of this character sanctioned the extension of the traditional

40 J.B. Henderson, *The development and decline of Chinese cosmology*, New York: Columbia University Press, 1984, p. 8.
41 Wright, *Buddhism*, p. 37.
42 Tang Caichang, when mentioning the ancient Chinese tribes, often used these symbolic colours; see for example Tang, *Juedianmingzhai*, p. 525.

world order beyond the four seas that customarily delineated the inhabited territories. China now assumed the central position in Asia, the 'Middle Continent'. Asia was surrounded by four continents, each belonging to a different tribe. The western one, symbolized by the colour white, was expanding. The red, brown and black lineages had already been conquered.

RACIAL HIERARCHY

In the sub-universe of the reformers, the white and yellow races were opposed to three darker races, doomed to racial extinction by hereditary inadequacy. Liang continuously dichotomized his five races into 'noble' (*guizhong*) and 'ignoble' (*jianzhong*), 'superior' (*youzhong*) and 'inferior' (*liezhong*), 'historical' and 'ahistorical'. Tang Caichang opposed 'fine' (*liangzhong*) to 'mean' (*jianzhong*) races.[43] Such binary constructions were part of the categorical thinking prevalent in China since antiquity. Yin and Yang Confucianism supported a dualistic view of the cosmos. Male and female, for instance, were theoretically equivalent, but inequality was constructed on the gender division: *nan gui nü jian*, 'male is noble, female is mean'. Binary classifications were extrapolated from the social hierarchy of the Qing dynasty. Citizens were divided into two groups: 'common', or 'fine people' (*liangmin*) and 'mean people' (*jianmin*). The latter comprised several groups: government servants and attendants; tenant-servants; entertainers (*lehu*), including prostitutes and actors; beggars, 'fallen people' (*duomin*), 'boat people' (*jiuxing yuhu*) and the Dan (fishers on the south-east coast); slave-servants.[44] This line of demarcation was legally abolished by the emperor Yongzheng in 1723, but social discrimination persisted until the twentieth century.[45]

43 Ibid., p. 501.
44 See Jing Junjian, 'Hierarchy in the Qing dynasty', *Social Sciences in China*, 1 (1982), p. 166; see also Ch'u T'ung-tsu, *Law and society in traditional China*, Paris: Mouton, 1965, pp. 128–35.
45 See H.A. Hansson, 'Regional outcast groups in late imperial China', unpubl. doctoral thesis, Harvard University, 1988.

The 'fallen people' of Shaoxing have been studied by James Cole. These hereditary outcasts were barred from taking part in examinations and were registered separately from commoners until 1911. Intermarriage between *duomin* and *liangmin* was inconceivable. A native of Shaoxing wrote an essay on the 'fallen people' justifying their inferior social position: 'Among all men there are the respected and the base, the noble and the mean, the great and the little, the gentleman and the small man.'[46] His argument was supported by Han Yu's (768–824) theory of three grades in human nature and by quotations from the *Analects*. Chinese attempts to classify human beings into categories, similar to the theories on humours in medieval Europe, were indeed widespread and intrusive.[47]

The reformers projected this native hierarchical model upon the world. Order was reconstructed by means of traditional classifications. No distinctions were established between the coloured races: they were all 'mean'. Cultural pride, aesthetic values, barbarian imagery and racial stereotypes converged in the conceptual debasement of the 'lower races'. The writer Tang Caichang constructed antithetical couplets using the notion of four races introduced by Yan Fu: 'Yellow and white are wise, red and black are stupid; yellow and white are rulers, red and black are slaves; yellow and white are united, red and black are scattered.'[48] This example illustrates perfectly how categorical thinking was embedded in the very structure of the classical language, with evenly balanced clauses succeeding one another in a rhythmic progression. However, not all racial prejudice achieved such levels of linguistic elegance. Much of Tang's account of mankind was suffused by vulgar stereotypes. Australian aborigines, for instance, 'are pitch-black, have emaciated limbs, resemble a macaque and are more repulsive than the

---

46 J.H. Cole, 'Social discrimination in traditional China: The To-min of Shaohsing', *Journal of the Economic and Social History of the Orient*, 25, part 1 (1982), p. 103.
47 See Derk Bodde, 'Types of Chinese categorical thinking' in *Essays on Chinese civilization*, Princeton University Press, 1981, pp. 141–60.
48 Tang, *Juedianmingzhai*, p. 468.

orang-utan one can see in Malaysia.'⁴⁹ Most reformers were equally imbued with a sense of racial superiority. Liang Qichao persistently denied any sense of equality with the coloured peoples: India did not flourish 'because of the limitations of her race. All the black, red and brown races, by the microbes in their blood vessels and their cerebral angle, are inferior to the whites. Only the yellows are not very dissimilar to the whites.'⁵⁰ Elsewhere he wrote that 'blacks and browns are lazy and stupid.'⁵¹ Darker races were driven only by instinctive desires for food and sex. During his trip through the United States in 1903, Liang thus explained the American lynching phenomenon: 'The blacks' behaviour is despicable. They only die without regret if they have succeeded in touching a white woman's skin. They often lurk in the darkness of woods to rape them. Thereafter these women are murdered so that they will not talk. Nine out of ten cases of lynching are due to this crime.'⁵² Racial prejudice was often extrapolated from regional stereotypes, which have always been rife in China. Liang Qichao, as Young Lung-chang has demonstrated, contributed several articles on regional differences within China, based on sweeping generalizations and absurd prejudices.⁵³

RACIAL FRONTIERS

In order to heighten racial awareness the reformers dramatized the construct of race, injecting into it a new emotional content. In the sub-universe of the reformers, China was being pulled apart by the conflicting forces of decline and renewal. It would either merge with the defeated hordes of degenerate breeds or join the ranks of

49 Ibid., p. 563. The macaque, *mihou*, had previously been assimilated to the 'blue-eyed, red-bearded barbarians' during the Han; see above, ch. 1, p. 14.
50 Liang Qichao, 'Lun Zhongguo zhi jiangqiang' (About the future power of China) in *YBSWJ*, 2, 2: 13.
51 Liang Qichao, 'Lun Zhongguo renzhong zhi jianglai' (About the future of the Chinese race) in *YBSWJ*, 2, 3: 52; see also 2, 3: 41; 3, 4: 8; 5, 22: 87.
52 Liang, 'Xin dalu' in *YBSZJ*, 5, 22: 87.
53 Young Lung-chang, 'Regional stereotypes in China', *Chinese Studies in History*, 21, no. 45 (Summer 1988), pp. 32–57.

the dominating races. A still loftier ideal beckoned: China could subjugate the white race and rule the world. Liang Qichao declared that the whites were arrogant and disliked hard work.[54] The yellows, on the contrary, were humble and diligent; they were the initiators of civilization, the descendants of the Yellow Emperor.[55] The darker races had already been eliminated from the stage of history. The Han race could unite the globe. Australia and America would become the colonies of the ruling yellow race.[56] Liang theatricalized the 'yellow peril': 'Our Chinese race is the most expansive and vigorous race on the earth. Both England and France are alarmed because our race cannot be restrained and will spread all over the world. They even fear that we will one day overflow and invade Europe.'[57] Articles on the 'yellow peril', taken from the foreign press, were translated and published in the reformers' main organ.[58]

The 'white race', however, remained a flexible category. Throughout his voluminous writings, Liang Qichao further classified the enemy. In the first issue of his 'New Citizen', for instance, he divided the whites into Latin, Slavonic, and Teutonic races. The Latins had reached their peak during the Middle Ages, but had perished under the Teutons, who had dominated Europe since the fall of Rome. The Teutons were further subdivided into Germans and Anglo-Saxons. The Anglo-Saxons had proved to be the only 'superior' 'race': they occupied a quarter of the globe and were present on all the five continents.[59]

54 Liang, 'Lun Zhongguo renzhong zhi jianglai' in YBSWJ, 2, 3: 52.
55 Liang Qichao, 'Zhongguoshi xulun' (About Chinese history), YBSWJ, 3, 6: 6; 'Lun Zhongguo xueshu sixiang bianqian zhi dashi' (About the general trend of the changes in Chinese scientific thought) in YBSWJ, 3, 7: 4 for example.
56 Liang, 'Lun Zhongguo renzhong zhi jianglai' in YBSWJ, 2, 3: 52–4.
57 Liang Qichao, 'Lun Zhongguo guomin zhi pinge' (About China's national quality) in YBSWJ, 5, 14: 5; see also 3, 6: 44.
58 Shiwubao (Current affairs), reprinted, Taipei: Zhonghua shuju, 1967, vol. 1, pp. 361–2; see also p. 311.
59 Liang Qichao, 'Xinminshuo' (About renewing the people) in YBSZJ, 3, 4: 7–8; see also 'Ouzhou dili dashi lun' (About the general trend of European geography) in YBSWJ, 4, 10: 101–6.

Classifications and charts were Liang's obsession; they lent an aura of scientific authenticity to his racial message. A more sophisticated analysis led him to distinguish between a Hamitic, a Semitic and an Aryan race. The Hamitic and Semitic races, assumed to be branches of the white race, had had their period of glory in ancient Europe, but only the Aryan race – comprising the Latin, Celtic, Teutonic and Slavonic sub-races – had contributed to modern European civilization. Through an inexorable process of struggle for survival, Liang claimed, the Teutons had emerged in recent times as the dominant power.[60]

The primary function of such tedious articles was to channel information about other peoples. Many Chinese intellectuals were discovering that the West encompassed many different life-styles, with values and norms widely at variance from those of their own country. But all these efforts to dissect the white race also served to belittle China's sole rival for supremacy. The notion of a white race was narrowed down to the Anglo-Saxons; all other Westerners simply receded into the background.

The white race was degraded by fragmentation, the yellow race was aggrandized by integration. Racial frontiers could easily be reassigned. The Vietnamese and the Filipinos provide a case-study of the phenomenon of inclusion and exclusion. Both peoples were usually classified as 'brown', but during the struggle against the French the Vietnamese suddenly found themselves described as 'real yellows' who would 'never allow themselves to become meat on the white race's chopping block'. They would fight the French devils (*fagui*) until not one single 'hirsute, ash-eyed white man' remained in their country.[61] The Filipinos, normally excluded as black savages,[62] were portrayed as the 'spearhead of the yellow race's fight against the white race' during their struggle against

60 Liang, 'Xin shixue' in *YBSWJ*, 4, 9: 19.

61 Liang Qichao, 'Yuenan zhi wangguo shi' (The history of Vietnam's national subjugation) in *YBSZJ*, 4, 19: 24–6.

62 Seamen from Luzon were named 'black devils' (*heigui*); see 'Bianzheng rengui lun' (About properly distinguishing men from devils), *Wangguo gongbao*, 15 (2 Dec. 1882), pp. 146–7.

the United States in 1898.[63] Japan's success in emulating the West was ascribed to the fact that its race had 'originated from China'.[64]

The discourse of race found institutional support after Liang's arrival in Japan in late 1898. After the *coup d'état* which abruptly ended the Hundred Days (the three months during which the emperor appointed reformers to official positions in an attempt to modernize the country), he escaped with the help of pan-Asianists Hirayama Shū and Yamada Ryōsei.[65] Some of Liang's closest friends in Japan were linked with pan-Asianist associations, for instance Miyasaki Torazō and Kashiwabara Bantarō. Pan-Asianism was based on the notion of a common race (*dōshu* or *tong-zhong*) and a shared cultural heritage (*dōbun* or *tongwen*), uniting Asia in its fight for independence from the West. Liang introduced pan-Asianism in the first issue of his *Qingyibao* (Upright discussions), which he started two months after his arrival in Japan. The aims of this journal included the 'exchange of information between China and Japan and the establishment of friendship'. He also proposed to 'expound the learning of East Asia in order to preserve Asia's essence [*yacui*].'[66] Japan was acclaimed as China's 'fraternal neighbour, as closely related as lips to teeth', an old saying which became proverbial after it was used by the last Jin emperor in a warning to the Song emperor against the Mongols.[67] Pan-Asianism was compatible with Liang's longing for a cosmopolitan world order, a notion typical of intellectuals emerging

---

63 Liang Qichao, 'Lun Mei Fei Ying Du zhi zhanshi guanxi yu Zhongguo' (About the effects of international conflicts on China) in *YBSWJ*, 4, 11: 2. See also Liang Qichao, 'Mieguo xinfa lun' (About a new way of exterminating a country) in *YBSWJ*, 3, 6: 38.

64 Liang, 'Lun Zhongguo zhi jiangqiang' in *YBSWJ*, 2, 2: 13.

65 P. Huang, *Liang Ch'i-ch'ao and modern Chinese liberalism*, Seattle: University of Washington Press, 1972, p. 47. For the influence of Japan on Liang, see Huang's third chapter; for an account of Liang's translation of Shiba Shirō's pan-Asian novel *Jiaren qiyu* (Strange encounters of elegant females), see pp. 49–52.

66 Liang, *Qingyibao* in *YBSWJ*, 2, 3: 31.

67 Liang, 'Lun xue Ribenwen zhi yi' (About the advantage of learning Japanese) in *YBSWJ*, 2, 4: 82.

from a Confucian ideal of universal harmony. It did not, however, exert a lasting influence on him, as he soon realized that this utopian vision was subordinated to Japan's military expansion. After little more than a year, on the occasion of the hundredth issue of the *Qingyibao*, the principles of pan-Asianism were no longer mentioned.[68] A subsequent analysis of Asia's racial composition would only confer the title of 'superior yellow race' on China. Other Asians were categorized as of 'inferior yellow race'.[69]

Liang also rejected the Western notion of a 'Mongolian race' and excluded China's minorities from the 'genuine yellows'. He distinguished ten different races in China, six of which were of relative importance. The Miao were described as China's aborigines, similar to America's reds or Australia's blacks. The comparison was symbolic: the Miao were doomed to rapid extinction and deserved no further attention. In contrast to this dismissal of the Miao, there followed a passionate panegyric to the Han race. They were the initiators of civilization and had civilized the whole of Asia. Also, they could claim divine origin and were illustrious all over the world. The Tibetan race, found in Tibet and Burma, were the descendants of the Jiang (during the Yin and Zhou dynasties), the Yue (during the Qin and Han dynasties), the Tufan (during the Tang dynasty) and the Xixia (during the Song dynasty). The Mongols, living in inner and outer Mongolia, were renowned for their military prowess and had founded the Yuan dynasty. The Xiongnu lived in Middle Asia and in the Xinjiang area; they also included several ancient barbarian tribes. The Tungus – the founders of the Qing dynasty – had originated in north Korea and spread over the Heilongjiang region. Although Liang found it difficult to determine the precise origins of a race, he concluded that the 'gigantic Han race' was quite unique and by no ways comparable to China's minorities.[70] He declared that the

68 Liang Qichao, 'Qingyibao zhi xingzhi' (The nature of the Qingyibao) in *YBSWJ*, 3, 6: 54.
69 Liang Qichao, 'Yazhou dili dashi lun' (About the general trend in Asian geography) in *YBSWJ*, 4, 10: 76.
70 Liang, 'Lun Zhongguo xueshu' in *YBSWJ*, 3, 7: 4.

terms 'Han race' and 'yellow race' were synonymous.[71] The racial frontiers of the 'genuine yellows' did not extend beyond the glorious Han.

RACIAL AMALGAMATION

Amalgamation of selected races was a key to reform. Yi Nai actively advocated interracial marriage (hezhong) as a means of strengthening the people of the empire. Although he anticipated intermarriage with the white race, unions with the inferior black and red races had to be discarded.[72] The diplomat Wu Tingfang also pronounced himself in favour of mixed unions: 'There is no doubt that mixed marriages of the white with the yellow races will be productive of good to both sides.'[73] Tang Caichang advocated the amalgamation of the white and yellow races,[74] for it was only through 'racial communication' (tongzhong) that China would flourish again. He advanced ten arguments in support of intermarriage:

(1) The exuberance of flowers and plants was the result of their original union. Giant prehistoric trees that had failed to merge with other varieties had disappeared after natural catastrophes.

(2) Bees and butterflies were the matchmakers of nature. They contributed to the blooming of flowers by transmitting the pollen from one variety to the other.

(3) Zoologists had proved that the nature of animals could be enhanced by environmental and dietary change. In the Age of Great Peace, the world would be open to exchange, the mean would be ennobled, and the unruly would become tractable. In

71 Ibid., 3, 7: 4.
72 Yi Nai, 'Zhongguo yi yi yi ruo wei qiang shuo' (China should take its weakness for strength) in Xiangbao leicuan (Classified compilation of articles from the Xiangbao), Feb. 1898–April 1898, Taipei: Datong shuju, 1968, vol. 1, pp. 23–4.
73 Wu Tingfang, America through the spectacles of an Oriental diplomat, New York: Stokes, 1914, p. 185.
74 The following is based on Tang Caichang, 'Tongzhongshuo' (About racial communication) in Tang Caichang ji (Works of Tang Caichang), Beijing: Zhonghua shuju, 1980, pp. 100–4.

times of trouble, people lived in insularity, devoured by envy and hatred for different people, debased by an evil nature.

(4) In ancient times, marriage within the lineage had been prohibited. This principle was in accordance with the idea of racial exchange. Only people isolated by high mountains and deep valleys were debarred from exogamy; their population could not flourish, and quickly disappeared.

(5) Between the five continents, there was a general flow of political, artistic, military and economic exchanges. Why would racial exchange not follow?

(6) The Japanese recognized the strength of the European race and the weakness of the Asian race: their government sanctioned the practice of intermarriage.

(7) In Hong Kong, Singapore and the Pacific islands, intermarriage between Chinese and foreigners had produced offspring of unparalleled intelligence and strength.

(8) Although England, Russia, France and Germany all maintained national borders and nurtured mutual distrust, their citizens were free to intermarry.

(9) Buddhism believed in a pervading spirit uniting all living creatures.

(10) Intermarriage was not confined to the treaty ports alone: even several high officials had taken Western wives.

Tang drew upon botany, zoology, history and even Buddhism in his defence of race contact. Thus far, however, his arguments lacked an essential element: an indigenous cultural trait on which the idea of racial exchange could be grafted. Tang continued his dissertation by opposing two foreign schools of learning. The school of evolution believed in the theory of natural selection and the elimination of the unfit. That of physiology, on the other hand, considered that with the progress of medicine and universal truth, the weak could be cured and the evil transformed. Evolution corresponded to Xunzi's theory of man's evil nature. Physiology was compared to Mencius' teachings on the innate goodness of man. Whereas Xunzi upheld justice (*yi*), Mencius supported humanity (*ren*). Only the latter, however, suited the 'One World' (*datong*), an age of equality in which racial communication would

inevitably follow other forms of communication. Mencius sanctioned racial amalgamation: only if the white and yellow races
merged would the strength of the yellow race be enhanced, in
accordance with Confucianism.

Kang Youwei, perhaps the most acclaimed Chinese philosopher
of the last hundred years, expounded a utopian vision of the world
in his *Datongshu*, or 'One World', completed in 1902. Kang was
an outstanding classical scholar from an influential gentry family
near Canton. Although many members of his lineage were traditional literati, some rose to official positions through military
service; others engaged in trade, and one of his uncles applied his
talents to industrial enterprise. Kang Youwei became the leader of
the reform movement and played a key role during the Hundred
Days in 1898. *One World* argued for the elimination of the darker
races in order to achieve universal harmony. Darker races were
unequal and should be eradicated. Kang proposed to whiten them
by dietary change, intermarriage, migration and sterilization.

Dietary change consisted of replacing 'indigestible insects,
grass' and other gastronomical oddities,[75] on which Africans were
thought to subsist, by properly cooked food. If several generations
of blacks were fed on a Chinese diet, they would at least lose their
fishy smell (*xingchou*). Intermarriage was difficult to realize. The
appearance of the blacks, 'with their iron faces, silver teeth, slant-
ing jaws like a pig, front view like an ox, full breasts and long hair,
their hands and feet dark black, stupid [*chun*] like sheep or swine',
was simply too frightening.[76] No refined white girl would ever
agree to mate with a 'monstrously ugly black'.[77] Whites and
yellows who married blacks as a contribution to the purification of
mankind should therefore be awarded a medal with the inscription
'Improver of the race'.[78] The migration method was founded
on environmental determinism. Kang had already observed that
British people born in India had a 'yellow-bluish' (*huanglan*) hue,

75 Kang Youwei, *Datongshu* (One World), Beijing: Guji chubanshe, 1956,
p. 122.
76 Ibid., p. 118.
77 Ibid.
78 Ibid., p. 121.

whereas Chinese born in Europe or in the United States evidenced a distinctive white colour. Old blacks should be shipped to Canada, South America and Brazil, the best of the Africans being relocated in Europe.[79]

The last method recommended by Kang was sterilization. 'Browns or blacks whose characteristics are too bad, whose physical appearance is too ugly or who carry a disease should be given a sterilizing medication to stop the perpetuation of their race.'[80] Some Western race theories ultimately proposed segregation or extermination, whereas Kang merely prescribed racial unity through assimilation. He transformed the traditional concept of cultural absorption into a vision of physical amalgamation. Westerners sought purity, the Chinese unity. The West's technological superiority had led to the discovery of the world, but Westerners soon realised that they were demographically in the minority: in their tortured imagination, they were confronted by hordes of uncivilized savages who would overflow and destroy their superior civilization. Despite exclusion acts, the West had been infiltrated and infested by impure elements; its search for purity was an expression of anxiety. China had less to fear. The reformers pointed to its huge land mass and vast population. They could safely surmise that yellow would emerge as the dominant type after an amalgamation of the races, much as Mao Zedong, half a century later, would contemplate atomic war, firmly believing that China would prevail by sheer weight of numbers.

Geographic determinism was important not only for Kang Youwei's migration plans. Xue Fucheng (1838–94), a high official and respected expert on foreign affairs often quoted by the reformers, stopped in Saigon, Singapore and Ceylon on his way to Europe, where he served as a minister from 1890 until his death in 1894. His diary was an eye-witness report: 'I have seen the aborigines of Saigon, Singapore and Ceylon. They are ugly and savage, similar to deer and swine. The various people from Vietnam, Burma, India, Malaya and Arabia are all black-faced, stocky and

79 Ibid.
80 Ibid., p. 122.

boorish. How could they be compared with the Chinese refinement and elegance and the Europeans' whiteness and tall stature?'[81] Climate was responsible for this racial inequality. Below the 'red line', or equator, the heat drained them of their *jingqi*,[82] or vital essence, leaving them without physical strength or mental energy. 'In the tropics, people propagate but have no spirit.'[83] Only in the temperate zones could *jingqi* be congealed and accumulated, setting the whites and yellows apart from the other races. Geographic determinism also helped Liang to explain the irreversible inferiority of the darker races. Africans lived in tropical regions: they had a 'muddled mind' and did not 'think of progress'.[84]

'WESTERN INFLUENCE'

As was underlined in the theoretical introduction to this chapter, the reformers interacted mainly with indigenous intellectual trends and had only minimal contact with foreign systems of thought. Liang Qichao's main source of inspiration was the *Yinghuan zhilüe* (Brief account of the maritime circuit), which he bought in Shanghai in 1894 after having failed the metropolitan examination. Only then did he 'start to discover that there were five continents and various nations'.[85] The *Yinghuan zhilüe*, introduced in the preceding chapter, was a world geography compiled from various sources by the New Text Confucianist Xu Jiyu in 1848. It presented Africa as a chaotic continent, inhabited by

81 Xue Fucheng, *Chushi Ying, Fa, Yi, Bi siguo riji* (Diary in four countries), Taipei: Wenhai chubanshe, 1966–7, p. 28. This part has been deleted in the 1981 edition; Xue Fucheng, *Chushi siguo riji*, Changsha: Hunan renmin chubanshe, 1981, p. 20; see also p. 14.
82 *Jing* is a medical term for a fundamental substance maintaining the function of the body; *qi* is the energy of life.
83 Xue, *Siguo riji*, p. 29.
84 Liang Qichao, 'Dili yu wenming zhi guanxi' (The relation between geography and civilization) in *YBSWJ*, 4, 10: 106–7.
85 Ding Wenjiang, *Liang Rengong xiansheng nianpu changbian chugao* (A first draft chronological biography of Liang Qichao), Taipei: Shijie shuju, 1959, p. 15.

backward black barbarians. Tang Caichang also drew upon the *Yinghuan zhilüe* in his description of Africa.[86] He introduced his 'Study of the races of the world' with a summary of Yan Fu's essays.[87] Tang's study was a compilation of quotations taken from Chinese and Western sources. Altogether, he cited thirty-three different sources, of which eighteen were Chinese.[88] Besides Xu Jiyu, the most often quoted was the *Wanguo shiji* (A world history) by the Japanese Okamoto Kansuke, translated in the 1890s. Of the fifteen Western publications cited, all translated by missionaries, eleven dealt exclusively with European history. Finally, of a total of ninety-seven quotations, only twenty-seven were derived from Western sources.

Robert Mackenzie's *Nineteenth century: A history* was often quoted by the reformers. Translated by Timothy Richard in 1894, it became popular among the new élites and was included in a selection of foreign books that Liang strongly recommended to students of the West.[89] Mackenzie's history was a vulgar hymn to the benefits of progress. The *Nineteenth century* depicted a state of barbarism and ignorance that was confronted by a reign of enlightenment and democracy. Within this universe, missionaries spent years of excruciating effort attempting to undermine heathenism and reclaim the world to God. A typical example was the Sandwich Islands. Before the arrival of Christianity and civilization, the inhabitants had 'sunk to the lowest depth of degradation. They

---

86 Tang, *Juedianmingzhai*, pp. 558–62.
87 Ibid., p. 467.
88 Chinese sources, besides contemporary material, also included the *Suishu* (622), the *Liangshu* (629), the *Jinshu* (645), the *Mingshi* (1735), Du You's (732–812) *Tongdian*, Ma Duanlin's *Wenxian tongkao* (1317), Gu Yanwu's (1613–82) *Tianxia junguo libing shu* and Wei Yuan's (1734–1856) *Shengwuji* (1842).
89 Liang Qichao, 'Xixue shu mubiao (zhaize)' (A choice of books to study the West) in Jian Bozan et al. (eds), *Wuxu bianfa* (The Hundred Days), Shanghai: Shenzhou guoguang she, 1953, vol. 1, pp. 447–62. A discussion of the complete list of books compiled by Liang can be found in Chen Chi-Yun, 'Liang Ch'i-ch'ao's missionary education: A case study of missionary influence on the reform', *Papers on China*, 16 (1962), pp. 111–14. Chen believes that 'the missionary influence upon Liang Ch'i-ch'ao seemed to be rather indirect'; ibid., p. 78.

fed on raw fish and the flesh of dogs . . . The family relation was unknown. Licentiousness was without limit or restraint of shame . . . Population was rapidly diminishing under the wasting influence of the vices which prevailed.'[90] With Christianity, however, the picture changed drastically. 'The people became quiet, orderly, industrious . . . [Christianity was] bringing in its train security to life and property, peace, industry, and progress; raising the wasteful and treacherous savage to the dignity of a God-fearing, law-abiding citizen, who bears fairly his contribution to the common welfare of the human family.'[91] The reformers blotted out the whole process of progress which had elevated the 'savage' to 'civilization', denying that the blacks could possibly be part of the 'human family'. They deliberately obliterated the 'enlightened' side of the picture in which most Western sources visualized foreign peoples. Notions such as 'equality among nations', 'human family' or 'coexistence of civilizations' were discarded. There had been one world, and the world would be one.

Another example is W.A.P. Martin's translation of Henry Wheaton's standard work, *Elements of international law*, first published in 1863. This treatise was used by Tang Caichang and the reformers in support of their views about minorities, who were considered to have no culture or religion and thus could not be regarded as equal to the 'civilized' 'races'. By quoting Wheaton, these opinions were given a pseudo-legal sanction. The reformers, however, considerably distorted the *Elements* by citing the only sentence concerning 'savages' in a 500-page treatise: 'A state is also distinguished from an unsettled horde of wandering savages not yet formed into a civil society.'[92] Kang Youwei had gained fame by drawing on his scholarship to reinterpret the classics: he attempted to demonstrate that Confucius had never resisted social change and that Confucianism was compatible with reform. Equally, the reformers manipulated Western sources in their

90 R. Mackenzie, *The nineteenth century: A history*, London: T. Nelson and Sons, 1889, p. 212.
91 Ibid., pp. 213–14.
92 H. Wheaton, *Elements of international law*, London: Stevens, 1889, part 1, para 17, line 3, p. 30.

efforts to reconstruct an alternative symbolic universe.

Extended contact with Western discrimination could activate defensive reactions. In a chapter entitled 'California, 1882-1885: Confrontation with racial antagonism', Noriko Kamachi has convincingly demonstrated how the reformer Huang Zunxian (1848–1905) developed an evolutionary world view of racial conflict after having experienced racial discrimination in the United States. Huang was shocked by the violence of American anti-Chinese sentiment and felt humiliated by the lowly position of the Chinese in California. He would later express his pride in his country in an aggressive military march with the words: 'Harmony among the five continents cannot be realized. Blacks and reds were humiliated by the whites. Now the whites are afraid of the 'yellow peril'. What is the yellow peril? It is we, we Asians! We! We! We!'[93] Belief in universal harmony was all too easily inverted into an opposite pole of racial conflagration.

Huang, however, had developed a racial consciousness even before his arrival in the United States. In Japan, he used the phrase 'same culture same race' (*tongwen tongzhong*) to construct a fictive sense of biological unity between Chinese and Japanese. Huang insisted that the Japanese were descendants of the Han, and reproached them for neglecting to mention their Chinese ancestry.[94] Moreover, before his arrival in the United States, Huang was already writing about the 'black slaves' and the 'yellow race' being endangered by the mounting white tide.[95] His ideas seemed to be in harmony with those of Okamoto Kansuke, the author of a world history that was popular with the reformers in the 1890s: 'There are five human races: the yellow, the white, the black, the purple and the copper. Their origins are all different.'[96] In any event, did white prejudice oblige Huang to denigrate what he called the 'stupid black slaves', or had blacks never been part of his

---

93 See Noriko Kamachi, *Reform in China: Huang Tsun-hsien and the Japanese model*, Cambridge, Mass.: Harvard University Press, 1981, p. 141.
94 Ibid., p. 55.
95 Huang Zunxian, *Renjinglu shicao qianzhu* (Collection of annotated poems by Huang Zunxian), Shanghai: Guji chubanshe, 1981, p. 238.
96 Ibid., p. 239, n. 4.

ideal of universal harmony (*datong*)?[97] Like Kang Youwei and other intellectuals, Huang perhaps confused harmony with unity. At the age of twenty, still immersed in a sinocentric universe, he wrote that 'all men are fashioned out of yellow mud'; at fifty-four, having discovered that there was more than yellow mud in the world, he wondered 'Why is the yellow race not the only race in the world?'[98]

ALTERNATIVES

The traditional élite tried to maintain its power by discrediting the reformers' competing body of knowledge. For the conservatives, 'race' was taboo, as it implied a degree of relativism that undermined the bases of their sinocentric universe.[99] In mid-1898 a group of scholars drew up a seven-point 'Scholars' Covenant' criticizing the reformers. The sixth point lambasted the vitiated language of Kang Youwei's followers and denounced the use of terms like 'yellow race' (*huangzhong*) and 'white race' (*baizhong*).[100] Ye Dehui also vehemently rebuked the reformers' proposals for racial amalgamation, which he could only describe as the 'wild barking of mad dogs'.[101] The construct of race remained the prerogative of the reformers.

The reformers constructed race as an extension of the patrilineal line of descent. *Baozhong*, or the 'preservation of the race', encapsulated contemporary anxieties and legitimized the need for reform. Confucianism, however, continued to exert an influence as a religious-moral faith. *Baojiao*, or the 'preservation of the faith', was an attempt to promote Confucianism as a national

97 Ibid., p. 362.
98 Kamachi, *Huang Tsun-hsien*, pp. 15, 141.
99 See however, S. Nagata, *Untersuchungen zum Konservatismus im China des späten 19. Jahrhunderts*, Wiesbaden: Otto Harrassowitz, 1978, pp. 118–200.
100 C.M. Lewis, *Prologue to the Chinese revolution: The transformation of ideas and institutions in Hunan Province, 1891–1907*, Cambridge, Mass.: Harvard University East Asian Research Center, 1976, pp. 64–5.
101 Ye Dehui (ed.), *Yijiao congbian* (Documents of the campaign against the 1898 reform movement), Taipei: Wenhai chubanshe, 1970, p. 442.

religion by giving it an institutional legitimation. Despite the many attacks on the traditional culturalist world view, Confucianism remained a powerful form of ethical-spiritual identity. *Baohuang*, or the 'preservation of the emperor', was also brandished by the reformers in their promotion of a constitutional monarchy. Most people, however, wanted neither a Confucius nor an Emperor. The revolutionaries would reject both in order to focus on the preservation of the race.

4

RACE AS NATION (1903-1915)

Race as nation was a conceptual extension of race as lineage. *Minzu*, or 'nation', integrated both the notion of people (*min*) and the fiction of descent (*zu*). The reformers first conceptualized *minzu* in 1903 in an attempt to find a political rationale for the state.[1] 'Nation' meant a lineage that shared a territory and an ancestor: it was both an organic and a corporate unit. The reformers' definition of 'nation' was opposed to that of the revolutionaries: whereas the former promoted a 'greater nationalism' (*da minzuzhuyi*) which included all 'yellow people' dwelling on the soil of empire, the latter narrowly focused on the 'Han descendants of the Yellow Emperor' (*xiao minzuzhuyi*). The reformers still hoped to preserve Confucius and the emperor (*baojiao* and *baohuang*), but the revolutionaries advocated only the preservation of the race and the state (*baozhong* and *baoguo*). In 1899, for instance, Kang Youwei formed a monarchist society to protect the emperor. Branches of this society were established in Chinese communities overseas, leading to a conflict with Sun Yatsen and the revolutionaries striving for the overthrow of the Qing dynasty. The revolutionaries were often educated in Japan and were generally younger than the generation of reformers.

This chapter is based on the periodical press and the political pamphlets circulated by the revolutionaries. The reformers elevated the press from an organ for trade news to a powerful social and literary force; the revolutionaries expanded the scope of the periodical press into a means of propaganda. They were generally better funded and better organized than the reformers, some making use of extraterritorial arrangements for the promotion of their journalistic activities. Moreover, whereas the older generation still wrote in a literary style that mainly addressed the educated

---

1 See Liang Qichao, 'Zhengzhixue dajia Bolunzhili zhi xueshuo' (The doctrine of the great political scientist Bluntschli) in *YBSWJ*, 5, 13: 67-89.

public, the younger revolutionaries wrote in various degrees of
vernacular, aiming at the largest possible readership. Finally, it
should be noted that despite official censorship and the imperial
ban on revolutionary journals, the printed word continued to
command a wide circulation in China as well as in Chinese communities abroad. Revolutionary ideas were spread within China
mainly by two new social groups: the students returned from
Japan, whose numbers dramatically increased from the turn of the
century onwards, and the new officers in the reformed army, who
often had close connections with the revolutionaries.

RACIAL EVOLUTION

The racial discourse that developed in China after the Sino-Japanese
War of 1894–95 has generally been reduced to a symbiosis of 'traditional ethnocentrism' with 'modern social Darwinism'. Social
Darwinism can be defined as the application of Charles Darwin's
biological theory of natural selection to the evolution of human
society. It has been used uncritically to characterize a variety of
evolutionary ideas that diverge significantly from Darwin's original theory. Peter Bowler has warned that 'little will be gained if
the term ''social Darwinism'' is extended to cover so many different ideas that it becomes virtually meaningless.'[2]
    It is difficult to describe Charles Darwin's concept of evolution
precisely, especially in view of the modifications he introduced in
subsequent editions of his *On the origin of species* (first published in
1859). Certain aspects of his work, however, should be highlighted in order to facilitate comparisons with different evolutionary views. First, Darwin never developed a systematic analogy
between the natural world and human society. He insisted repeatedly that he was not competent to discuss the social application of
his theory. He did, however, contribute to the rise of what would
later be called social Darwinism by using highly metaphorical concepts in the theoretical exposition of natural selection. The adop-

2 P.J. Bowler, *Evolution: The history of an idea*, Berkeley: University of California Press, 1984, p. 267.

tion of metaphorical concepts, derived from Malthus and Spencer, reinforced the tendency to theorize in social rather than biological terms.[3] The expression 'survival of the fittest' originated only in the 1860s as a synonym for natural selection, not in the early 1850s, before the publication of *On the origin of species*, as is commonly assumed.[4] Secondly, *On the origin of species* underlined the individual basis of human evolution. The emphasis was on selection between individuals, as opposed to selection between groups: 'Owing to this struggle for life, any variation, however slight and from whatever cause proceeding, if it be in any degree profitable to an individual of any species, in its infinitely complex relations to other organic beings and to external nature, will tend to the preservation of that individual, and will generally be inherited by its offspring.'[5] The struggle for existence arose between individuals of the same species, with individuals of other species, or with the environment, but Darwin admitted that 'the struggle almost invariably will be most severe between the individuals of the same species.'[6] In *The descent of man* (1871), Darwin maintained his individualistic approach to evolution but also pointed to intergroup competition. Competition between groups, however, was combined with cooperation within groups. Thirdly, Darwin emphasized that development was a branching and adaptive process, as opposed to the neo-Lamarckian theory of linear ascent. Darwinism saw evolution as an open-ended process governed by natural selection, adaptation and random change. Growth and development represented a process of specialization, leading to new branches on the evolutionary tree. Neo-Lamarckism viewed evolution as an inevitable ascent through a preordained hierarchy of developmental stages on a ladder. Design and progress guided the Lamarckian paradigm: from invertebrates to fish, reptiles,

3 On this, see J.A. Rogers, 'Darwinism and social Darwinism', *Journal of the History of Ideas*, 33, no. 2 (1972), pp. 265–80.
4 See D.B. Paul, 'The selection of the "survival of the fittest" ', *Journal of the History of Biology*, 21, no. 3 (Fall 1988), pp. 411–24.
5 C.R. Darwin, *On the origin of species* (reprint of the 1st edn), with a foreword by C.D. Darlington, London: Watts, 1950, p. 53.
6 Ibid., p. 65.

mammals and man, the embryo developed in a purposeful way towards maturity. Finally, Darwin did not believe that social progress could be transmitted through inheritance. The theory of the inheritance of acquired characteristics was also part of the Lamarckian paradigm. Darwin emphasized random variation and selection. Lamarck assumed that phenotypical changes imposed by altered habits could be inherited by the next generation: the giraffe, for instance, stretches its neck to reach higher leaves. Structural modifications had gradually been accumulated over many generations, producing the long neck which characterizes the species.

As soon as it appeared, Darwin's theory of natural selection was raided by authors of the most divergent political convictions. Many searched to enshrine their preconceived opinions in an evolutionary frame. In France, for instance, right-wing politicians appropriated Darwinian slogans to equate economic competition with the struggle for survival. The dominant tendency, however, was to downplay the 'struggle for life' and to emphasize the progressive implications of evolution, such as social solidarity and cooperation.[7] In the Arab world, some Christian intellectuals adopted popular slogans of struggle for survival.[8] Generally, however, the theory of evolution was interpreted in terms of Quranic authority: most intellectuals rejected the evolutionist justification of war. Shibli Shumayyil translated Büchner's commentary on Darwin into Arabic, replacing struggle and competition by cooperation and striving for the happiness of the whole;[9] Ismail Mazhar supported Kropotkin's views of mutual aid; Jurji Zaydan appealed to Henri Drummond's idea of cooperation.[10]

In the context of modern Chinese intellectual history, 'social

---

7 See L.L. Clark, *Social Darwinism in France*, Tuscaloosa: University of Alabama Press, 1984.

8 H.B. Sharabi, *Arab intellectuals and the West: The formative years, 1875–1914*, Baltimore: Johns Hopkins University Press, 1970, p. 69.

9 A. Hourani, *Arabic thought in the liberal age, 1798–1939*, Cambridge University Press, 1983, pp. 248–50.

10 A.A. Ziadat, *Western science in the Arab world: The impact of Darwinism*, Basingstoke: Macmillan, 1986, pp. 57–60.

Darwinism' is a myth. The predominant evolutionary theories in China from the end of the nineteenth century until the middle of the twentieth century were non-Darwinian. Complete translations of Charles Darwin's work were not even available until 1919.[11] The cliché of 'social Darwinism' also conveys a simplified view of evolutionary theories that reduces a significant part of Chinese intellectual activity to a passive regurgitation of Western thought. Chinese intellectuals received the theory of evolution in a socio-political context very different from that of the West. They operated within a symbolic universe that led them to reinforce different aspects of the evolutionary paradigm. As Mary Rankin noted, 'although the idea of struggle for survival could be used in almost any context, the 1911 revolutionaries tended to apply it particularly in racial terms.'[12] The predominant interpretation of the theory of natural selection was one of racial competition (*zhongzu jingzheng*) and racial survival (*baozhong*). The main external source of inspiration was the synthetic philosophy of Spencer and the linear model of Lamarck.

Yan Fu brought Herbert Spencer's work to the attention of the Chinese public in a series of short essays written in 1895; and in 1898 Zhang Binglin (1869–1936), together with Zeng Guangquan, the grandson of Zeng Guofan, published an introduction to the English philosopher in the reformist journal *Changyanbao*.[13] The first sociology text published in Chinese was Zhang Binglin's translation of a Japanese work inspired by Spencer.[14] It appeared in

11 Ma Junwu, *Wuzhong yuanshi* (C.R. Darwin, *On the origin of species*), Shanghai: Zhonghua shuju, 1919. See also R.B. Freeman, 'Darwin in Chinese', *Archives of Natural History*, 13, no. 1 (1986), pp. 19–24, and P.J.P. Whitehead, 'Darwin in Chinese: Some additions', *Archives of Natural History*, 15, no. 1 (1988), pp. 61–2.

12 M.B. Rankin, *Early Chinese revolutionaries: Radical intellectuals in Shanghai and Chekiang, 1902–1911*, Cambridge, Mass.: Harvard University Press, 1971, p. 30.

13 *Changyanbao*, nos 1–8 (July–Sept. 1898), photolithograph, Taipei: Zhonghua shuju, 1967.

14 See Tang Zhijun, 'Zhang Taiyan de shehuixue' (Zhang Binglin's study of sociology) in Zhang Nianchi (ed.), *Zhang Taiyan shengping yu xueshu* (The life and work of Zhang Binglin), Beijing: Sanlian shudian, 1988, pp. 532–42. It is

1902, the same year in which Yan Fu finished his influential translation of Spencer's *The study of sociology* (1872).[15] The following year, Ma Junwu's *A guide to sociology* included a chapter of Spencer's *Principles of sociology*;[16] Giddings' compendium on Spencer was also made available in Chinese.[17]

An important feature of Spencer's synthetic philosophy was his metaphysical belief in the unity of evolution. All processes of change were explained as the manifestations of a global cosmic evolution. Spencer's belief in the necessity of a universal principle appealed to Chinese intellectuals, who were emerging from a symbolic universe that stressed the interrelation of human and cosmic processes. The reformers attempted to insert their ideas of socio-political transformation into a wider global framework of evolutionary cosmology. Analogous thinking correlated natural, spiritual and social phenomena as the manifestations of a single cosmic principle. Spencer also focussed on group selection. His holistic approach to the idea of evolution stands in contrast to the individualistic basis of Darwin's theory. In Spencer's view, the individual citizen was embedded in a social aggregate that evolved organically. The object of sociology was to study these aggregates: 'In every case its object is to interpret the growth, development, structure, and functions, of the social aggregate, as brought about by the mutual actions of individuals whose natures are partly like those of all men, partly like those of kindred races, partly distinctive.'[18] Societies were aggregates of men, groups whose properties were determined by the properties of their parts. Correlative to

---

worth noting that Darwin's writings were available in Japanese as early as 1881. Meiji Japan's interpretation of Darwinism was heavily nationalistic. It also used Darwin as a weapon against Christianity; see Eikoh Shimao, 'Darwinism in Japan', *Annals of Science*, 38 (1981), pp. 93–102.

15 Yan Fu, *Qunxue siyan* (H. Spencer, *The study of sociology*), Beijing: Shangwu yinshuguan, 1981 (1st edn 1902).

16 Ma Junwu, *Shehuixue yinlun* (A guide to sociology), Shanghai: Xijiang ouhuashe, 1903.

17 Wu Jianchang, *Shehuixue tigang* (An outline of sociology), Shanghai, 1903.

18 H. Spencer, *The study of sociology*, London: Williams and Norgate, 1907, p. 53.

this holistic approach was Spencer's comparison of society to an organism. This analogy was essentially opposed to the other main social theory of the nineteenth century, namely the mechanistic analogy, which viewed human intervention as independent from the social structure. Whereas the organismic view implied a collectivistic political theory, the mechanistic approach supported individualism and atomism.[19] Contemporaries like Lester Ward were quick to point out the incompatibility of Spencer's organismic view of society with his almost fanatical belief in *laissez-faire*. As Stanislaw Andreski noted, 'Rather than to fundamentalist liberalism, Spencer's theory of society should have led him to espouse some form of authoritarian collectivism because the organisms regarded as higher display a greater centralization of the nervous system, and a greater subordination of the parts to the whole.'[20]

The notion of group, however, was also inspired by the Ming loyalists, whose writings were revived by both reformers and revolutionaries. Wang Fuzhi's concept of *qun* (group), used in association with *zu* (lineage) or *lei* (type), was particularly influential. Liang Qichao published a study on the concept of *qun*, 'group', 'flock', in 1897. His 'Shuoqun' (About groups) centred around the problem of integration and organization of the political community.[21] For Liang, processes of change and evolution were directed by the cosmological principle of grouping. Huang Zunxian also perceived China's lack of national cohesion as the country's greatest weakness. He noted that in the West, individuals united in groups to cooperate. Xunzi's idea of *qun* supported his views: 'Heaven created men without the ability to fly like birds or run as fast as beasts. Nonetheless, men are superior in the world. The reason is that men can pool their strength, which beasts cannot do. In the world nothing is stronger than the power

19 See W.M. Simon, 'Herbert Spencer and the social organism', *Journal of the History of Ideas*, 21, no. 2 (April–June 1960), p. 299.

20 S. Andreski, *Herbert Spencer: Structure, function and evolution*, London: Nelson, 1971, p. 28.

21 On Liang Qichao's concept of *qun*, see Chang Hao, *Liang Ch'i-ch'ao and intellectual transition in China, 1890–1907*, Cambridge, Mass.: Harvard University Press, 1971, pp. 95 ff.

of unified force. It is like burning coal: if the pieces are scattered, even a child can kick and extinguish them; if they are put together in a stove, the heat is so intense that no one can even approach it.'[22] Huang developed a concept of national association evolving around the idea of *qun* by 1897. Yan Fu linked the concept of *qun* to Spencer's idea of group by translating sociology as *qunxue*, 'the study of groups', 'for', as he explained, 'Xunzi said that man is superior to animals by his ability to group.'[23] Yan Fu's racial bias was clear in his brief presentation of Darwin, which focused exclusively on the theory of struggle for survival. Instead of conveying the individualistic approach of Darwin, Yan pictured evolution as a process of constant struggle between groups: 'By struggle of species, it is meant struggle for survival. By natural selection, it is meant the survival of the fittest race [*zhong*]. The idea is that people and living organisms appeared in the world and coexisted in all their variety, feeding together on the benefits of nature. When they came in contact with each other, they struggled for their own survival. In the beginning, races struggled with races [*zhong-zheng*], then groups struggled with groups. The weak constantly became the prey of the strong, the stupid constantly became the slaves of the intelligent. Those who survived and perpetuated their species had to be resistant and valiant, agile and ingenious.'[24] Yan Fu shifted the emphasis from individual competition to racial struggle. Group cohesion, he argued, was the principle by which 'the race is strong and the group can stand.'[25] Zhang Binglin associated the principle of *qun* with racial strength. In his article 'On bacteria' (1899), he explained that racial power was proportional to the ability to group (*hequn*): the inferior black, brown and red races, he believed, had become prostrate before the yellow race because they had failed to group. On the other hand, the yellow race was dominated by the whites. The whites had vanquished the yellows because of their greater ability to group.[26]

22 Kamachi, *Huang Tsun-hsien*, p. 166.
23 Yan, *Yan Fu shiwen xuan*, p. 15.
24 Ibid., p. 14.
25 Ibid., p. 17.
26 Tang Zhijun (ed.), *Zhang Taiyan zhenglun xuanji* (Selected political writings

Spencer's cosmological vision of evolution and his concept of group survival attracted Chinese intellectuals. Struggle between groups, however, was not a salient characteristic of his philosophy. Spencer deprecated struggle, abhorred the growth of militarism and disliked biological justifications for war. In his view, cooperation gained a clear preponderance over struggle in the industrial stage of society. Spencer was influenced by Lamarck long before the publication of Darwin's work, and believed firmly in the theory of inheritance of acquired characteristics. From a Lamarckian point of view, the development of altruism was central to the process of adaptation to the environment. Natural selection and struggle for survival were no more than a passing phase of evolution, gradually replaced by cooperation.[27]

In 1898 Yan Fu also translated T.H. Huxley's *Evolution and ethics*. In his lecture of 1893 on evolution and ethics, Huxley had vigorously attacked *laissez-faire* policies and had defended the need to curtail self-interest. Social cooperation was seen as superior to social competition: 'I have termed this gradual strengthening of the social bond, which, though it arrests the struggle for existence inside society, up to a certain point improves the chances of society, as a corporate whole, in the cosmic struggle – the ethical process.'[28] For Huxley, competition was paramount only in the primitive 'state of nature'. Human intervention had led to the construction of a 'state of art', protecting mankind from the antagonism of the cosmic process.[29] Yan Fu paraphrased Huxley: 'The reason why those who want to form a group suppress competition within that group is so that they can withstand the natural forces without the group.'[30] Even among the lower orders,

---

of Zhang Binglin), Beijing: Zhonghua shuju, 1977, p. 139.

27 See J.D.Y. Peel, *Herbert Spencer: The evolution of a sociologist*, London: Heinemann, 1971, pp. 151–2.

28 T.H. Huxley and J. Huxley, *Evolution and ethics*, London: Pilot Press, 1947, p. 54.

29 See J.G. Paradis, *T.H. Huxley: Man's place in nature*, Lincoln: University of Nebraska Press, 1978, pp. 142 ff.

30 Yan Fu, *Tianyanlun* (T.H. Huxley and J. Huxley, *Evolution and ethics*), Beijing: Shangwu yinshuguan, 1981, p. 33.

Huxley detected the fundamental principle of group cohesion which exerted such a strong appeal on his Chinese interpreters: 'Within it [the beehive], the struggle for existence is strictly limited. Queen, drones, and workers have each their allotted sufficiency of food; each performs the function assigned to it in the economy of the hive, and all contribute to the success of the whole co-operative society in its competition with rival collectors of nectar and pollen and with other enemies, in the state of nature without.'[31] The Huxleian dichotomy between 'artificial' and 'natural' society was convergent with the *nei-wai* opposition, or inner-outer dualism, so characteristic of Chinese social philosophy. The writings of Yan Fu and other leading reformers represented an internal state of art opposed to an external state of nature. Spencer's idea of inter-group competition was combined with Huxley's concept of intra-group cooperation to form a social policy of group cohesion that adequately fitted the needs of the time.

In the comments Yan Fu intermingled with his translation of Huxley, the concern with the construct of race was evident.[32] The terms 'group' and 'race' were interchanged,[33] the simian origin of mankind was expounded at length and the imminent racial extinction of the red and black races was announced. Yan Fu even perceived the power to colonize and open up new territories as indicative of the 'inferiority or superiority of a people's race'.[34] The influence of these comments was considerable. One radical writer, for instance, used them to legitimize his own theory on the sub-human origins of the Manchus. The author, writing in the radical magazine *Jiangsu*, compared the difference that had existed between the first man and the primates to the chasm separating

31 Huxley, *Evolution*, p. 47.

32 On this, see also Hao Xiang, 'Lun Zhongguo jindai zichan jieji zhexue dui jinhualun xueshuo de gaizao' (The transformation of the theory of evolution by bourgeois philosophy in modern China), *Zhongguo zhexue shi yanjiu*, 1 (1988), pp. 79–84.

33 Compare *baozhong jinhua* at p. 5 with *baoqun jinhua* at p. 12; see *baozhong* combined with *hequn* at p. 16, etc., in Yan, *Tianyanlun*.

34 Ibid., pp. 30, 14, and 20.

civilized people from 'inferior races of nomads', and went on to urge the Chinese to distance themselves from these 'inferior races' and to join the 'civilized nations' in their advance towards the Pure Land (*jile shijie*, a translation of the Buddhist Sukhavati).[35] The conceptualization of an evolutionary paradigm that was closely correlated to the social and political considerations of the intellectuals was essentially non-Darwinian.[36] The individual basis of evolution was replaced with the concept of *qun*. Darwin's emphasis on the branching process of evolution was also ignored. Reformers and revolutionaries adopted a theory of linear evolution which converged with the Lamarckian paradigm. The evolutionary dimension was rearticulated along a temporal axis with two poles: progress and degeneration. The idea of progress was embedded in language: *jinhua*, or 'evolution', meant 'transformation forwards', whereas its antipode *tuihua*, or 'devolution', meant 'transformation backwards'. Devolution faced evolution: both concepts rapidly infiltrated the public debate, particularly during the first decades of the twentieth century, which were marked by the dissolution of the Confucian symbolic universe, the disintegration of the imperial system, and the dislocation of traditional values. Neurotic concern with degeneration and racial survival became the counterpoint of the cult of progress.[37]

RACIAL PRESERVATION

Nationalism was perceived as a key to racial survival by the Chinese students in Japan during the first decade of the twentieth century.[38]

35 'Renzu' (Ancestors of mankind), *Jiangsu*, 3 (June 1903), pp. 141–3.
36 On the non-Darwinian theories of evolution in Europe, see P.J. Bowler, *The non-Darwinian revolution: Reinterpreting a historical myth*, Baltimore: Johns Hopkins University Press, 1988.
37 Collective neurosis about degeneration was of course widespread in Europe too; see Daniel Pick, *Faces of degeneration: A European disorder, c. 1848–c. 1918*, Cambridge University Press, 1989.
38 This section probes the discourse of race among radical students by focusing mainly on three periodicals, *Tides of Zhejiang* (*Zhejiangchao*), *Jiangsu* (*Jiangsu*) and *Hubei Student* (*Hubei xueshengjie*). These are generally considered to have

The number of students in Japan increased steadily after 1900 to exceed 10,000 by 1906. Although most students initially grouped according to their province of origin, they were quick to develop a strong feeling of national identity and group loyalty.[39] The concept of nationalism was couched in terms borrowed from the Japanese. *Minzuzhuyi*, from the Japanese *minzokushugi*, exerted a lasting influence on the political terminology of the Chinese students. The term literally meant 'racism', and expressed a nationalist vision based on race.[40] Race and nation overlapped in the term *minzu*.[41] The constant juxtaposition of *guo*, 'country', to

---

been the most influential of the scores of periodicals published by students in Japan from 1902–11. Other journals, of course, also included numerous articles pertaining to the construct of race. The *Jingshi wenchao* (Literary tides of statecraft) had a special section on race in each issue ('Renzhongbu') from April 1903 onwards. The *Juemin* charted the history of human races (Zhong Guang, 'Renzhongshi' (History of human races), *Juemin* (Awake the people), 8 (July 1904)); a periodical founded by Hunanese students listed the various origins of mankind and investigated human races ('Wanguo zhongzu yuanshi biao' (Table of the origins of the various nations' races), 'Geguo renzhong leikao' (Study of the types of human races), *Hunan tongsu yanshuobao* (Hunan journal of popular speeches), 12 (Sept. 1903)); one of the main vernacular journals included articles on the Yellow Emperor, human races, and on racial struggles since ancient times ('Renzhong' (Human races), 'Huangdi zhuan' (Biography of the Yellow Emperor), 'Pangu yilai zhongzu jingzheng de dashi' (General trend of racial struggles since Pangu), *Zhongguo baihuabao* (The China vernacular), no. 1 (Dec. 1903) *et seq.*; many other examples could be given.

39 For an introduction to the influence of Japan on Chinese radicals, see M.B. Jansen, 'Japan and the Chinese Revolution of 1911' in D. Twitchett and J.K. Fairbank (eds), *The Cambridge history of China*, Cambridge University Press, 1980, vol. 11, part 2, pp. 339–74.

40 See R.A. Scalapino and G.T. Yu, *Modern China and its revolutionary process: Recurrent challenges to the traditional order, 1850–1920*, Berkeley: University of California Press, 1985, p. 172.

41 The term *minzu* is usually rendered as 'nation', or 'people', but there is an area of overlap with 'tribe' and 'race'. Lexicographic problems were first discussed at official level in the 1950s. In 1954, Fan Wenlan published a study arguing that the Han's *minzu* had taken shape as early as the Qin and Han periods. Fan's thesis was the starting point for a series of heated debates on the exact definition of *minzu*. These culminated in a conference in 1962 that examined the use of the term in translations of Marx, Engels and Stalin. It

zhong, 'race', in set phrases like 'love the race and love the country' (*aizhongaiguo*), or 'national boundaries and racial boundaries' (*guojiezhongjie*) also contributed to the integration of the construct of race into the nationalist vision. The *guo*, as one nationalist explained, was not merely a geographical expression: it had a racial

---

appeared that the German terms *Nation*, *Volk* and *Völkerschaft* as well as the Russian terms *natsia*, *narod* and *narodnost'* had all been translated by *minzu* (Zhang Lu, 'Guanyu "minzu" yici de shiyong he fanyi qingkuang' (About the situation of the use and translation of the term *minzu*), *Minzu tuanjie*, 7 (July 1962), pp. 34–9). It was implicitly recognized that the term embraced a biological as well as a political meaning. An ill-advised translator, however, had rendered Stalin's *narodnost'* by *buzu*, or 'tribe'. *Natsia*, or *minzu*, was used exclusively to describe a community that had already reached a certain level of capitalist development and of political awareness. The conferees finally agreed upon consistently employing the term *minzu* in all cases, thereby ascribing a political status to all the minorities, whatever their stage of development (on this, see G. Moseley, 'China's fresh approach to the national minority question', *The China Quarterly*, 24 (Dec. 1965), pp. 15–27; see also T. Heberer, 'Probleme der Nationalitätentheorie und des Nationsbegriffs in China', *Internationales Asienforum*, 16, nos 1–2 (May 1985), pp. 109–24).

Another result of the conferees' terminological inquiry was to reveal a state of confusion between the terms *zhongzu* (race) and *minzu* (nation). Lin Yaohua, in a lengthy article analyzing the concept of *minzu*, quoted several contemporary historians who used both terms indiscriminately, and urged social scientists to be more attentive to terminology (Lin Yaohua, 'Guanyu "minzu" yici de shiyong he yiming de wenti' (About the problems of the synonyms and the use of the term *minzu*), *Lishi yanjiu*, 2 (Feb. 1963), p. 175). His remonstrations had little effect, as historians in the 1970s still used both terms interchangeably (J.A. Fogel, 'Race and class in Chinese historiography', *Modern China*, 3 (July 1977), p. 351). Such confusion had existed since the adoption of the concept *minzu* from the Japanese (*minzoku*) before 1900. Some researchers have traced the first appearance of the term *minzu* back to Liang Qichao in 1898 (see Jin Tianming and Wang Qingren, '"Minzu" yici lai woguo chuxian ji qi shiyong wenti' (The appearance of the term *minzu* in our country and the problems of its use), *Shehui kexue jikan*, 4 (1981), quoted in Wang Lei, 'The definition of "nation" and the formation of the Han nationality', *Social Sciences in China*, 4, no. 2 (June 1983), p. 167). More recent research goes back to a 1895 issue of the reformist journal *Qiangxuebao* (Han Jinchun and Li Yifu, 'Hanwen "minzu" yici de chuxian ji qi zaoqi shiyong qingkuang' (The first appearance of the term *minzu* in Chinese and the circumstances of its early use), *Minzu yanjiu*, 2 (1984), pp. 36–43). This has been challenged by

connotation.[42] Even Yan Fu publicly declared that 'the sentiment of patriotism is rooted in racial nature'.[43]

Racial survival lay at the root of the radical students' concern with group cohesion. The first issue of the *Tides of Zhejiang*, a nationalist journal published in Japan by Chinese students, stated that 'those who are able to group their own tribe into an organized body able to resist other groups will survive.' In an era dominated by racial competition, the key to survival lay in the cohesive force of the group (*qunli*). Nationalism fostered unity, as it 'erects borders against the outside and unites the group inside'.[44] A contributor to the journal *Yunnan* attributed the decline of the 'barbarian red and the savage black races' to their ignorance of the racial principles of nationalism: a nation needed a 'group strategy and group strength' (*quncequnli*).[45]

World politics were expounded in terms of racial cohesion. India, for instance, had been conquered by the 'white race' because its class system inhibited racial homogeneity.[46] Russians were a 'crossbreed between Europeans and Asians and nothing else', claimed another polemicist. A cranial analysis and a detailed racial investigation revealed that the Russians had Asian blood running in their veins. This racial heterogeneity was responsible for Russia's inability to group.[47] The naval superiority of the United

Peng Yingming, who believes that the reformer Wang Tao first introduced the term from the English in the early 1870s (Peng Yingming, 'Guanyu woguo minzu gainian lishi de chubu kaocha' (Preliminary investigation with respect to the history of the concept of nation in our country), *Minzu yanjiu*, 2 (1985), pp. 5–7).

42 Yuanyun, 'Sike zhenglun' (Four political views), *Zhejiangchao*, 7 (Sept. 1903), p. 43.

43 Zhang Nan and Wang Renzhi, *Xinhai geming qian shinian jian shilun xuanji* (Selected material on debates of the ten years preceding the 1911 Revolution), Beijing: Sanlian shudian, 1963, vol. 1, p. 110.

44 Yuyi, 'Minzuzhuyi lun' (On nationalism), *Zhejiangchao*, 1 (Feb. 1903), p. 3.

45 *Yunnan*, 1 (Aug. 1906), pp. 7–12.

46 'Yindu miewang zhi yuanyin' (The reasons for the extinction of India), *Zhejiangchao*, 1 (Feb. 1903), pp. 4–6.

47 Feisheng, 'Eren zhi xingzhi' (The Russians' nature), *Zhejiangchao*, 1 (Feb. 1903), pp. 4–5, 2 (March 1903), pp. 77–9.

States, on the other hand, was ascribed to its racial quality: were not the Americans an inch taller than the English?[48]

The discourse of race as nation gradually spread to infect most of the writings of the young radicals. Education, for instance, was seen unanimously as a means of uniting the race in its struggle for survival.[49] An article entitled 'Iron-blooded education' blamed the traditional education system for having lost its 'racial nature' (zhongxing): excessive assimilation of alien races had led to the dilution of Han blood. A new iron-blooded education would have to develop a 'racial ideology' (zhongzu sixiang).[50] Ye Xuesheng echoed the educator's concern by deploring the excessively universalistic orientation of Chinese thought, which had to be replaced by 'racial thought'.[51] Another utopian proclaimed that physical education would prevent the 'withering of the race',[52] whereas an enthusiastic reviewer praised physical exercise as beneficial to 'the strengthening of the race and the protection of the country'.[53] Medicine was also viewed as instrumental in China's racial renaissance.[54] Even sexual equality, a major blow against Confucian puritanism, was envisaged as a means of struggling against the white race: had not the Ming loyalist Gu Yanwu written that 'husband and wife both have a share of responsibility for the fate of the country'?[55]

Despite the mounting tide of anti-Manchuism,[56] the student

48 Taosheng, 'Haishang de Meiren' (The Americans on the sea), Zhejiangchao, 6 (Aug. 1903), p. 2.
49 See, for instance, Shulou, 'Jiaoyuhui wei mintuan zhi jichu' (Education associations as a foundation for civil corps), Jiangsu, 1 (April 1903), pp. 13–19.
50 Lincang, 'Tiexuezhuyi zhi jiaoyu' (Iron-blooded education), Zhejiangchao, 10 (Dec. 1903), pp. 64–6.
51 Ye Xuesheng, 'Zhongguo kaifang lun' (About the opening of China), Zhejiangchao, 6 (Aug. 1903), pp. 1–12.
52 Bolin, 'Tiyu' (Physical education), Yunnan, 1 (Aug. 1906), p. 40.
53 Review of Tiyuxue (Physical education), Zhejiangchao, 4 (May 1903), p. 18a.
54 'Xing yixue tong' (On promoting medicine), Hubei xueshengjie, 2 (Feb. 1903), pp. 61–72.
55 Jiangsu, 4 (July 1903), p. 144.
56 On anti-Manchuism before the 1911 Revolution, see Li Liangyu, 'Xinhai geming shiqi de paiman sixiang' (Anti-Manchuism during the 1911 Revolution), Nanjing daxue xuebao, 2 (1989), pp. 67–77.

journals continued to focus on the 'white race'. A characteristic biography of Koxinga, the famous warrior-general who opposed the Manchus in the seventeenth century, concluded with a panegyric to his racial achievements:

> The whites are the proud sons of heaven [a title normally reserved for 'the descendants of the Yellow Emperor']. They press on the blacks, and the blacks decline; they push down the reds and the reds are destroyed; they raze the browns and the browns die out. Now they display their devilish tricks and lie in wait for us yellows; they are on the watch for us the yellow Han race. Some centuries ago, Genghis Khan was the only one who could resist them. I disdain to worship him: the Mongol race was the public enemy of the Han race. I disdain to worship him, and only adore Zheng Chenggong [Koxinga]. He was able to make the Dutch, who launched European power, hold back and give way. He was able to make the Manchus, after they enslaved the Han race, engage in battle.[57]

The racial imagery woven into their writings by the radical students was not fundamentally different from the notions that had been developed by the reformers. There was a distinct continuity between the discourse of race as lineage to that of race as nation. People were categorized according to a strict racial taxonomy; history became a battlefield for contending races; politics was an arena for struggling nations. Tales of the white peril were counterbalanced by myths of yellow domination: one contribution assessed the possibility of a 'yellow peril',[58] another presented a translation from the Japanese about the imminent extinction of the 'white race' and the advent of a 'yellow age of One World' (*datong*).[59] Speculations about a white peril (*baihuo*) or

57 Yalu, 'Zheng Chenggong zhuan' (A biography of Zheng Chenggong), *Jiangsu*, 4 (July 1903), pp. 70–1.
58 'Huanghuo yuce' (Forecast of the yellow peril), *Jiangsu*, 1 (April 1903), pp. 103–7, based on a Japanese article.
59 Zhang Zhaotong, review of *Weilai shijie lun* (About the future world), *Jiangsu*, 3 (June 1903), p. 20a.

a yellow peril (*huanghuo*), however, remained variations on the more general theme of 'racial peril' (*zhonghuo*).

An increased sense of racial pride distinguished the revolutionaries from the reformers. Student writings consistently reported the humiliating treatment and derogatory pronouncements to which the Chinese were subjected. Europeans, it was revealed, claimed that the Chinese would soon degenerate into animals.[60] The Japanese called them an 'ignoble race' (*jianzhong*) and 'inferior animals' (*liedeng dongwu*).[61] Westerners laughed at the Chinese 'pigtail'; Japanese referred to the Chinese as *chanchanbotsu* ('chink'[62]). The most notable event reported in the press was perhaps the students' successful opposition to an 'Exhibition of the Races of Man' at Osaka in 1903. The exhibition initially planned to group the 'inferior races' of China, Korea, the Ryukyu Islands, India, Hawaii, Taiwan and Java under the heading of 'raw barbarian races' (*shengfanzhong*). Student outrage culminated in an official protest against the inclusion of China in the exhibition. 'Although we Chinese are inferior, why should we have to be classified together with these six races?', lamented one protester.[63] The theme of humiliation still pervades nationalist writings to this day. It emerged as a consciously constructed emotion sometime during the second half of the nineteenth century, and was given an emotional content through a long and complex process of internalization and habituation. Humiliation implied a sense of collective responsibility: the causes of failure could be attributed to the people's lack of effort or ability, not to external factors independent of the human will. It was voluntaristic, and it was opposed to

60 Zhongkan, 'Zizhipian' (On self-government), *Zhejiangchao*, 6 (Aug. 1903), p. 2.
61 *Hubei xueshengjie*, 2 (Feb. 1903), pp. 135–6.
62 'Tong ding tong' (Sorrow calms the sorrow), *Jiangsu*, 3 (June 1903), p. 124. *Chanchanbotsu* is an onomatopoeia associated with the slight ringing sound produced by glasses or coins striking together: chink. Whereas the English word chink primarily means a narrow opening or a slit, the Japanese translation opted for a different kind of association. I am indebted to C.-A. Bois for this information.
63 *Zhejiangchao*, 2 (March 1903), p. 134.

fatalism. Self-accusation completed the idea of causal attribution. The ingroup exacerbated the feeling of humiliation by accusing itself of failure: 'We Chinese are less than black slaves' was a common expression. Once infused with an emotional content, the feeling of humiliation was used as a catalyst. It mobilized patriotism, promoted ingroup solidarity, and addressed the sense of collective responsibility; it fostered outrage and created resentment favourable to voluntarist action.

To boost the morale of the 'race', the radicals pointed to peoples who fared even less well than the Chinese. The Jew often compensated for the injured pride of the Han:

Alas! How could I falsely pity the Jew? I cannot but pity the Jew. I do not pity the Jew of the past, I pity the Jew of the future. Jew! Jew! Tiny reflection of the prospect of our own country. The old Jew goes, the new Jew comes, but the misery of the new Jew surpasses the misery of the old Jew. Alas, when I write these words, the tear stains want to father traces of blood [sic], the traces of blood want to dry up in black marks.'[64]

Clearly, Chinese interest in the fate of the 'stateless Jews' was justified only if it could reflect the imaginary prospect of their own people. In reality, students actually 'warned themselves to refrain from looking down upon the Jews'.[65] Contempt for the Jews, and even a feeling of hatred towards them, remained vivid for decades. Wu Zelin, an outstanding anthropologist active in the 1930s, recently recalled that he and his colleagues used to find the Jews 'laughable, despicable, pitiable, admirable, enviable, and hateful'.[66]

The fact that the construct of race was more than just 'a propaganda tactic' – as a leading expert on the revolutionary movement

64 'Wuhu youtai' (Alas the Jew), *Zhejiangchao*, 7 (Sept. 1903), p. 165; the reformers also lamented the Jews; see for instance 'Youtairen zhi canzhuang' (The miserable condition of the Jew), *Xinmin congbao*, 20 (1903).
65 Ch'en, *China and the West*, p. 160.
66 S. Shapiro, *Jews in old China: Studies by Chinese scholars*, New York: Hippocrene Books, 1984, p. 160. Compare this recent statement with the writings of Wu, presented in the next chapter.

maintains[67] – becomes evident when one abandons the main body of political texts to venture into the short anecdotes and notes scattered through student publications. A qualitative analysis of such a seemingly inoffensive miscellany can provide illuminating insights into the radicals' sub-universe. A genuine interest in the biological processes of human evolution was reflected in short reports on new anthropological findings. A note entitled 'A strange race of men', for instance, described a tribe newly discovered in New Guinea. They were unable to walk, moved about by swinging from liana to liana, had atrophied feet and resembled apes.[68] One compiler established statistics on the comparative height of different nationalities.[69] Another anecdote misinterpreted a traditional African rite of passage: 'We know that if a black's blood mixes with another race, his black colour will gradually diminish. They dislike the ugliness of blackness, and often smear their faces with white powder.'[70] Many anecdotes described how foreigners humiliated the Chinese. Westerners regarded the Chinese as an inferior and uneducated race of slaves. But even the 'black slaves' in the United States were lettered: was this not a source of shame for the civilized Han?[71] In these jottings patriotism was mobilized to castigate those Chinese who betrayed the race: Chinese merchants in Yokohama who had applied for Japanese nationality, for instance, were covered with opprobrium.[72]

67 M. Gasster, 'The Republican revolutionary movement' in D. Twitchett and J.K. Fairbank (eds), *The Cambridge history of China*, Cambridge University Press, 1980, vol. 11, part 2, p. 497.

68 'Qiguai renzhong' (A strange race of men), *Zhejiangchao*, 9 (Nov. 1903), p. 113.

69 'Shijie geguo bingshi shenti zhi changduan' (Comparative height of soldiers from different countries of the world), *Youxue yibian*, 3 (Jan. 1903), pp. 276–7.

70 'Heiren zhi baifen' (The black's white powder), *Zhejiangchao*, 7 (Sept. 1903), p. 172.

71 'Heinu xuexiao' (Schools for the black slaves), *Jiangsu*, 7 (Oct. 1903), p. 168.

72 'Hengbin Huashang ru Ribenjizhe sishi yu ren!' (More than forty Chinese merchants in Yokohama enter the Japanese nationality!), *Jiangsu*, 7 (Oct. 1903), pp. 152–7.

RACIAL ANCESTRY

The myth of blood was sealed by elevating the figure of the Yellow Emperor to a national symbol. The Yellow Emperor (*Huangdi*) was a mythical figure thought to have reigned from 2697 to 2597 BC. He was hailed as the first ancestor (*shizu*) of the Han race, and his portrait served as the frontispiece in many nationalist publications.[73] From mid-1903, the radical magazines started using dates based on the supposed date of birth of the Yellow Emperor. Liu Shipei's (1884-1919) first published article advocated the introduction of a calendar in which the foundation year corresponded to the birth of the Yellow Emperor. 'They [the reformers] see the preservation of religion [*baojiao*] as a handle, so they use the birth of Confucius as the starting date of the calendar; the purpose of our generation is the preservation of the race [*baozhong*], so we use the birth of the Yellow Emperor as a founding date.'[74] Liu Shipei estimated that the Yellow Emperor had ascended the throne in his eleventh year. The Mongolian barbarians had destroyed the Song in 3993, the Manchus had captured Shanhaiguan in 4359, and the international expedition had entered Beijing in 4611: all were foreign races that had forcibly occupied the territory of the descendants of the Yellow Emperor, the Han race. The Yellow Emperor remained a powerful figure for many decades. Despite the historian Gu Jiegang's severe criticism of the myth in the 1920s,[75] he was still officially revered in 1941 as the founder of the nation and initiator of the race.[76]

73 For instance in *Jiangsu*, 3 (1903), *Ershi shiji zhi Zhina*, 1 (June 1905), *Minbao*, 1 (Nov. 1905), and others. The opening issue of the *Minbao* proclaimed that the Yellow Emperor was 'the first great nationalist of the world'.
74 Liu Shipei, 'Huangdi jinian shuo' (About a calendar based on the Yellow Emperor), *Huangdi hun* (The soul of the Yellow Emperor), 1904, p. 1; reprinted, Taipei: Zhonghua minguo shiliao congbian, 1968.
75 Gu Jiegang, 'Huangdi' (Yellow Emperor) in *Shilin zashi* (Miscellaneous historical studies), Beijing: Zhonghua shuju, 1963, pp. 176-84.
76 Zhang Qiyun, 'Huangdi zisun' (Sons of the Yellow Emperor, speech given during the National Festival of Grave Sweeping, 5 April 1941) in *Minzu sixiang* (Nationalist thought), Taipei: Zhengzhong shuju, 1951, p. 1. One of the latest scholarly contributions to the myth of the Yellow Emperor is Qian Mu,

Traditional ideas reinforced the construct of race. Confucian values of filial piety and ancestor worship paved the way for the cult of the Yellow Emperor. Racial loyalty was perceived as an extension of lineage loyalty. The revolutionary Chen Tianhua (1875–1905) integrated traditional values into a pattern of racial solidarity in his influential pamphlets, read throughout the Yangzi valley:[77] 'As the saying goes, a man is not close to people of another family [xing, 'surname']. When two families fight each other, one surely assists one's own family, one definitely does not help the foreign [wai, 'exterior'] family. Common families all descend from one original family: the Han race is one big family. The Yellow Emperor is the great ancestor, all those who are not of the Han race are not the descendants of the Yellow Emperor, they are exterior families. One should definitely not assist them; if one assists them, one lacks a sense of ancestry.'[78] Kin terms were infused into a racial rhetoric that called forth emotional expressions usually reserved for close relatives: 'Racial feeling begins at birth. For the members of one's own race, there is surely mutual intimacy and love; for the members of a foreign race, there is surely mutual savagery and killing.'[79] Such terms fostered the much needed bonds of association and loyalty within the group.

The young revolutionary Zou Rong also regretted the absence of a strong 'racial consciousness' (zhongxing) in China capable of uniting the people in their struggle against the oppressors. Zou Rong greeted the 'peasants with weatherbeaten faces and mud-caked hands and feet' as his genuine countrymen, the proud

Huangdi (The Yellow Emperor), Taipei: Dongda tushu youxian gongsi, 1944 (reprinted, 1987). The religion of the Yellow Emperor was formally established in Taiwan in March 1957 with government approval; see C. Joachim, 'Flowers, fruit, and incense only: Elite versus popular in Taiwan's religion of the Yellow Emperor', Modern China, 16, no. 1 (Jan. 1990), p. 7.

77 On Chen Tianhua, see E.P. Young, 'Ch'en T'ien-hua (1875–1905): A Chinese nationalist', Papers on China, 13 (1959), pp. 113–62.

78 Chen Tianhua, Chen Tianhua ji (Collected works of Chen Tianhua), Changsha: Hunan renmin chubanshe, 1982, p. 82.

79 Ibid., p. 81.

descendants of the Yellow Emperor.[80] Race was the catalyst of group homogeneity; it created clear boundaries by binding the ingroup and distancing the outgroup: 'When men love their race, solidarity will arise internally, and what is outside will be repelled. Hence, to begin with, lineages were united and other lineages repelled; next, villages were united and other villages repelled; thereafter, tribes were united and other tribes were repelled; finally, the people of a country became united, and people of other countries were repelled. This is the general principle of the races of the world, and also a major reason why races engender history. I will demonstrate to my countrymen, to allow them to form their own impression, how our yellow race, the yellow race of which the Han race is part, and I refer you to the history of China, is able to unite itself and repel intruders.'[81] It was the unchanging norm of race which distinguished 'the kinsmen and fellow countrymen of our great Han race' from 'barbarians',[82] in particular the Manchus. The Manchus were to be excluded from the unsullied Han race: 'What you, fellow countrymen, today call court, government or emperor are what we once called barbarians (of North, South, East or West), Hsiung-nu or Tartars. These tribes, living beyond the Shanhaikuan, were not by origin of the same race as the illustrious descendants of our Yellow Emperor. Their land is foul land, they are of a furry race, their hearts are beast's hearts, their customs are the customs of the users of wool, their writing is different from ours, and their clothes are different from ours.'[83]

Classification accentuated the original differences between the Han and the Manchus. Zou divided the yellow race into two main branches, the 'races of China', including the Han, the Tibetan and the Cochinese races; and the 'races of Siberia', composed of the Mongolian, the Tungus and the Turkic peoples.[84] The principal enemy was the 'white race':

80 Tsou Jung, The revolutionary army: A Chinese nationalist tract of 1903, intro. and transl. by J. Lust, Paris: Mouton, 1968, p. 72.
81 Ibid., p. 106.
82 Ibid., p. 109.
83 Ibid., p. 80.

The yellow and white races which are to be found on the globe have been endowed by nature with intelligence and fighting capacity. They are fundamentally incapable of giving way to each other. Hence, glowering and poised for the fight, they have engaged in battle in the world of evolution, the great arena where strength and intelligence have clashed since earliest times, the great theatre where for so long natural selection and progress have been played out.[85]

RACIAL ORIGINS

The nationalists had divergent interpretations of the origins of the human species. Liu Yazi, for instance, believed that racial differences corresponded to various origins of mankind.[86] Most, however, portrayed the Yellow Emperor as the progenitor of the Han race. One particular line of thought associated the Yellow Emperor with Westerners. The National Essence circle borrowed extensively from the historian Terrien de Lacouperie to corroborate the belief in a common origin between Westerners and Chinese. In his *Western origins of the early Chinese civilisation*, Lacouperie had put forward a theory on the derivative nature of the 'Chinese race':[87] a small number of families in possession of a comparatively advanced civilization arrived in China around the twenty-third century BC. These immigrants were the Bak Sings, who had originated in the vicinity of Elam and Babylonia and were directly connected with the Sumero-Akkadians. The Bak Sings were headed by the Yellow Emperor, whose name was similar to Kudur Nakhunti, the generic title of the kings of Susiana. The Yellow Emperor led his people to the south-west of present-day Gansu, where he eventually founded the Chinese Kingdom. The Baks were initially hemmed in by native states inhabited by the *limin*, or black-headed

84 Ibid., pp. 106–7.
85 Ibid., p. 106.
86 Liu Yazi, in Zhang and Wang, *Xinhai geming*, vol. 2, p. 813.
87 The following is based on Albert Etienne Jean-Baptiste Terrien de Lacouperie, *Western origins of the early Chinese civilisation from 2300 B.C. to 200 A.D.*, London: Asher, 1894.

people, but these were gradually forced into submission by conquest and intermarriage until the eventual establishment of a Chinese dominion on both sides of the Yellow River.

Apart from Herbert Spencer, the principal Western influence on Liu Shipei's *Book of expulsion (Rangshu)* was Lacouperie. Liu had consulted Lacouperie's theory in a Japanese *History of Chinese culture* readily available to Chinese students in Japan.[88] As noted in the preceding chapter, key sections of the *Western origins of the early Chinese civilisation* were eventually translated by Jiang Zhiyou and published between October 1903 and January 1905 in Liang Qichao's *New People's Journal*.[89] Terrien de Lacouperie's hypothesis about the Western origins of the Chinese was also introduced in the first issue of the *National Essence Journal*. This periodical was dedicated to the preservation of the national essence (*guocui*) of the Chinese civilization, which was thought to be threatened with extinction. For the National Essence group, the Yellow Emperor represented the Chinese race, but it was underlined that 'the race did not start with the Yellow Emperor'.[90] Huang Jie introduced Lacouperie in his 'Yellow History' and identified the Yellow Emperor as the father of the race, an offshoot of Western stock.[91] Lacouperie's theory remained influential at least until the 1930s.

Zhang Binglin was one of the more complex figures among the nationalists.[92] His philosophical approach, inspired mainly by

88 Liu's views on race have been treated by Martin Bernal, 'Liu Shih-p'ei and National Essence' in C. Furth (ed.), *The limits of change: Essays on conservative alternatives in Republican China*, Cambridge, Mass.: Harvard University Press, 1976, pp. 96 ff.
89 Jiang Guanyun, 'Zhongguo renzhong kao' (Inquiry into the Chinese race), *Xinmin congbao*, 38–9 (Oct. 1903) to 60 (Jan. 1905).
90 *Guocui xuebao*, 6 (1904), p. 3b.
91 See L.A. Schneider, 'National essence and the new intelligentsia' in C. Furth (ed.), *The limits of change*, p. 66.
92 One of the most useful introductions to the thought of Zhang Binglin is Wang Fansen, *Zhang Taiyan de sixiang (1868–1919) ji qi dui ruxue chuantong de chongji* (Zhang Binglin's thought from 1868 to 1919 and his attack on the Confucian tradition), Taipei: Shibao wenhua chuban shiye youxian gongsi, 1985. Shimada Kenji's *Pioneer of the Chinese revolution: Zhang Binglin and Confucianism*,

Yogacara Buddhism and Daoism, questioned the objective reality of Western values such as progress and social evolution. As a politically engaged intellectual, one of his main contributions was a vision of nationalism expressed in terms of blood and soil. It should be emphasized, however, that the racial element was but one strand of thought in a very complex whole, the discussion of which is beyond the scope of the present study. Until 1898, Zhang's overriding concern was the confrontation between the so-called superior white race and the yellow race.[93] Zhang only recognized the cultural value of the white race, and perceived Europe as another Middle Kingdom. The racial equivalence of Chinese and Western civilization was supported by Terrien de Lacouperie's theory of a common origin in the ancient Near East.[94] In convergence with Terrien de Lacouperie, Zhang upheld the belief that mankind had originated from one race, but he inverted the Western perspective by suggesting that the original race had been yellow and had migrated to China under the Yellow Emperor. Zhang's perspective underlined the biological continuity

Stanford University Press, 1990, is invaluable. See also Chang Hao, *Chinese intellectuals in crisis: Search for order and meaning, 1890-1911*, Berkeley: University of California Press, 1987, and C. Furth, 'The sage as rebel: The inner world of Chang Ping-lin' in C. Furth (ed.), *The limits of change*, pp. 113–50.

93 See Kondō Kuniyasu, 'Shō Heiren ni okeru kakumei shisō no keisei' (On the formation of Zhang Binglin's revolutionary thought), *Tōyō bunka kenkyūjo kiyō*, no. 28 (March 1962), pp. 207–24. From 1898 onwards, this concern was gradually superseded by a violent anti-Manchuism. As emphasized in the introduction, this study is not concerned with the Han perception of minorities in China. For an introduction to Zhang Binglin's anti-Manchu thought, see Onogawa Hidemi's 'Zhang Binglin de paiman sixiang' (Zhang Binglin's anti-Manchu thought), *Dalu zazhi*, 44, no. 3 (March 1972), pp. 39–60. For a study that refutes the importance of Zhang's racialist and anti-Manchu thought, see Wong Young-tsu, *Search for modern nationalism: Zhang Binglin and revolutionary China, 1869-1936*, Hong Kong: Oxford University Press, 1989; for a review of this work see Frank Dikötter, *Bulletin of the School of Oriental and African Studies*, 53, part 3 (Oct. 1990), pp. 559–60. See also Kauko Laitinen, *Chinese nationalism in the late Qing dynasty: Zhang Binglin as an anti-Manchu propagandist*, London: Curzon Press, 1990.

94 Zhang Binglin, *Qiushu* (Book of raillery), Shanghai: Gudian wenxue chubanshe, 1958, pp. 41–56.

of the yellow race and pointed to the derivative nature of the white race. The white race was as virtuous, intelligent and skilled as the yellow race: had not the ancients called Rome the Great Qin (*Daqin*)?[95] Zhang's concept of race was based on the traditional distinction between the civilized (*wen*) and the uncultured (*ye*). Both the white and the yellow races were surrounded by barbarian tribes. He compared the backward tribes within China to the degenerate coloured races beyond its borders.[96] The culturalistic opposition between civilized Han and untamed Rong, derived from the *Spring and autumn annals*, was reinforced by Zhang's personal view of evolution.[97] Zhang opposed culturally evolved human beings (*ren*) to biologically degenerated animals (*shou*). Fashionable Western terminology was blended with traditional imagery to make the formulation of a conceptual link between animals and barbarians easier: 'The size of blood vessels is big only in animals, whereas the facial angle is only high among raw barbarians; this is what civilized races have in common.'[98] Barbarian tribes, unlike the civilized yellow and white races, were the biological descendants of lower species: the Di had been generated by dogs, and the Jiang could trace their ancestry back to sheep.[99]

Zhang's strong interest in the Yogacara concept of man led him to adopt an evolutionary vision that emphasized the innate tendency of people to be morally good as well as evil. Refuting the unilinear approach of popular Lamarckism, he viewed evolution as a malleable phenomenon capable of both reversals and advances. Zhang admitted that all people had originally evolved from the primates, but claimed that from the outset they had been unequal.

95 Ibid., p. 38.
96 See for instance Zhang Binglin, 'Menggu shengshuai lun' (About the rise and fall of the Mongols), *Changyanbao*, 9 (Sept. 1898), p. 1a.
97 On Zhang's concept of evolution, see also Wang Yu, 'Zhang Taiyan jinhuaguan pingxi' (An appraisal of Zhang Binglin's view of evolution) in Zhang, *Zhang Taiyan*, pp. 232–99.
98 Zhang Binglin, 'Lun xuehui you yi yu huangren ji yi baohu' (About the benefit of study societies for the yellows and that they should urgently be protected), *Shiwubao*, 19 (March 1897).
99 Zhang, *Qiushu*, p. 38.

Four processes of increased differentiation determined the degree of evolution: 'Environmental differentiation made the skin colour change, sexual differentiation made the skeleton change, social differentiation made the customs change, contractual differentiation made the language change.' Race and culture, often separated in Western thought, were seen as mutually dependent in the process of transformation. 'Differences between tribes exist as a result of the time of civilization, differences between the civilized people and the barbarians exist as a result of a cultured or uncouth nature.' Cultural degeneracy would have its biological consequences: 'People who are indolent in the use of their intelligence will waste away and become macaques and long-tailed monkeys.'[100]

RACIAL NATIONALISM

The leading group of political nationalists was that of the Tongmenghui, founded by Sun Yatsen in 1905.[101] Sun Yatsen (1866–1925) was considered the leader of the Republican revolution in 1911; he came to direct the Guomindang and is still known as the 'father of the country'. However obtuse his writings may have been, it is imperative briefly to consider his principle of racial nationalism (minzuzhuyi), since it exerted a lasting influence on Chinese politics and was adopted as official policy under the Guomindang. Racial nationalism was one of the 'Three Principles of the People' (Sanminzhuyi) Sun elaborated throughout his life. The Sanminzhuyi embodied the programme of the national government; it is also the title of the national anthem of the Republic of China. The principle of racial nationalism embodied the discourse of race as lineage as well as the discourse of race as nation.

Sun's principle of racial nationalism rested on the idea of 'racial solidarity'. Raising the spectre of racial extinction, 'Sun Yat-sen

100 Ibid., pp. 41, 38 and 58.
101 I do not intend in this section to discuss the handful of Tongmenghui nationalists and other '1911 revolutionaries' whose writings and deeds have already been treated at considerable length elsewhere. It will suffice here to indicate the connection between race and nation in the writings of Sun Yatsen.

made his appeal to an emerging national consciousness, strongest
in its racial form of prejudice against foreigners; he appealed also to
fear.'[102] Sun's claim that only nationalism could forestall racial
destruction was a belief he shared with other reformers and revolutionaries, including the Italian fascists. Both used a standard biological conception of race, perceived the country's population as
the strength of the race, and rejected individualism and cosmopoli-
tanism as inimical to the survival of the nation-race.[103]

Sun Yatsen, in common with most reformers and radical students, portrayed the Han as a pure biological entity:

> Considering the law of survival of ancient and modern races, if
> we want to save China and to preserve the Chinese race, we
> must certainly promote Nationalism. To make this principle
> luminous for China's salvation, we must first understand it
> clearly. The Chinese race totals four hundred million people;
> of mingled races there are only a few million Mongolians, a
> million or so Manchus, a few million Tibetans, and over a
> million Mohammedan Turks. These alien races do not number
> altogether more than ten million, so that, for the most part, the
> Chinese people are of the Han or Chinese race with common
> blood, common language, common religion, and common cus-
> toms – a single, pure race.[104]

Sun's world view – one shared by many political activists in
China – was dominated by the idea of a confrontation between
the yellow and the white races.[105] In unison with the reformers,
Sun declared that:

102 L. Sharman, *Sun Yat-sen, his life and its meaning*, Stanford University Press,
1968, p. 288.
103 See A.J. Gregor, 'National-fascismo and the revolutionary nationalism of
Sun Yat-sen', *Journal of Asian Studies*, 39, no. 1 (Nov. 1979), pp. 21–37.
104 Sun Wen (Sun Yatsen), *Sanminzhuyi* (The three principles), Shanghai:
Shangwu yinshuguan, 1927, pp. 4–5; this translation follows F.W. Price, *San
min chu i: The Three Principles of the People*, Shanghai: China Committee, Institute of Pacific Relations, 1927, pp. 11–12.
105 See Kobayashi Toshihiko, 'Sun Yatsen and Asianism: A positivist
approach' in J.Y. Wong (ed.), *Sun Yatsen: His international ideas and international*

Mankind is divided first into the five main races – white, black, red, yellow, brown. Dividing further, we have many sub-races, as the Asiatic races – Mongolian, Malay, Japanese, Manchurian and Chinese. The forces which developed these races were, in general, natural forces, but when we try to analyze them we find they are very complex. The greatest force is common blood. Chinese belong to the yellow race because they come from the blood stock of the yellow race. The blood of ancestors is transmitted by heredity down through the race, making blood kinship a powerful force.[106]

Sun Yatsen's writings were never particularly original, and there is no need to consider his principle of racial nationalism further. It embodied the main strains of thought described in the last two chapters and expressed in simple terms the racial perception prevalent among the revolutionaries whom we have been considering.

In contrast to the reformers, who expressed their ideas of sociopolitical renewal in a framework still dominated by reference to the past, the nationalists successfully broke away from the cultural tradition. They elaborated a construct of race that focused narrowly on the Han, who were envisaged as a perennial biological unit engendered by a mythological ancestor. Until 1915, however, the nationalist vision of blood and soil remained confined to the political arena. With the New Culture Movement, the discourse of race would reach a much wider audience. This forms the starting-point of the next two chapters.

---

connections, with special emphasis on their relevance today, Sydney: Wild Peony, 1987, pp. 15–37.
106 Sun, *Sanminzhuyi*, pp. 4–5; Price, *San min chu i*, pp. 8–9.

5

RACE AS SPECIES (1915–1949)

INTRODUCTION

The New Culture Movement. Up till 1915, Chinese discussions of racial matters were confined mainly to the political arena. Races were perceived as competing biological groups striving for survival. Even after the fall of the Manchu dynasty in 1911, writings on race merely elaborated on the themes expounded by the reformers and the revolutionaries. However, further developments were generated by the New Culture Movement, which emerged around 1915 and lasted for several years. This movement of intellectual renewal was essentially urban-based, and answered the needs of the new social classes that had emerged with the disintegration of traditional social structures.

The First World War was a prosperous period for the economy of the Chinese coastal regions, which benefited both from the replacement of the imperial dynasty by a Republic and from the decline of European trade. During this 'golden age' of economic expansion,[1] cities like Beijing, Tianjin, Nanjing, Shanghai, Wuhan and Canton became the outposts of modernization, growing into large metropolises that harboured new social classes. In the citadels of the Chinese coastal civilization, the urban élite rubbed shoulders with the petty bourgeoisie (*xiao shimin*). Affluent compradors, influential scholar-intellectuals, wealthy merchants and *nouveaux riches* mingled with petty bureaucrats, artisans and labourers, teachers and journalists.

Nationalism was an important characteristic of urban culture. Both the merchant-entrepreneur class and the new intelligentsia were imbued with a sense of national renewal which encompassed questions of social order and collective identity. The reconstruc-

---

1 M.-C. Bergère, *The golden age of the Chinese bourgeoisie, 1911–1937*, Cambridge University Press, 1989.

126

tion of a national identity was a vital aspect of the New Culture Movement. New forms of artistic expression emerged with the *baihua* vernacular style of writing. History was rethought, the classics were reappraised, superstition and traditional ethics were attacked.

Occidentalism. The urban public's need for a new culture, distinct from the Confucian heritage yet able to provide a sense of continuity, was largely articulated by the intelligentsia. Many young intellectuals (*zhishifenzi*, a newly coined term), often educated in either Japan or the West, were determined to integrate foreign science and culture into Chinese society. They urged the people to part with what they called the 'stagnant elements' of 'traditional culture' and to accept foreign democracy, science and culture as the founding elements of a new order. Western thought thus came to play a central role in the effort of cultural reconstruction. If opinions diverged about the extent to which the country should be westernized (*xihua*), most intellectuals agreed that the West was the ultimate norm by which change should be measured.

Through a process of polarization, the West was forced into an artificial relationship of opposites with Confucianism. This binary vision rested largely upon the substance-application school (*tiyong*) formulated by the 1860 generation of reformers. It was expanded during the New Culture Movement: similarities between China and the West were discarded, continuities were ignored, analogies were rejected; the common elements in mankind were often disregarded, whereas the diversity of human experience was forcibly channelled into opposed directions. The radical reformer Chen Duxiu, like so many of his contemporaries, focused only on what he perceived as the 'fundamental' differences between China and the West, the 'yellow' and the 'white' 'races': the West was individualistic, China was communalistic; the West was utilitarian, China was ritualistic, Westerners emphasized struggle, the Chinese preferred tranquillity.[2] This dichotomized vision was

2 Chen Duxiu, 'Dong Xi minzu genben sixiang zhi chayi' (Fundamental differences in thought between the peoples of the East and the West) in *Chen Duxiu wenji*, Shanghai: Yadong tushuguan, 1922, pp. 57–62.

given its quintessential expression by the conservative Liang Souming: the East was 'spiritual', the West was 'materialistic'. Whether as an idealized version of itself or as a polluted alien, the West became China's *alter ego*.

Projection was another characteristic of Occidentalism. Native ideas were projected upon the West. The Chinese notion of 'Western thought' was erected as a totem:[3] it encapsulated all frustrated ideals, it incorporated visions of the future, it sanctioned change; it became the ritualized expression of hope. With the decapitation of the imperial system and the disintegration of the Confucian world order, 'Western thought' was used as an external source of legitimation. The reformers of the nineteenth century had used the *tiyong* concept: the *ti* (substance) applied to China, the *yong* (application) to the West: 'Chinese learning for substance, Western learning for practical application' (*Zhong wei ti, Xi wei yong*). By placing China and the West in a dialectical relation of *ti* and *yong*, the reformers had exposed the authority of Confucianism to doubt. In his *Kongzi gaizhi kao* (Confucius as a reformer) of 1897, Kang Youwei manipulated the classics of Confucianism to represent Confucius as a progressive reformer. With the fading away of Confucian authority at the beginning of the twentieth century, 'Western thought' had to fulfil the same purpose as Confucianism had done: it was compelled to cover cultural iconoclasm with a cloak of authority. The relationship to 'real' Western thought was thus indirect and oblique, and at times minimal. Attitudes towards it of course varied from author to author, and it would be wrong to stress unduly the phenomenon of Occidentalism. Hu Shi, for instance, was a renowned intellectual, genuinely attracted by certain schools of Western philosophy, such as Dewey's pragmatism. But some authors merely attributed their own thoughts to Westerners, much as Abelard of Bath ascribed his own ideas to Islamic thought during the Middle Ages when there was an infatuation with Islamic science.

3 Werner Meissner also points at totemistic thinking in China, but uses the term in a different way; see his fascinating *Philosophy and politics in China: The controversy over dialectical materialism in the 1930s*, London: C. Hurst, and Stanford: Stanford University Press, 1990, p. 8.

Fragmentation was the third feature of Occidentalism. Chinese habits of thought often accommodated Western thought only in the most fragmentary form. The latter underwent simplification and deformation, with quotations being taken out of context. To ease assimilation, Western thought was impoverished, dissected or mutilated; it was introduced to China in the forms of primers, summaries and digests.

Polarization, projection and fragmentation were some of the more negative aspects of a creative and innovative movement of cultural renewal. Despite the limitations of Occidentalism, many aspects of Western thought still found their way to the Chinese reading public, just as water seeps through parched earth. Western thought, by its sheer existence, also introduced a comparative perspective that stimulated the development of original ideas. The New Culture Movement was more than a period of cultural reconstruction; it was also a period in which the need to satisfy the human quest for truth became even more compelling. Republican China was the orphan of certitude: in an age of anxiety, people were searching for a meaning to life.

The rise of the press. Spurred on by the New Culture Movement, the discourse of race made rapid progress, infiltrating many domains of intellectual activity. The most striking developments took place in the social sciences, especially anthropology, ethnology, biology, human geography and demography.

This chapter discusses the discourse of race in the Republic of China from 1915 to 1949, the sources for which include daily newspapers, popular periodicals, introductions to biology, medicine, evolution, anthropology and genetics, primers on science, medical handbooks, marriage guides, schoolbooks and caricatures. Most of these publications were written in simplified vernacular Chinese, produced as cheaply as possible, and widely distributed in all major cities. They addressed the largest possible sector of the social spectrum, and became highly popular among the urban-based middle class. The periodical press, which had been launched by the reformers in the 1890s, played a particularly important role. A wide variety of specialized periodicals were introduced during the New Culture Movement, managed by established publishing companies or by independent associations. Many sought to popularize science, to introduce Western thought and to spread education. Periodicals became so popular that writers generally chose to contribute articles rather than write books. The spread of the periodical press was facilitated by the rise of publishing houses, the introduction of modern printing methods, the growth of a modern education system after the abolition of the imperial examination system in 1905, the institutionalization of educational associations, and by a general increase in functional literacy. The *Eastern Miscellany* (*Dongfang zazhi*), for instance, achieved a circulation of 45,000 in 1931, and a single issue might be consulted by ten to twenty readers.[4] Copies were deposited in public libraries and reading rooms, and were frequently rented, resold or loaned.

Many of the books consulted for this study were published as part of popular self-study series, or *congshu*. *Congshu* books were written by members of the academic community, yet they reached a large readership; some used only a limited vocabulary and an elementary grammar to ensure the widest possible circulation. Wang Yunwu, who from 1921 onwards became editor-in-chief of the huge Commercial Press, applied the notion of 'mass production' to *congshu* books, lowering production costs and extending the distribution network.[5] These books became very popular during the 1930s, and had a significant influence on the shaping of urban culture in Republican China.

Many authors had participated in the Republican revolution of 1911, were active during the New Culture Movement, and filled prominent positions in the institutions for higher learning established during the 1920s and '30s. They maintained close contact with one another, created *guanxi* networks and drew on per-

---

4 Lin Yutang, *A history of the press and public opinion in China*, London: Oxford University Press, 1933, p. 122.
5 See J.-P. Drège, *La Commercial Press de Shanghai, 1897–1949*, Paris: Presses Universitaires de France, 1978, pp. 54–5.

sonal configurations for mutual support.[6] The returned-student élite was as small in proportion as had been the metropolitan graduates (*jinshi*) in imperial China. Some foreign-educated students were direct descendants of reputable scholar families: Pan Guangdan, for example, was a graduate of Columbia University; his father was a member of the prestigious Hanlin Academy. Like their imperial predecessors, the newly-educated élite firmly believed that the scholar should operate on behalf of the whole of society. Having grown up in an age of transition, they were convinced that national reconstruction was the responsibility of the intellectual class. They tackled the task of promoting science and bringing knowledge to the uneducated classes. China, wrote Hu Shi in 1915, needed a form of government that would 'enable the enlightened class of people to utilize their knowledge and talents for the education and betterment of the ignorant and indifferent'. Jiang Menglin, a prominent educator, commented that 'our motto is government of the people, for the people, and by the educated class.'[7] From benevolent Confucian scholar to activist Republican intellectual was only a small step.

More important historically, this specialized élite was instrumental in restructuring the dominant symbolic universe. They delimited social reality, redefined group membership, recreated hierarchy and reorganized history. They sought meaning and order in a time of chaos. Race was one of the leading concepts in the reconstruction of reality.

ORIGINS

Theories of evolution fostered the search for original purity. Visions of an unpolluted race were projected into an idealized past to compensate for the nation's degraded position in the new world

6 On the academic community in Republican China, see E-tu Zen Sun, 'The growth of the academic community 1912–1949' in J.K. Fairbank and A. Feuerwerker (eds), *The Cambridge history of China*, vol. 13, part 2, Cambridge University Press, 1986, pp. 361–420.
7 Both quotations are taken from C.W. Hayford, *To the people: James Yen and village China*, New York: Columbia University Press, 1990, p. 12.

order created by the West. Science and myth wove a fabric on which the frustrated mind could visualize its fantasies. Wei Juxian, for instance, published an important article in the journal *Forwards* on the origins of the Han race. Wei was born in 1898, was attached to the Beijing Normal University as a researcher, and accepted a professorship at Jinan University in Shanghai in 1933. He had numerous official positions and was considered a specialist in the conservation of antiquities. After the communist takeover in 1949 he moved to Taiwan, where he distinguished himself by writing a study on the Chinese discovery of America and a work on anthropology. In his 1933 article, Wei identified the Xia as the genuine descendants of the Yellow Emperor. The Xia were closely related to the Caucasians; many historical documents were produced to demonstrate that they had deep-set eyes, high noses and beards similar to that of the Aryans. 'The Xia race's physical appearance, language, customs and clothes are all similar to those of the Aryan race, of which those who are heavily bearded are Caucasians.'[8] The Yin descended from the Emperor Yan and had intermarried with the Xia to generate the Han race. Wei situated the Xia's original homeland in the Caucasus; they were a white and pure race. The Yin were red barbarians from an area of China now known as Sichuan province. The mixing of white and red had given birth to the yellow Han. Wei Juxian maintained the myth of purity by locating the source of pollution in an alien group: southern barbarians had undermined the original purity of the divine descendants of the Yellow Emperor.[9]

Chinese scientists of international repute were also in search of purity. Li Chi published *The formation of the Chinese people: An*

---

8 Wei Juxian, 'Zhongguo minzu qiantu zhi shi de kaocha' (Study on the future of the Chinese race), *Qiantu*, 1, no. 10 (Oct. 1933), p. 7.
9 A circumspect comment on Wei's methodological approach appeared in the same journal five months later. The author, Wang Boping, cautiously referred to Wei's abuse of mythology, his unhistorical methods of analysis and his partiality; see Wang Boping, 'Zai lun Zhongguo minzu qiyuan wenti' (Again about the question of the origins of the Chinese race), *Qiantu*, 2, no. 3 (March 1934).

anthropological inquiry with the Harvard University Press in 1928.[10]
Li contested the idea that the Chinese had been an unchanging and
homogeneous race. He began by gathering all the data available on
Chinese skulls, and found that 14.41 per cent were dolichocephalic
(a long and narrow shaped head), 42.12 per cent mesocephalic (an
intermediate shape) and only 43.47 per cent brachycephalic (a
broad shaped head). Li also measured noses, and discovered that
the platyrrhinic type (flat nose) was a minor element in the physical make-up of Chinese physical traits. Results were distributed
by province. Li then reconstructed the routes along which cities
had evolved in order to follow the historical movements of the
'We-group'. This painstaking exercise was based on the records
of 4,478 city walls, thus enabling building activity in different
provinces at different periods to be charted. In a chapter on surnames Li assumed that Chinese surnames of the same origin
denoted a blood-relationship. The term 'We-group' came to sig-
nify the 'Descendants of the Yellow Emperor': Li attempted to
disentangle the original surnames created by the Yellow Emperor
from the surnames of other tribes. He classified 4,657 names on
the basis of ethnic and geographical significance in sixty-two
maps. Finally, he took the study of the migration of the Yellow
Emperor's descendants further by investigating the census figures
appearing in the official dynastic histories of China. The conclusion Li Chi drew from all the evidence he had gathered so meticu-
lously was that the prevalent type of the 'original race' was
brachycephalic-leptorrhine (small nose). A group of narrow-
headed Tungus were responsible for diluting the divine race of the
Yellow Emperor by intermarriage. The Tungus were a group of
peoples from Siberia, of which the Manchus were thought to be a
branch. Li Chi ended his inquiry on a note of hope: 'In the future
one may expect a continued leptorrhinization of the south and a
rebrachycephalization of the north', a process by which the pure
type of the Yellow Emperor would come to replace the inferior
elements of China's racial composition. The cruder discursive

10 This paragraph is based on Li Chi, *The formation of the Chinese people: An
anthropological inquiry*, Cambridge, Mass.: Harvard University Press, 1928.

levels of race as lineage and race as nation were legitimized and transformed into theories by Li Chi.

Archaeologists, too, sought evidence of human beginnings in China. Lin Yan, for instance, carefully examined all the theories that traced the origins of the 'Chinese race' to alien migrations: all lacked 'scientific proof'. Like many of his contemporaries, he cited the discovery of Beijing Man at Zhoukoudian as evidence that the 'Chinese race' had existed on the soil of the Middle Kingdom since the earliest stage of civilization. Excavations supported his hypothesis by demonstrating that migrations had taken place only within the empire. It was concluded that China was inhabited by 'the earth's most ancient original inhabitants'.[11] Science was infused into age-old myths to revitalize sinocentric beliefs that could provide the sense of continuity that was so essential in an age of anxiety: it rationalized the construct of race.

Zhang Junjun's search for purity revolved around the concept of blood. Zhang was born in 1897 in Hunan province, taught anthropology at Jinan University in Shanghai, and became a popular writer on the idea of racial degeneration. He studied psychology with Woodworth at Columbia University, but read anthropology and eugenics – the pseudo-science of race improvement – in his spare time. The premise of Zhang's approach was that all the ancestors of the Han race had O group blood flowing in their veins, a purity subsequently vitiated by racial mixing with inferior barbarians.[12] Each province was analyzed and classified according to blood type. The A group was predominant in the north, where the original O group had been bastardized by frequent barbarian invasions. In Jiangsu and Zhejiang provinces, however, the O group was found in more than 50 per cent of the population, whereas in the south it hovered around 40 per cent. The results of Zhang's inquiry into Chinese blood composition demonstrated

---

11 Lin Yan, *Zhongguo minzu de youlai* (Origins of the Chinese race), Shanghai: Yongxiang yinshuguan, 1947, p. 27.

12 The following is based on Zhang Junjun, *Zhongguo minzu zhi gaizao* (The reform of the Chinese race), Shanghai: Zhonghua shuju, 1935. See also his *Zhongguo minzu zhi gaizao, xubian* (Sequel to the reform of the Chinese race), Shanghai: Zhonghua shuju, 1936.

that the nation was a mixed association of an original race, pre-served mainly in the region of the Yangzi River (Jiangsu and Zhejiang), and a variety of barbarian tribes.

The topographical mapping of purity led to the localization of genius. 15,089 famous historical personages, supposed to be repre-sentative of the Chinese intellect, were classified by province. The majority, unsurprisingly, came from Jiangsu (2,428) and Zhejiang (1,974), the two provinces where the original race was supposed to be best preserved, ranking far above other regions (Hunan held third place with 1,200 historical figures; at the bottom was Heilongjiang province with a pathetic dozen). Zhang thus recon-structed the itinerary of the Han race: the first branch of healthy and superior (*youxiu*) Han, taught by the Gods and blessed by Heaven, had moved into the Yellow River region. Barbarian invasions, famine and internecine wars had caused migrations towards the region around the Yangzi River. During both phases, the original race had degenerated by intermarriage with inferior races.

Like many other intellectuals of the 1930s, Zhang Junjun was inspired by the pioneering study of Liang Boqiang on the Han race's blood. Liang took the blood's 'index of agglutination' as an indicator of purity. He maintained that the Han race was 'purer' in the south, where it had never intermarried with barbarians. The index of Guangdong province, for instance, was the highest in the country.[13]

The idea of degeneration by infusions of inferior blood was not universally accepted. The historian Gu Jiegang emphasized the potential contributions of non-Han peoples through both cultural admixtures and biological amalgamation.[14] Lin Yutang, professor of literature, journalist and writer of popular books, was also a typical exponent of the theory of 'blood infusion'. In his widely read *My country and my people* he could certify that each foreign

13 Liang Boqiang, 'Yixueshang Zhongguo minzu zhi yanjiu' (Medical research on the Chinese race), *Dongfang zazhi*, 23, no. 13 (July 1926), pp. 93 and 98. Liang equated the 'Chinese nation' with the 'Han race'.
14 L.A. Schneider, *Ku Chieh-kang and China's new history*, Berkeley: Univer-sity of California Press, 1971, p. 164.

invasion had been conducive to 'a kind of phylogenetic monkey-gland grafting [sic], for one observes a new bloom of culture after each introduction of new blood.'[15] The nation's racial vigour was explained by the periodic addition of fresh plasma, a phenomenon thought to have occurred with striking regularity in Chinese history.

COLOUR

The discourse of race was institutionalized only after the Republican revolution of 1911. Chen Yinghuang, who was born in Hunan in 1877 and became a radical student in Japan around the turn of the century, was appointed as the first professor of physical anthropology at Beijing University. In 1918 he produced a comprehensive survey of 'human races' which perpetuated the Confucian tension between hierarchy and unity.[16] In his preface he claimed that all peoples contributed equally to mankind, regardless of their skin colour or 'degree of evolution'. The imposition of a hierarchical vision on the conceptual unity of mankind (datong) was embedded in his definition of anthropology: 'Anthropology studies all races, from the Chinese and the English down to the dwarf slave and the black slave.'[17] Like most anthropological studies in Republican China, Professor Chen's book was oriented towards the deconstruction of Western racial theories. Whiteness as a factor in racial differentiation was dismissed as a myth. Chen noted that the Caucasian skin was rarely white; it was often stained by impure brown particles. A genuine white skin was to be found only among the northern Europeans, but even these turned dark under the tropical sun: their skin peeled and became freckled. He quoted a

15 Lin Yutang, My country and my people, New York: John Ray, 1935, p. 27.
16 Chen's work was republished eight times, and was reprinted in Taiwan in 1971 as part of a series of scientific books for young people. The book was described on the back cover of this reprint as the most illuminating work ever written on anthropology by a Chinese scientist. Chen Yinghuang, Renleixue (Anthropology), Taipei: Xueren yuekan zazhi she, 1971.
17 Chen Yinghuang, Renleixue (Anthropology), Shanghai: Shangwu yinshuguan (1st edn 1918), 1928, p. 5.

Japanese scientist who had apparently demonstrated that whites, too, had spotted buttocks.[18] Chen's work was echoed by a popular *Précis of human physiological health science*, published in 1921, which explained how the quantity of 'pigment granules' in the epidermis accounted for the 'different colours' of the human race.[19] This explanation was adopted by some writers critical of skin colour as a criterion for racial superiority. Too few authors, unfortunately, realized that the construct of race was based only on a spoonful of melanin.

The impermanence of skin colour was often underlined. In his *History of the progress of mankind and culture* (1926), Gong Tingzhang asserted that even some blacks could become white. Southern Europeans were in fact dark, whereas Nordics revealed a faint red complexion: blood vessels ran underneath a translucent skin. The United States was undergoing an integral racial mutation: blacks were turning white, whereas whites were becoming 'slightly red, the hair increasingly dark, the cheekbones more protuberant and the under-jaw larger'.[20] Gong Tingzhang was a professor of literature in various institutes of higher learning, including Beijing Normal University. His book was published by the Commercial Press as part of a cheap *congshu* series written in the vernacular for mass consumption.

Higher spheres of academic research also toyed with the concept of skin colour. Zhu Xi, professor at Sun Yatsen University in Canton and a specialist in the field of artificial parthenogenesis in Chinese frogs, published a study on the ancestry of mankind. He distinguished ten shades of skin colour: pure white (no example was given), red-white (Scandinavians, North Germans, English), ash-white (Mediterranean), dark yellow (American Indians, Indo-Malaysians, Polynesians), yellow-brown (Malaysians), red-brown, black-brown (Australians), deep brown, black, and pure yellow,

18 Ibid., p. 81.
19 Xue Deyu, *Renti shengli weishengxue tiyao* (Précis of human physiological health science), Shanghai: Shangwu yinshuguan, 1921, p. 14.
20 Gong Tingzhang, *Renlei yu wenhua jinbu shi* (History of the progress of mankind and culture), Shanghai: Shangwu yinshuguan, 1926, pp. 54–66.

reserved for the Chinese. Zhu Xi reclassified the American Indians as 'American yellows'.[21] Racial frontiers remained flexible.

HAIR

Pruner-Bey's classic article 'Chevelure comme charactéristique des races humaines' was published in 1863, but hair remained relatively unimportant in European physical anthropology. Skin colour and headshape were the cornerstones of racial typology. In the Chinese discourse of race, however, hair was a physical trait which determined racial differentiation. Professor Chen Yinghuang questioned the scientific validity of skin colour, which he regarded as a myth manipulated by arrogant Westerners. His anthropological survey began with a detailed analysis of hair systems. Three pages were devoted to the classification of different types of beards, whiskers and moustaches (see illus. 3, between pp. 160–1).[22] Chen Yinghuang subscribed to the neo-Lamarckian paradigm, viewing evolution as an inevitable ascent through a preordained hierarchy of developmental stages. Haeckel's concept of recapitulation was central to this belief: embryological growth was thought to pass through the earlier stages of evolution, starting with the amoeba and ascending to the level of fish, reptile and, finally, mammal. In its ascent to mankind, the human foetus gradually lost its hair after the first seven months. Some barbarians had never evolved beyond the ape-man stage, and retained an over-developed hair system: the *wonu* was given as example. *Wonu*, or 'dwarf slave', was an age-old derogatory term applied to the Japanese; it was also an approximate phonetic transliteration of Ainu, the name of a minority from the Hokkaido region. A drawing depicted a naked *wonu*, heavily bearded and covered with hair from top to toe (see illus. 4). Zhang Zuoren, professor of zoology at Sun Yatsen University and a colleague of Zhu Xi, also considered the absence of body hair to be the most striking feature of mankind. Like Chen Yinghuang and the majority of Chinese

21 Zhu Xi, *Women de zuxian* (Our ancestors), Shanghai: Wenhua shenghuo chubanshe, 1940, pp. 226, 252.
22 Chen, *Renleixue*, pp. 66–9.

scientists of that period, Zhang was not a Darwinian but a neo-Lamarckian; he too referred to 'Professor Haeckel' in his search for Occidental authority. Zhang noted that regression to a previous level of evolution was always possible, and reprinted a picture of a hirsute man 'born in Russia'. Chinese examples were also provided: in 1921, a certain Miss Wang had given birth to a hairy baby, later exhibited at the Agricultural Experimental Ground in Beijing.[23] Racial atavism highlighted the fragile nature of the delineation between man and beast: behind civilized man lurked a hideous animal. You Jiade's *Origins of mankind* (1929) also drew extensively on the recapitulation theory of evolution. The 'fine and long hair' covering the foetus was similar to that of a monkey: it normally fell out at the moment of birth.[24]

Recapitulation was one of the principal arguments in support of racial discrimination in the West. Coloured people, it was argued, were inferior because they retained certain juvenile traits. Lin Yutang, who addressed an English-reading public in his *My country and my people* (1935), was aware of the misuse of recapitulation theory in Western science, and defended the Chinese by distinguishing between race and culture. The Chinese, according to Lin, were culturally old but racially young. Havelock Ellis, who had characterized the Asiatics as racially infantile, was misleading: Lin preferred the term 'prolonged childhood'.[25]

The non-Darwinian model of unilinear evolution infused meaning and order in a shifting universe: it legitimized the cult of progress and the need for hierarchy. Progressivism dominated Republican China. From the communist theories of historical stages to the fascist vision of the millennium, time was articulated as running along a temporal axis with one direction: forwards. The theory of evolution (*jinhualun*), or 'theory about the transformation forwards', replaced the Confucian dichotomy between centre and periphery. Gong Tingzhang, like so many others,

23 Zhang Zuoren, *Renlei tianyan shi* (History of human evolution), Shanghai: Shangwu yinshuguan, 1930, pp. 51–2.
24 You Jiade, *Renlei qiyuan* (Origins of mankind), Shanghai: Shijie shuju, 1929, p. 7.
25 Lin, *My country*, p. 40.

140   RACE AS SPECIES (1915–1949)

divided mankind into three stages of civilization. The lowest stage was reserved for the *shengfan*, or 'raw' barbarians: they fed on raw meat, blood, grass and roots, and dwelt in the dark forests of the mountains.[26] These raw barbarians were coated with thick hair, a feature that betrayed the beast. Gong reproduced Chen Yinghuang's drawing of the 'dwarf slave' by way of illustration. 'Cooked' barbarians attained the second level of evolution. The final stage was civilization. English and Chinese had patches of body hair only on the chest and on the legs. In his *Evolution of organisms*, Zhu Weiji also asserted that the yellows and whites alone had attained the level of civilization.[27]

The discourse of race was theorized at the academic level and popularized by the *congshu* series mentioned above. Zhang Ziping, for instance, was a Japanese-educated mineralogist turned novelist. He wrote several books on geography and evolution for the Commercial Press, as well as a pamphlet on 'Haeckel'.[28] His widely read *Human geography* (1924) selected hair as the most reliable criterion for racial taxonomies. Skin colour was not a genuine racial feature: some yellows were white, whereas Europeans in Africa could have a 'pure black colour'.[29] Craniology was also debunked: the interracial variability of head shape was insignificant. Zhang produced a drawing of different hair textures that corresponded to his fivefold classification of mankind. Borders between science and popularization were not always distinct: six years later, Zhang listed the straight-haired races (i.e. Chinese) and the curly-haired races as two distinct branches in the genealogy of organisms. Popular aesthetic norms guided his inquiry: straight hair was judged 'more beautiful' than curly hair.[30] In nineteenth-century Europe, hair was sometimes divided into a 'leiotrichous'

26 Gong, *Renlei*, p. 11.
27 Zhu Weiji, *Shengwu de jinhua* (Evolution of organisms), Shanghai: Yongxiang yinshuguan, 1948 (1st edn 1945), p. 72.
28 Zhang Ziping, *Hekeer* (Haeckel), Shanghai: Kaiming shudian, 1934.
29 Zhang Ziping, *Renwen dilixue* (Human geography), Shanghai: Shangwu yinshuguan, 1926 (1st edn 1924), pp. 32, 34.
30 Zhang Ziping, *Renlei jinhualun* (The theory of human evolution), Shanghai: Shangwu yinshuguan, 1930, pp. 84, 74.

type (straight and wavy, i.e. European) and a 'ulotrichous' type (crisp, woolly, or tufted): each universe clearly constructed its own taxonomy under the guise of 'science'.

Recapitulation corroborated the traditional association of hair with savagery. Absence of hair from face and body was considered a sign of racial development. Lin Yutang searched even further for evidence of racial superiority:

> A study of the hair and skin of the [Chinese] people also seems to indicate what must be considered results of millenniums of civilized indoor living. The general lack or extreme paucity of beard on man's face is one instance of such effect, a fact which makes it possible for most Chinese men not to know the use of a personal razor. Hair on men's chests is unknown, and a moustache on a woman's face, not so rare in Europe, is out of the question in China. On good authority from medical doctors, and from references in writing, one knows that a perfectly bare mons veneris is not uncommon in Chinese women.[31]

Racial prestige, it seemed, justified splitting hairs.

The association of hairiness with bestiality became a major feature of anti-Japanese caricature during the 1930s.[32] The midget's kimono concealed a coat of bristles and hair, embodying the beast-like attributes of the invader. In many caricatures, the stubbly and furry dwarf was a molester of virginal Chinese girls, personifying the rape of civilization by barbarism. The clog and the furry leg, trampling on Chinese sovereignty, became a widely used symbol of Japanese imperialism during the 1930s. Women in kimonos used international treaties to wipe their hairy bottoms, revealing both the island nation's disdain for law and the subhuman features of the female sex. Where claws, fangs and horns emerged, the unregenerate dwarf receded from bestiality into the darkness of devilry. In the pictorial world of war-time China, ghoulish hobbits roamed lands laid waste by the forces of

31 Lin, *My country*, p. 26.
32 The following draws freely on Frank Dikötter, 'La représentation du Japon et des Japonais dans la caricature chinoise (1923–1937)', unpubl. MA thesis, Dept. of History, University of Geneva, 1985.

evil. Westerners also partook in the iconography of malevolence. Drunken, debauched, brutish and loathsome, crouching among moneybags and armaments, the unshaven capitalist became a popular stereotype of Chinese socialist caricature in the 1930s.

ODOUR

Odour was seen as the result of race. In a popular introduction to human races, Gu Shoubai wrote that blacks could be recognized by their smell. They had a 'protruding jaw, very thick lips, a narrow forehead' and emitted an offensive stench.[33] In holding this view, Gu was certainly not an isolated figure on the academic scene. Professor Gong Tingzhang claimed that even the slightest physical contact with the black man was enough for the olfactory organs to be repelled by his 'amazing stench'. Each race exuded its peculiar odour: 'Africans have a smell of rotten meat one can detect from far away. Browns from America also have a specific odour; they also accuse the whites of having a bad smell.'[34] Zhou Qichang, whose textbook on the origins of mankind contained remarkably few derogatory remarks by Chinese standards, could not refrain from commenting on the 'negroes' foul odour'.[35] Even Lin Huixiang, a reputable professor of anthropology at the University of Xiamen, remarked that the Sudanese had 'an unusual stink, perhaps due to their living conditions'.[36]

BRAIN

The myth of skin colour, the cornerstone of Western racial theories, was only dismantled in order to reconstruct native stereotypes and categorizations. Features of Western anthropological

---

33 Gu Shoubai, *Renleixue dayi* (Main points of anthropology), Shanghai: Shangwu yinshuguan, 1924, p. 51.
34 Gong, *Renlei*, pp. 1 and 55.
35 Zhou Qichang, *Renlei de qiyuan he fenbu* (Origins and distribution of mankind), Shanghai: Dadong shuju, 1927, p. 49.
36 Lin Huixiang, *Shijie renzhong zhi* (Records on the races of the world), Shanghai: Shangwu yinshuguan, 1933 (1st edn 1932), p. 142.

theory that did not accord with the Chinese framework of racial perceptions were eliminated. Phrenology, a Western belief that had no cultural counterpart in China, was rarely mentioned. Craniology was used only for methodological purposes.

Wu Dingliang was perhaps an exception. As director of the Institute of Physical Anthropology, he had obtained 358 skulls from a public graveyard north-west of Kunming, and was struck by the high proportion of metopism, a cranial anomaly consisting of a separation of the two lateral halves of the frontal bone. Wu noted that metopism was generally attributed to a greater development of the frontal lobe and was associated with racial superiority. He compared his findings with cases occurring among other 'races', found that all had inferior rates, and concluded that the Chinese were 'at least as superior as the Europeans'.[37] But those who, like Wu Dingliang or Zhang Liyuan, fully accepted the Western idea of a relation between intelligence and cranial capacity were rare.[38] Many authors mentioned cranial measurements but doubted their accuracy.

Zhang Junjun accepted the idea that the cranial capacity of the Chinese race could be measured. Most Western sources, however, indicated that the Chinese brain weighed slightly less than that of the average Caucasian. Zhang did not believe that such small differences were sufficient to establish the inferiority of the 'Chinese race'. He correlated the weights of body and brain to obtain a figure indicative of the relative brain capacity of different races: 'The average body weight of our race is less compared to that of the Europeans, but the cranial weight, by contrast, is almost the same, so the relative cranial weight of our people is superior to that of the Europeans. Thus one can deduce that the cranial coefficient of the Chinese race is very high, and one may conclude that the development of our race's cranial strength is not inferior to that of

37 Wu Dingliang, 'On metopism of Chinese skulls and its relation to the size of cranial measurements', *Renleixue jikan*, 1 (Collected papers on anthropology), Zhongyang yanjiuyuan lishi yuyan yanjiusuo, 1941, vol. 2, pp. 84–6.
38 Zhang Liyuan, *Renleixue dayi* (Main points of anthropology), Shanghai: Shenzhou guoguangshe, 1931, p. 19.

any other race!'³⁹ Zhang Junjun also challenged Western intelligence quotient tests. He contended that most tests like Goddard Binet, Stanford Binet and Army Beta were biased: the number of tested specimens was too small, a significant variation in age appeared in interracial comparisons, and the tests failed to take cultural differences into account. The authority of colleagues was also invoked: Lu Zhiwei had proved by means of the Binet and Pintner-Paterson Performance tests that Chinese children were as intelligent as their American counterparts.⁴⁰ Zhang Junjun never dismissed the myth of 'race': his critical attitude was only oriented towards the reconstruction of an endogenous discourse. He concluded that the 'Chinese race' belonged to the 'superior category'.

Tong Runzhi, writing in the prestigious *Eastern Miscellany*, also expressed concern about the intelligence of the 'Chinese race'. Westerners scorned the Chinese, called them 'yellow dogs' and proscribed intermarriage: but were the yellows really as inferior as other coloured races? A review of various IQ tests revealed the pathetic scores of blacks and reds. Tong fully endorsed the results, and ascribed a 'feeble intelligence' to coloured people. Achievements of Chinese children were rarely inferior to those of American children, except when tests did not take into account their cultural background. Moreover, Tong noted, most tests were based on immigrants, whose intellectual capacity did not reflect the vast potential of the Chinese mind. Tong proposed the cultivation of talents, the spread of education and the implementation of eugenic policies in order to exploit the hidden resources of the superior Chinese intellect.⁴¹

Not all social scientists indulged in detailed comparative studies. Was not the superiority of Chinese civilization the result of a unique intelligence? For Chen Jianshan, a popular writer on the idea of evolution, the ordinary European brain was simply

39 Zhang Junjun, *Minzu suzhi zhi gaizao* (The reform of the race's quality), Shanghai: Shangwu yinshuguan, 1943, p. 34.
40 Lu Zhiwei's results originally appeared in the *Shehui xinli zazhi*, 2 (1931), pp. 402–8.
41 Tong Runzhi, 'Zhongguo minzu de zhili' (The intelligence of the Chinese race), *Dongfang zazhi*, 26, no. 3 (Feb. 1929), pp. 67–74.

smaller than the Chinese.[42] The author of *Research on the human body* boldly postulated that the degree of civilization was the only indicator of cranial weight: 'If we compare the cranial weights of different people, the civilized are somewhat heavier than the savages, and the Chinese brain is a bit heavier than the European's.'[43] Jiang Xiangqing, in a popular introduction to the 'science of body measurements' for athletes, related civilization to height and intelligence. Savages were on the whole smaller than civilized people. Chinese and Japanese were relatively taller than Europeans: 'the more stupid (*yu*), the smaller'. The construct of race was often an extension of class differentiation: the upper classes were assumed to be taller than the lower classes.[44] Lin Yutang, China's crusader for racial rehabilitation, thought that his people's only fault was that they suffered from 'an overdose of intelligence'. Unlike most of his contemporaries, he did not believe that intelligence was confined to the educated élite: 'One rarely sees in the slums and factory districts that type of big, husky animal of a similar class in the West, distinguished only by his big jaw, low forehead, and brute strength. One meets a different type, with intelligent eyes and cheerful appearance and an eminently reasonable temperament.'[45]

BARBARIANS

In contrast to Western racial discourse, when Chinese writers associated darker people with apes they did so only superficially. Western anthropology was characterized by a fixation on the link between African and ape, legitimized by comparative studies that had begun with Peter Camper in the 1770s. For Sir William Lawrence, a major figure of British racial science, 'the Negro

42 Chen Jianshan, *Renlei naosui zhi jinhua* (The evolution of the human brain), Shanghai: Zhengzhong shuju, 1947, p. 76.
43 Chen Yucang, *Renti de yanjiu* (Research on the human body), Shanghai: Zhengzhong shuju, 1937, p. 180.
44 Jiang Xiangqing, *Renti celiangxue* (The science of body measurements), Shanghai: Qinfen shuju, 1935, pp. 97–8.
45 Lin, *My country*, pp. 78 and 80.

structure approximates unequivocally to that of the monkey. It
not only differs from the Caucasian model; but is distinguished
from it in two respects; the intellectual characters are reduced, the
animal features enlarged and exaggerated.'[46] Belief in the graded
series of races made the link even more compelling. Western
anthropology, however, merely gave the lustre of a pseudo-science
to an ancient prejudice. Despite the Christian doctrine of man's
biological uniqueness, analogies between man and animal had
existed for centuries. Popular mythology blurred the boundary
between them. According to Keith Thomas, the early modern
period abounded with half-man, half-animal 'missing links'. 'It
was also believed that offspring could be engendered by sexual
unions between man and beast.'[47] The black was related to the ape
in modern anthropology as a result of a lasting belief in the fragility
of human separateness from nature.

Chinese analogies between man and animal proceeded from a
different perspective. A study of theriology – the belief that man
partakes of the nature of the animal which he resembles – may
illuminate the difference. William Lessa notes that Chinese
theriology seldom has a morphological basis, whereas animal comparisons in the West are all based on physical resemblances between
humans and animals: 'neither descriptions nor the drawings of
features which are associated in appearance with this or that
animal species seem to bear much resemblance to these particular
animals.'[48] Whereas Western comparisons are suggestive, Chinese
analogies are merely allegorical. Westerners downgraded blacks
on a fictive biological scale. In the Middle Kingdom, mankind was
ranked in a social hierarchy. Since the earliest phase of Chinese
civilization, blackness symbolized the slave.

Africans were categorized as the 'black slave race' until the end

46 Nancy Stepan, *The idea of race in science: Great Britain, 1800–1960*, London:
Macmillan, 1982, p. 15; for the common association of blacks with apes, see
pp. 15–18.
47 Keith Thomas, *Man and the natural world: Changing attitudes in England,
1500–1800*, Harmondsworth: Penguin Books, 1984, pp. 134–5.
48 W.A. Lessa, *Chinese body divination, its forms, affinities and functions*, Los
Angeles: United World, 1968, p. 138.

of the 1920s. Gu Shoubai, in his popular introductions to the peoples of the world, divided blacks into a 'black slave race' (*heinu zhongzu*), a 'little black slave race' (*xiao heinu zhongzu*) and a 'standard black slave race' (*zhun heinu zhongzu*).[49] Professor Gong Tingzhang reproduced a picture of a black in suit and tie: the caption read 'black slave from Africa'.[50] Elite perceptions of the subordinate classes were projected upon the outside world. Gong remarked that blacks and Australian aborigines had 'small brains' and had attained the level of civilization of 'stupid peasants' (*yunong*) in China.

Where ape-like features appeared, differences in biological origins were highlighted. Chen Jianshan, the popular evolutionist, classified the 'black slave' with the chimpanzees, gorillas and Australians as a branch of the propithecantropus.[51] A popular zoology textbook first published in 1916 included a paragraph on the differences between man and ape. The 'inferior races' (*liedeng zhongzu*) had a facial index similar to that of the orang-utan. Polygenism accounted for the inequality of mankind. The 'black slave' was classified in the gorilla branch, and Malays were descendants of the orang-utan.[52]

The discourse of race was spread to more popular levels by the use of stereotypes.[53] One of the earliest anthropological studies to

49 Gu, *Renleixue*, p. 51. Gu Shoubai published a second slim volume on anthropology the same year; Gu Shoubai, *Renleixue* (Anthropology), Shanghai: Shangwu yinshuguan, 1924.

50 Gong, *Renlei*, p. 53.

51 Chen Jianshan, 'Shi renlei' (Explaining mankind), *Minduo zazhi*, 5, no. 1 (March 1924), p. 7.

52 Chen Darong, *Dongwu yu rensheng* (Animals and life), Shanghai: Shangwu yinshuguan, 1928 (1st edn 1916), pp. 8–13. The author thus echoed the 'polyphyletic theory' first expounded by Carl Vogt in 1865, in which he identified a different anthropoid ape with each human race; see L. Poliakov, *Le mythe aryen. Essai sur les sources du racisme et des nationalismes*, Bruxelles: Editions Complexe, 1987, p. 316.

53 Blacks in China became the victims of such stereotypes. An early example is an article published in the November 1904 issue of *Eastern Miscellany*. The author reported how an American black had sneaked into a train in Foshan. He had forced his way into a second class carriage, physically assaulted the

be published in China, written during the first decade of the twentieth century and still bound in the traditional way, described the Burmese as lazy, the Thai as cowards and the Vietnamese as frivolous and dishonest.[54] Gu Shoubai continued to propagate traditional barbarian imagery into the 1920s. His books were published in cheap and widely distributed home-study series. Blacks were 'racially inferior'; only the aborigines of Australia and South America could be 'more barbarous'. Abyssinians ate meat from living horses, Australian aborigines were cannibals, Taiwanese barbarians went about decapitating people 'when they are idle' (Gu distinguished between 'raw barbarians' and 'cooked barbarians'), and Malays existed on mud and human flesh.[55] Sets of stereotypes new to China were invoked: the Jew had an eagle-nose and loved money, the 'yankee type' (in English) was reddish and arrogant, the Slav was brutish.[56] The *Great dictionary of zoology* (1923), the first reference work of its kind, analyzed human races according to their hair-type. The 'woolly-haired' had 'a rather long head, many protruding teeth, and a quite low forehead, so that their face is inclined towards the back. This type of people have a shameful and inferior way of thinking, and have no capacity

---

conductor, and called the Chinese 'dog tails' (*gouwei*). In a sudden urge for sexual intercourse, he had then turned to the two females present in his compartment. His impulse, however, had been cut short by the rapid intervention of four valiant railway workers, who apprehended the offender and threw him off the train. (Presumably, this unfortunate black sailor, unaware of being in a second-class coach, and having experienced American segregation laws at first hand, had simply perceived the gesticulations of the ticket collector and the hostile attitude of the other travellers as racial harassment and then started to shout 'go away!', heard as *gouwei*.) The journalist explained that there were five races on earth: gold, silver, copper, iron and lead. The yellows were the noblest, the 'proud sons of Heaven' (*tian zhi jiaozi*), not even equalled by the whites, let alone the blacks, 'the most vile and ugly of all races'; see 'Heinu yi yu qi wo huaren ye' (The black slave also wants to humiliate the Chinese), *Dongfang zazhi*, 1, no. 11 (Nov. 1904), p. 80.

54 Anonymous, *Renzhongxue* (Anthropology), n.d., pp. 36–8; copy consulted at the Capital Library of Beijing.

55 Gu, *Renleixue*, pp. 51, 41, 65, 67, 68.

56 Ibid., pp. 42, 50.

to shine in history.' Australian aborigines were 'the most inferior race on earth'.[57] Liu Huru, in his widely-used treatise on human geography, published in 1931 as part of the New Age Historical and Geographical Series, proclaimed that most blacks 'like to sing and dance and love ornaments'. Their customs, however, were judged 'low and ugly', and their character 'ferocious'. In New Guinea and Australia, blacks had a 'vulgar and low intelligence', and ate grass and insects.[58] Scientism and age-old stereotypes constantly intermingled to accommodate ethnocentric feelings of superiority.

Popular aesthetic norms facilitated the conceptual debasement of the Japanese. When they were not referred to as 'dwarf slaves', their size was ridiculed: Zhou Qichang called these 'yellow or darkish' people a 'race of tiny men' (*airenzhong*).[59] An anonymous early work entitled *Anthropology* dichotomized the Japanese into a 'beautiful race' and an 'ugly race', the latter characterized by a 'fat body, large and square heads, protruding cheeks, slant eyes, a flat nose and a big mouth'.[60]

It would be wrong to assume that these clichés have been gathered here simply by sieving printed material through a filter that retains racial utterances. A dredger would be needed to gather up all the racial clichés, stereotypes and images which abounded in China as well as in the West during the period between the two world wars. These clichés were the more salient features of a racial discourse that was pervasive and highly influential; moreover it was rarely challenged. They were adopted and perpetuated by large sections of the intelligentsia. The seriousness with which the discourse of race was constructed is further reflected by the preoccupation with classification.

57 Du Yaquan *et al.* (eds), *Dongwuxue da cidian* (Great dictionary of zoology), Shanghai: Shangwu yinshuguan, 1927 (1st edn 1923), p. 15.
58 Liu Huru, *Rensheng dili gaiyao* (General principles of human geography), Shanghai: Shangwu yinshuguan, 1931, pp. 47–8.
59 Zhou, *Renlei*, p. 45.
60 Anonymous, *Renzhongxue*, p. 33.

RANK

Preoccupation with classification pervaded most Chinese anthropological treatises. 'For the Chinese, to engage in scholarship
meant to record and classify. Whatever the phenomenon, it was
duly noted and put in one of the several compartments set up for
classification purposes. Once this had been done, however, the
scholar's job was done.'[61] Although Shigeru Nakayama is referring
here only to the inhibition of analysis in astronomy in ancient
China, the same impression emerges from the endless lists of
'races' compiled by Chinese anthropologists, from the amateurish
tabulations of the reformer Tang Caichang to the sophisticated
inventory of Lin Huixiang. Anthropology described, classified
and ranked; it was not concerned with analysis. It integrated
newly-discovered peoples into a symbolic universe dominated by
hierarchy. The West's abuse of science to legitimize discrimination in their colonies was of less relevance in China. Anthropology
was taxonomic: once a 'race' was classified, the intellectual's job
was done.

The fivefold system of racial classification elaborated by the
reformers at the end of the nineteenth century remained virtually
unchanged in Republican China. This system incorporated both
the tense relationship with the West and the traditional contempt
shown towards the periphery. The system was legitimized by
reference to the West. Most writers quoted Blumenbach, the
German anthropologist mentioned above. The *Great dictionary of
zoology* introduced the works of Brinton, who associated five races
with five continents.[62] Zhou Qichang adopted the former's fivefold pattern after reviewing alternative methods of classification.[63]
'Brinton' was no more than a Western label attached to an
endogenously developed system. Reformers and revolutionaries

61 Shigeru Nakayama, *Academic and scientific tradition in China, Japan, and the
West*, Tokyo: University of Tokyo Press, 1984, pp. 58–9, quoted in Francesca
Bray, 'Essence et utilité. La classification des plantes cultivées en Chine',
Extrême-Orient – Extrême-Occident, 10 (1988), p. 13.
62 Du, *Dongwuxue*, p. 17.
63 Zhou, *Renlei*, p. 29.

had classified races by five continents well before Brinton was introduced to China. Professor Zhu Xi mentioned Huxley's division into Negroid, Australoid, Mongoloid, Xantochroid and Melanochroid races, a system similar to that of the reformers.[64] The term 'Huxley' conveyed academic prestige, indispensable to the status of a university professor. Lower levels of culture also classified mankind into five races. *Riyong baike quanshu*, or popular daily encyclopedias, were a direct continuation of the *riyong leishu* evoked in chapter 2. Popular almanacs, however, did not merely transcribe the discourse of race from the higher spheres of theorization into more accessible language. An early encyclopedia of 1919 divided mankind into a yellow, white, black, red and 'kite' (*yuan*) race,[65] the latter being a popular term for a skin colour ranging from dark brown to light black. From 'Huxley' to 'kite', the discourse of race remained singularly homogeneous.

Li Xuezeng's presentation of the origins of mankind deserves special mention, since it highlights how age-old mental patterns intermingled with modern concepts. Li placed Asia at the centre of a graph that represented the origins and development of human races. The centre was occupied by the 'Mongoloids'. The first concentric circle remained empty, the second circle was assigned to the Nordics, the third to a tribe from the Canary Islands, the fourth to the 'Negroids'. Three more circles followed, dedicated respectively to the 'Australoids', the Negrillos and Neanderthal man.[66] Li's graphic representation bore a striking resemblance to the cosmological plan of the *Tribute of Yu*, which, as we saw in the first chapter, had divided the world into five concentric configurations more than two millenia earlier.

64 Zhu, *Women de zuxian*, p. 225.
65 Chen Duo *et al.* (eds), *Riyong baike quanshu* (Daily encyclopedia), Shanghai: Shangwu yinshuguan, 1919, part 3, pp. 93–6. See also Huang Shaoxu *et al.* (eds), *Riyong baike quanshu* (Daily encyclopedia), Shanghai: Shangwu yinshuguan, 1934, pp. 183–7.
66 Li Xuezeng, *Yazhou zhongzu dili* (Racial geography of Asia), Shanghai: Zhengzhong shuju, 1947, p. 10.

CONVERGENCES

With the decapitation of the imperial system in 1911, the social basis, political power and ideological function of the Confucian élite vanished. The traditional symbolic universe disintegrated. Confucianism lost its authority as an all-encompassing frame of reference. The West was increasingly perceived as an alternative source of authority, and a sophisticated referential system was gradually reconstructed. Foreign labels such as 'Huxley' or 'Professor Haeckel' were attached to indigenous strains of thought perceived to be convergent with those in the West. Once a label gained sufficient acceptance, its authority could be further promoted by the adjunction of an 'ism', or *zhuyi*, doctrine:[67] *Hekeer*, 'Haeckel' could become *Hekeerzhuyi*, 'Haeckelism'. An intellectual would first harness the label 'Haeckel' to establish his own authority,[68] and then construe 'Haeckelism' to buttress his position in the academic community.[69] The work of Ernst Haeckel was translated into Chinese only very rarely.

Translations did not constitute a significant part of this referential system. The substitution of an indigenous label by a foreign one as a means of reidentification did not need to be based on a body of translated texts. Fewer than twenty Western works on physical anthropology were translated into Chinese between 1897 and 1949.[70] Some of them were never integrated into the dominant

67 Hu Shi attacked infatuation with abstract representations and launched the famous debate on 'problems and isms' (*wenti yu zhuyi*) in 1919. See Jerome B. Grieder, *Intellectuals and the state in modern China: A narrative history*, New York: Free Press, 1981, pp. 326-31.

68 Hu Jia, 'Hekeer zhi zhushu yu Hekeer yanjiu zhi cankaoshu' (The work of Haeckel and reference material on Haeckel), *Xuedeng*, 10 Aug. 1922; Hu Jia, 'Hekeer duiyu jinhualun zhi gongxian' (Haeckel's contribution to the theory of evolution), *Minduo*, 3, no. 4 (April 1922).

69 Hu Jia, 'Hekeerzhuyi yu Zhongguo' (Haeckelism and China), *Xuedeng*, 9-10 Aug. 1922.

70 They were Zhang Mingding, *Renleixue xiaoyin* (R.R. Marett, *Mankind in the making*), Shanghai: Shangwu yinshuguan; Lü Shuxiang, *Renleixue* (R.R. Marett, *Anthropology*), Shanghai: Shangwu yinshuguan, 1931; Ma Junwu, *Renlei yuanshi ji leize* (C.R. Darwin, *The descent of man*), Shanghai: Shangwu

referential system, while others were used in the construction of sub-systems. Qi Sihe, for instance, referred readers to two translations of Marett in his lonely attack on the notion of race in China published in 1937.[71] Translations were scanned in the search for 'proof'. A neatly taken note recently forgotten by a Chinese student referred to Taylor's *Racial geography*, whose author 'advocated with all his force the superiority of the yellow race over the white race.'[72]

Returned students who had studied in Japan and the West were active in restructuring the symbolic universe by integrating references to Western authors. By so doing, they demonstrated their specialized knowledge and legitimized their positions of power

yinshuguan, 1932; Hua Rucheng, *Renlei zai ziranjie de weizhi* (T.H. Huxley, *Man's place in nature*), Shanghai: Shijie shuju; Yu Deling, *Renlei shengwuxue* (J.G. Needham, *Anthropobiology, speech delivered in China*), Shanghai: Zhongguo kexue gongsi, 1930; Jin Shuliu, *Ren yu dongwu* (W.M. Smallwood, *Man, the animal*), Shanghai: Shangwu yinshuguan; Du Zengrui, *Renlei zhi jinhua* (G.A. Baitsell, *The evolution of man*), Shanghai: Shangwu yinshuguan; Qian Bohan, *Renlei shengming de jinhua* (G.A. Dorsey, *Nature of man*), Shanghai: Beixin; *Cong hou dao ren* (F. Engels, *Role of labour in the process of the humanising of the apes*), Shanghai: Taidong shuju; Wu Zhihui, *Huanggu yuanren* (J. McCabe, *Prehistoric man*), Shanghai: Wenming shuju; Yu Songli, *Shijie youzhi shidai* (E. Clodd, *The childhood of man*), Shanghai: Shangwu yinshuguan; *Renlei de texing yu fenbu* (C.G. Seligman, *Characteristics and distribution of human races*), Shanghai: Shangwu yinshuguan; Gong Te, *Shijie renzhong yu minzu* (J. Deniker, *Les races et les peuples de la terre*), Shanghai: Wenjiaoguan; Xue Yiheng, *Huo jiqi* (A.V. Hill, *Living machinery*), Shanghai: Shangwu yinshuguan, 1936; Huang Xibai, *Zhongzu yu lishi* (E. Pittard, *Les races et l'histoire*), Changsha: Shangwu yinshuguan, 1940; Ge Suicheng, *Renzhong dilixue* (G. Taylor, *Racial geography*), Shanghai: Shangwu yinshuguan, 1937; references from Guoli tushuguan, *Jin bainian lai Zhong yi xishu mulu* (Catalogue of Western works translated into Chinese during the last hundred years), Taipei: Zhonghua wenhua chuban shiye weiyuanhui, 1958, pp. 73–4; *Shangwu yinshuguan tushu mulu* (1897–1949) (Catalogue of books edited by the Commercial Press, 1897–1949), Beijing: Shangwu yinshuguan, 1981, p. 148.
71 Qi Sihe, 'Zhongzu yu minzu' (Race and nationality), *Yugong*, 7, nos. 1–2-3 (April 1937), p. 32.
72 I found this note, dated 1988, by accident in the Capital Library in Beijing. It referred to Ge Suicheng, *Renzhong dilixue* (G. Taylor, *Racial geography*), Shanghai: Shangwu yinshuguan, 1937, p. 284.

within the community. Anthropologists such as Fei Xiaotong, Wu Dingliang and Lin Yaohua, for instance, would disseminate the theories of their respective schools.[73] During their sojourn in the West, however, students were exposed to a broad array of anthropological concepts. The integration of a particular trend of thought was limited by the cultural background and personal experience of the individual student, for they operated in a symbolic universe that constrained the exercise of choice within a definite framework. An illuminating example is Pan Guangdan, whose work on mainline eugenics will be considered in the next chapter. In a review of *The American negro*, edited by Donald Young in 1928, Pan Guangdan expressed his disappointment in the contributors' unwillingness to speak in terms of racial inequality:

> But to be true to observable facts, in any given period of time sufficiently long for selection to take effect, races *as groups are* different, unequal, and there is no reason except one based upon sentiment why we cannot refer to them in terms of inferiority and superiority, when facts warrant us. It is to be suspected that the Jewish scholars, themselves belonging to a racial group which has long been unjustly discriminated against, have unwittingly developed among themselves a defensive mechanism which is influencing their judgements on racial questions. The reviewer recalls with regret that during his student days [in the United States] he had estranged some of his best Jewish friends for his candid views on the point of racial inequality.[74]

Extended periods of exposure to Western thought were necessary to induce change in an individual's intellectual orientation. Fei Xiaotong, for example, studied anthropology at Qinghua University under Pan Guangdan and Chen Da, two social scientists notorious for their belief in the virtues of eugenics. Fei became

73 See He Liankui, 'Sishi nianlai zhi Zhongguo minzuxue' (Forty years of Chinese ethnology) in Li Ximou (ed.), *Zhonghua minguo kexue zhi* (Records on science in the Republic of China), Taipei: Zhonghua wenhua chuban shiye weiyuanhui, 1955, pp. 1–21.
74 Pan Guangdan, review of Donald Young (ed.), *The american negro* (1928), *The China Critic*, 28 Aug. 1930, p. 838.

interested in anthropometry: armed with calipers and anthropo-
meters, he roved Beijing prisons in search of the biological measure
of crime. It was only after having studied under Bronislaw
Malinowski at the London School of Economics in 1936 that he
abandoned anthropometry and went on to write several classic
studies of the Chinese peasantry.[75]

COMPLEXES

It would be an oversimplification to portray the intelligentsia of
the Republican era as universally prejudiced. A few writers openly
denied the existence of racial differences between peoples. Zhang
Junli, for instance, wisely excluded 'common blood' from his
definition of the nation. The Han had intermarried with different
tribes since the Tang dynasty and had lost their 'racial purity'.[76] Qi
Sihe criticized the use of racial categories in China, and pointed out
how 'race' was a declining notion in the West.[77] The very idea of
racial inequality, however, was challenged only rarely. Many intellectuals adopted a vision of racial hierarchy that was close to the
Confucian idea of social order. What they contested was the belief
in white superiority. 'In Shanghai, for instance, many of the most
mediocre Englishmen despise noble-minded, erudite scholars.
They believe that a race with a yellow skin and straight hair is
absolutely not of their kind and can definitely not surpass their
level of superiority!,'[78] exclaimed professor Wu Zelin.

In the absence of a concept of equality, the prevailing sentiment
of superiority was all too easily inverted, allowing a feeling of
inferiority to creep into the Chinese mind:

> Most of the [Chinese] people, however, continue to think of
> our race as inherently superior to that of our neighbors of

75 R.D. Arkush, *Fei Xiaotong and sociology in revolutionary China*, Cambridge,
Mass.: Harvard University Press, 1981, pp. 37–46.

76 Zhang Junli, *Minzu fuxing zhi xueshu jichu* (The scientific foundations for
national revival), Beijing: Zaishengshe, 1935, pp. 10, 22.

77 Qi, 'Zhongzu yu minzu', pp. 25–34.

78 Wu Zelin, *Xiandai zhongzu* (Contemporary races), Shanghai: Xinyue
shudian, 1932, pp. 2–3.

lighter or darker skin. Indeed there is very often a set of superiority and inferiority complexes stirring within those who have constant or occasional contacts with foreigners. He constantly persuades himself of his unexplainable superiority over the foreigner, but frequently has to rationalize in order to disperse the inferiority complex.[79]

It was whispered that not only the whites but even the 'inferior races' despised the Chinese. Stereotypes were inverted: in India, remarked one observer, people regarded the Chinese as thieves.[80] Many writers compared the Chinese to 'black slaves'; for one, 'Chinese are less than black slaves' because at least Africans struggled for independence.[81] Such exercises in self-abasement undermined the confidence necessary to adapt to a changing world. Professor Lu Xinqiu denounced the Chinese inferiority complex: 'Naturally we cannot categorically state that the Chinese have a long history and civilization and that they are the most superior race of mankind, but it is not necessary to lower oneself.' He reassured the insecure reader: 'From a scientific point of view, the constitution of our body has also many superior points.'[82] Another writer could guarantee that 'the Chinese are not an inferior race. The intellectual and physical strength of the Chinese people are not inferior to that of other races [. . .] We should resolutely not be too proud, but we need not have an inferiority complex and despise our own creative ability.'[83]

79 Frederick Hung (Hong Yuan), 'Racial superiority and inferiority complex', The China Critic, 9 Jan. 1930, p. 29.
80 'Yindu zhi huaqiao' (India's overseas Chinese), Qiantu, 2, no. 11 (Nov. 1934), pp. 2–3.
81 'Ai tongbao zhi jiangwang' (Grieving for the perishing of overseas Chinese), Dongfang zazhi, 1, no. 12 (Dec. 1904), p. 88.
82 Lu Xinqiu, Jinhua yichuan yu yousheng (Evolutionary heredity and eugenics), Shanghai: Zhongguo kexue tushu yiqi gongsi, 1949, p. 42.
83 Huang Wenshan, 'Fuxing Zhonghua minzu de jiben yuanze' (Fundamental principles for reviving the Chinese nation) in Minzu zhi shang lun (About the nation going up), Hankou: Duli chubanshe, 1938, p. 52; see also Huang Wenshan's 'Zhongzuzhuyi lun' (About racism), in Huang Wenshan xueshu luncong (Collected studies on society), Taipei: Zhonghua shuju, 1959,

Some intellectuals underwent a heightening of their racial consciousness while in the West. Students abroad often complained of Western paternalism and arrogance. Although some Chinese genuinely suffered from racial discrimination, an element of self-victimization and self-humiliation often entered into the composition of such feelings. Alienation abroad could easily be compensated for by the projection of superior feelings on to the homeland,[84] a trait which found expression in the poet Wen Yiduo.

Wen sailed for the United States in 1922 but even on board ship his courage ebbed away as he felt increasingly apprehensive of racial discrimination in the West. In America he felt lonely and homesick: he described himself as the 'Exiled Prisoner'. 'Homesickness led him to over-idealize his country and prejudiced him against anything non-Chinese,' notes his biographer.[85] Wen wrote home: 'For a thoughtful young Chinese, the taste of life here in America is beyond description. When I return home for New Year, the year after next, I shall talk with you around the fire, I shall weep bitterly and shed tears to give vent to all the accumulated indignation. I have a nation, I have a history and a culture of five thousand years: how can this be inferior to the Americans?'[86] His resentment against the West cumulated in a poem entitled 'I am Chinese':

---

pp. 225–54, first published in 1942. It may be noted that Huang, a professor at Lingnan University, was one of the ten signatories of the notorious 'Manifesto on cultural construction on a Chinese base', published in 1934, which criticized the westernizing tendencies of the New Culture Movement and called for study of the nation's cultural heritage.

84 On the theme of alienation, see Jerome Ch'en, 'Yiguo, "yihua": liangci dazhan jian Yingyu guojia Zhongguo liuxuesheng taidu he xingwei de bianqian' (Estrangement in strange lands: Attitudinal and behavioural changes of Chinese students in English-speaking countries between the two world wars), manuscript presented at the Institute of Modern History, Beijing, Summer 1990. See also his *China and the West*, pp. 151–72.

85 Hsu Kai-yu, *Wen I-to*, Boston: Twayne Publishers, 1980, p. 61.

86 Wen Yiduo, *Wen Yiduo quanji* (Complete works of Wen Yiduo), Hong Kong: Yuandong tushu gongsi, 1968, vol. 1, p. 40.

I am Chinese, I am Chinese,
I am the divine blood of the Yellow Emperor,
I came from the highest place in the world,
Pamir is my ancestral place,
My race is like the Yellow River,
We flow down the Kunlun mountain slope,
We flow across the Asian continent,
From us have flown exquisite customs.
Mighty nation! Mighty nation![87]

A feeling of inferiority in some cases was linked to a sense of sexual inadequacy. As demonstrated in a previous chapter, sexual fear of the foreigner was an important element of anti-Christian propaganda during the nineteenth century. Although the extreme prudery of much Chinese writing makes it difficult to find any material pertaining to the relation between sex and race, the negative image of the Westerner in nineteenth-century literature was of a hairy, meat-eating, libidinous, tall, white devil against whom the virgin should be protected. Mixed feelings of fear, disgust, secret admiration and envy led to an ambivalent attitude towards foreign sexuality that continues to this day. Chinese students felt inferior about their appearance and were hypersensitive on this score.[88] Some Chinese could be overwhelmed by a sense of physical inferiority in the presence of Westerners.

---

87 Wen Yiduo, 'Wo shi Zhongguoren' (I am Chinese), *Xiandai pinglun*, 2, no. 33 (July 1925), pp. 136-7.
88 Hsien Rin has reported a revealing clinical case involving a Chinese undergraduate who went to the United States to study engineering after the Second World War. The student resided in a dormitory shared by many Americans. He rapidly developed an inferiority complex and started disparaging himself, for he felt 'that he was short and weak as compared with American students, and that his genital organ was shorter than those of other students he observed in the shower room.' (Hsien Rin, 'The synthesizing mind in Chinese ethnocultural adjustment' in G. de Vos and L. Romanucci-Ross, *Ethnic identity: Cultural continuities and change*, Palo Alto: Mayfield, 1975, p. 149). The student soon developed paranoia and was sent back to Taiwan.

STRUGGLE

The Republican era in China was one of almost constant violence. The country was ravaged by terrorism, militarism, factionalism and warlordism. The rural areas suffered from oppression, famine and banditry; the urban centres endured corruption and maladministration. Socially the country was fractured, politically it was divided. Foreign encroachments further increased fragmentation. The awarding of rights in Shandong to Japan at the Versailles Peace Conference in 1919 was seen as the end of the country's territorial integrity: demonstrations on May the Fourth in protest at the treaty terms became the political core of the New Culture Movement. Initially led by students, it quickly won the support of merchants, businessmen, shop-owners and industrial workers. The search for unity found its quintessential expression in racial nationalism.

The belligerent dimension of the discourse of race underwent little change in Republican China. The threat of extinction was quantified. Tao Menghe, a professor at Beijing National University and future director of the Institute of Social Sciences, produced tabulations on the geographical progression of the 'white race' over the five continents. The whites, 'eternal rulers of all races', ruthlessly destroyed the feeble and weak races in the course of their expansion. Tao Menghe anticipated a major tenet of the communist period by integrating the 'coloured races' into one group. A new era in racial warfare had begun with the Abyssinian defeat of the Italian army in 1896: 'This is only the first thunderclap of the coloured races' attack on the white race.'[89] The biggest blow was the Japanese victory over the Russians in 1905. Professors Wu Zelin and Ye Shaochun compiled various statistics and tables on the comparative growth of the 'human races'. The future looked bleak: 'The Caucasian race expands every day, the coloured races will decline; if we look at the future, we actually cannot but

89 Tao Menghe, 'Zhongzu wenti' (Racial problems), *Xiandai pinglun*, 3, no. 63 (Feb. 1926), p. 208.

shudder and fear.' The whites were 'the turtle-dove occupying the magpie's nest'.[90]

The discourse of race was institutionalized at university level. Notions of racial war were also habitualized by vulgarization and repetition. Zhou Qichang's popular study on human races was dominated by visions of a racial Armageddon: 'Readers, do you understand the key to the problem? The crux of the matter is not struggle between states, but struggle between races! Have not the other three races already lost in the battle?'[91] Military vocabulary undergirded an aggressive discourse. Hu Huanyong, in a book which was part of a Youth Elementary Knowledge Series, claimed that the Chinese had 'the longest history, the highest culture, the largest population, a great and proud country', and were now 'reinforced' by Japan and Turkey, 'two yellow upcoming young-sters'. Together, they would fight against the whites, whose 'main camp' was situated in Europe.[92] A popular *ABC of human geography* deconstructed the white race as follows: 'Latins are the advance forces, Teutons are the central army, Slavs are the rearguard.'[93] Others described Asia as the 'great barracks' of the yellow race.[94] Such phraseology is not without affinity to contem-porary militant black writings. Garvey and Du Bois, for instance, considered American blacks to be the 'advance guard' of the 'black race' in its historic struggle against the 'whites'.[95]

Some nationalist writers advocated pan-Asianism. A contribu-tor to the *Contemporary Critic* proclaimed that racial survival would depend on cooperation between the Chinese and the Japanese. Only these two countries, along with some isolated

90 Wu Zelin and Ye Shaochun, *Shijie renkou wenti* (Problems of the world population), Shanghai: Shangwu yinshuguan, 1938, p. 84.

91 Zhou, *Renlei*, p. 61.

92 Hu Huanyong, *Shijie dili* (World geography), Shanghai: Zhengzhong shuju, 6th edn 1947 (1st edn 1942), pp. 43–4.

93 Li Zongwu, *Renwen dili ABC* (ABC of human geography), Shanghai: Shijie shuju, 1929, p. 24.

94 Wu and Ye, *Shijie renkou*, p. 92.

95 E.U. Essien-Udom, *Black nationalism: The rise of the black Muslims in the U.S.A.*, Harmondsworth: Penguin Books, 1966, p. 40.

ILLUSTRATIONS

1. 'Although they know white, Africans prefer the colour black.' *Dianshizhai huabao*, Shanghai, 1890s.
2. Racial geography in a schoolbook translated from the Japanese. The Chinese version has a picture of a Confucian scholar glued over the narrow-headed, flat-nosed Manchu included in the original. *Rensheng dilixue* (Human geography), Shanghai, 1907.
3. Hair systems classified by Professor Chen Yinghuang, *Renleixue* (Anthropology), Shanghai, 1918.
4. A depiction of the *wonu*, or 'dwarf slave', a derogatory term applied to the Japanese from the Han dynasty onwards. Chen Yinghuang, *Renleixue*, Shanghai, 1918.
5. An example of 'racial atavism': a dumb and blind child with a tail. Chen Yinghuang, *Renleixue*, Shanghai, 1918.

知白守黑

世之論美者曰雪膚曰玉貌皆貴其白獨亞非利
加洲則反是亞洲黑種故以黑為美其富翁女
黑甚歎深閨中推為純色不當中國之有毛嬙年及
許來宇近有其國商人公其地作小負販翁見其
精會計善居積然招為婿商利其射先之肖
來美少年面為商游客曰翁族福誼以輪代
佳人贅其白息其白面于眼命孫安之店年餘拳子繪
雜心厭其白色于眼命孫安之店年餘拳子繪
體斑斕黑白皆商不雅之謀諸醫曰凡物皆
易做惟做人之最難做之道由白而染之使黑剝
易由黑而灌之使白則難諸為其易可也乃用上
刮破清以黑水諸銀汞小銀刀薄以紙將其白膚得面
潤之餘居是膚受旬日其身不見立在炭爐邊
翁喜覺之為其類母也

馬子明

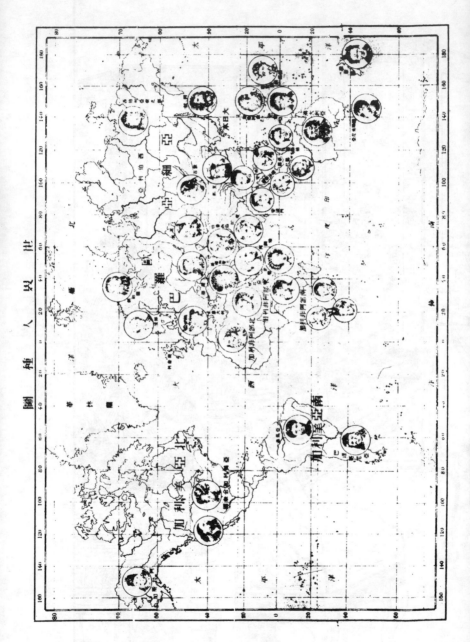

3

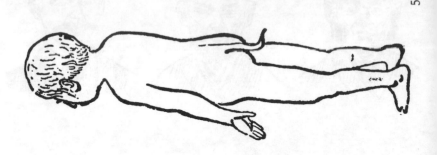

5

4

islands, had not yet been seized by the white man. 'Thinking from the point of view of racial survival, one cannot but hope that the Japanese, who have the same faces as we, will fully sympathize with us.'[96] He despaired, however, at the thought that the Japanese had followed the ways of the 'yellow-haired and blue-eyed' by forcefully occupying Shandong province. Pan-Asianism was adopted as an official policy of the Guomindang in the early 1930s. A 'nationalist literature' movement was initiated to cover up the Guomindang's capitulation to the Japanese. 'Its writers', recounts the famous author Lu Xun, 'after studying the colour of different peoples, decided that those of the same colour should take concerted action: the yellow-skinned proletariat ought not to fight the yellow-skinned bourgeoisie but the white proletariat instead. And they took Genghis Khan as their model, describing how his grandson Batu Khan led yellow hordes into Russia to destroy its civilization, enslaving its nobles and common people alike.'[97] Morbid visions of racial revenge were projected upon the figure of Batu Khan, magnified as the historical leader of the yellow race in the destruction of Western civilization. An extract from Huang Zhenxia's 160-page poem 'Blood of the yellow race' is representative of this type of literature:

> Hide, frightened European dogs!
> Topple, Muscovites imposing high buildings!
> Roll, Caucasian yellow-haired heads!
> Fearful, the oil oozing from burning corpses,
> The horror of putrid bodies strewing the ground;
> The God of Death seizes white girls in frenzied embrace,
> Beauties are turned into fearsome skeletons;
> Cannibals struggle like beasts in ancient palaces;
> A foul stench wafts from coffins a thousand years old;
> There is sorrow on the faces of the Crusaders;

96 Li Zhongkui, 'Huangren hai you shengcun de yudi ma?' (Is there still a territory where the yellow race can subsist?), *Xiandai pinglun*, 3, no. 60 (Jan. 1926), p. 148.
97 Lu Xun, *Selected writings*, Beijing: Foreign Languages Press, 1980, vol. 4, p. 149.

Iron hooves trample broken bones,
Camels utter wild howls;
God has fled; vengeful devils have raised the scourge of fire.
The Yellow Peril is here! The Yellow Peril!
Asian warriors' bloody maws are devouring men.[98]

SCHOOLBOOKS

The discourse of race cut across most political positions, from the fascist core of the Guomindang to the communist theories of Li Dazhao.[99] It was also internalized by young students.

Racial discourse was infused in schoolbooks immediately after the abolition of the imperial examination system in 1905. One of the first textbooks on human geography, compiled in 1907 from Japanese sources, introduced the human species in a special chapter. A paragraph entitled 'Each race's superiority or inferiority and its future' correlated skin colour to spiritual development: the 'most superior white race' dominated the planet, but the Chinese were the elect of nature, chosen to replace the whites in the future world.[100] Illustrations of the most 'characteristic races' were also provided. The original Japanese version, however, displayed a narrow-headed, flat-nosed, dreary Manchu for the 'Chinese race' (see illus. 2, between pp. 160-1). The illustration was judged offensive by the Chinese editors: a picture of a noble-featured Confucian scholar was glued over the original in every copy.[101]

Racial discourse filtered down to lower levels of education after

98 Huang Zhenxia, 'Huangren zhi xue' (Blood of the yellow race), *Qianfeng yuekan* (Vanguard monthly), 1, no. 7 (July 1931), p. 6; for this translation I have relied upon Yang Xianyi and Gladys Yang (transl.), Lu Xun, *Selected writings*, vol. 3, pp. 146-7.

99 See 'Class, nation, and race' in M. Meisner, *Li Ta-chao and the origins of Chinese Marxism*, New York: Atheneum, 1970, pp. 188-94.

100 *Rensheng dilixue* (Human geography), Shanghai: Qunyi shuju, 1907, pp. 147-9.

101 The sticker may be observed by slowly passing a finger over the illustration; the original picture becomes visible when the page is held against the light.

the foundation of the Republic in 1911. The opening sentence of a chapter on 'human races' in a 1920 textbook for middle schools declared that 'among the world's races, there are strong and weak constitutions, there are black and white skins, there is hard and soft hair, there are superior and inferior cultures. A rapid overview shows that they are not of the same level.' Among the five races, the young student was told, the whites were the most powerful, but the yellows were the most fertile, spreading gradually to all five continents.[102] In primary schools, readings on race politics became part of the curriculum:

> Mankind is divided into five races. The yellow and white races are relatively strong and intelligent. Because the other races are feeble and stupid, they are being exterminated by the white race. Only the yellow race competes with the white race. This is so-called evolution [. . .] Among the contemporary races that could be called superior, there are only the yellow and the white races. China is [i.e. belongs to] the yellow race.[103]

Another schoolbook, *Essentials of world geography*, inculcated notions of a 'white race' against which the 'four coloured races' had to fight.[104] Poems on racial self-determination were read daily, calling for national unity and help for the 'weak and backward races'.[105]

102 Fu Yunsen, *Renwen dili* (Human geography), Shanghai: Shangwu yinshu-guan, 1914, pp. 9–15.
103 L. Wieger, *Moralisme officiel des écoles, en 1920*, Hien-hien, 1921, p. 180, original Chinese text.
104 Cao Bohan, *Shijie dili gangyao* (Essentials of world geography), Shanghai: Dongnan chubanshe, 1943, pp. 4–5; see also Cao Bohan, *Shijie dili chubu* (Elementary world geography), Shanghai: Shenghuo shudian, 1948, pp. 6–7. Both were standard schoolbooks.
105 *Anti-foreign teachings in text-books of China*, supplement to the *International Gleanings from Japan*, no. 16 (Oct. 1932), Tokyo: Sokokusha, p. 12.

6

RACE AS SEED (1915–1949)

BACKGROUND

This chapter concentrates on the pseudo-science of eugenics, analyzing the discourse of race as a biological entity open to short-term alteration through artificial manipulation.[1] Whereas the species was thought to be subject to long-term evolution through natural mechanisms of selection and adaptation, it was believed that the genes could be controlled by human intervention. Eugenics created the myth of a superior 'race' bred by the artificial control of the genetic structure of the population.[2]

An interest in eugenics arose first in late nineteenth-century Britain, spreading rapidly to most industrialized countries. It reflected a concern about the biological standards of the population. *Laissez-faire* theories of modern civilization, it was argued, had interfered with the natural laws of selection with the result that unfit people proliferated at the bottom level of society. Unhealthy slums generated hordes of deficient people that drained the race of its vitality. Visions of an infectious *lumpenproletariat* submerging the fit elements of society plagued the upper classes. It was believed that breeding principles, such as assortative mating and artificial selection, could be applied to the population in order to put a halt to further degeneration. 'Positive eugenics', a term coined by Francis Galton (1822–1911), would ensure that individuals with above-average abilities would breed at a higher rate than ordinary people. 'Negative eugenics' would restrict the reproduction of inferior people; those having subnormal abilities would have to

1 Parts of this chapter have been published as Frank Dikötter, 'Eugenics in Republican China', *Republican China*, 15, no. 1 (Nov. 1989), pp. 1–17.
2 This chapter is confined to mainline eugenics, but I hope to approach other fields affected by 'race' in my forthcoming 'The yolk and the ticks: Birth, sex and death in modern China (1895–1949)', which deals in detail with the impact of the biological paradigm in modern China. For details, see Frank Dikötter, 'The yolk and the ticks', *Republican China*, 17, no. 1 (Nov. 1991).

be physically prevented from perpetuating their infirmities. Main-line eugenists assumed that intellectual capacity and behavioural traits were inherited and could not be enhanced by education. Those defined as being at the bottom of the mental scale became the main target of eugenic movements, which campaigned for their segregation or sterilization. Although eugenics never achieved a significant degree of institutional organization in Republican China, the discourse of race improvement was wide-spread and pervasive.

INCEPTION

Well before Darwin's time, the Chinese had attained a sophisti-cated level of knowledge about selection and breeding, particularly in botany.[3] Wang Guan wrote about peonies during the Song: 'Herbaceous peonies grow with the breath of heaven and earth. Their size and colour can be controlled by changing their nature born of heaven and earth so that rare shapes and colours are produced in our human world.' The universality of variation and its use to breed new varieties through artificial selection was well understood. The application of sporting selection was evident in the breeding of goldfish. The *Illustrated Book on Goldfish*, dated 1848, explained that 'in choosing fish for mating, select a male of excellent variety that complements the female in colour, type and size.' The development of botanical knowledge may have contrib-uted to the rise of eugenics in Republican China. The semantic isomorphism between 'seed' (*zhong*) and 'race' (*zhong, zhongzu*), characteristic of other rice-growing societies,[4] was also a signifi-cant factor in the development of racial discourse. 'To reproduce', or *chuanzhong*, meant to 'pass on the seed', or 'to spread the race'. Whereas eugenics in the West grew out of a long tradition of animal breeding, eugenics in China found a precursor in botany.

3 The following is based on Zhang Binglun, 'Researches in heredity and breeding' in *Ancient China's technology and science*, Institute of the History of Natural Sciences (ed.), Beijing: Foreign Languages Press, 1983, pp. 281–91. See also D. Leslie, 'Early Chinese ideas on heredity', *Asiatische Studien*, 7 (1953), pp. 26–46.

Another influential notion preceding the eugenic discourse was that of *taijiao*. Traditional medicine interpreted the conception of a child as the mixture of female blood with male semen. During pregnancy, menstrual blood was retained in the body of the mother to nourish the foetus. After the birth, yin blood was transformed into breast milk, which was believed to transmit the moral and physical qualities of the mother.[5] Diseased babies, as well as infants with major physical defects, were often eliminated in traditional China.[6] *Taijiao*, or 'prenatal education', was concerned with the effect of external influences on the development of the foetus. It assumed that the nature of the baby could be altered by emotional or physical shocks from the outside world. The *Lienüzhuan* thus prescribed some of the basic rules of prenatal education to the pregnant mother: 'The eyes will see no evil colours, the ears will hear no evil sounds, the mouth will speak no evil words: this is the meaning of *taijiao*.'[7] Prenatal education spread among the upper classes during the Western Han (206 BC–23 AD). Elite bias was implicit in the principles of *taijiao*. Jia Yi (200–168 BC), who wrote a treatise on *taijiao*, explained a fundamental rule: 'One must be cautious in marrying off one's children, and choose partners who have a sense of filial piety and fraternal duty, who always behave righteously. Thus one's posterity will be caring and filial; they will not dare to be loose or violent. Among relatives, none will be bad; all the lineages will assist one another. Indeed, the phoenix gives birth to the idea of humanity and justice, the tiger and the wolf give birth to the rapacious and perverse

4 *Zhong* is equivalent to *giông* in Vietnamese, *chùng* in Sino-Vietnamese, *shu* in Japanese, and *chong* in Korean.

5 A.K. Leung, 'Autour de la naissance: La mère et l'enfant en Chine aux XVIe et XVIIe siècles', *Cahiers Internationaux de Sociologie*, 76 (Jan.–June 1984), pp. 53, 56 and 64. See also C. Furth, 'Concepts of pregnancy, childbirth, and infancy in Ch'ing dynasty China', *Journal of Asian Studies*, 46, no. 1 (Feb. 1987), pp. 7–35, and C. Furth, 'Blood, body and gender: Medical images of the female condition in China, 1600–1850', *Chinese Science*, 7 (Dec. 1986), pp. 43–66.

6 Gudula Linck, *Frau und Familie in China*, Munich: C.H. Beck, 1988, p. 64; D. Elisseeff, *La femme au temps des empereurs de Chine*, Paris: Stock, 1988, p. 17.

7 *Taiping yulan* (Song encyclopaedia), 'Lienüzhuan', Taipei: Xinxing shuju, 1959, p. 1694 (360: 8).

mind: both are unequal, as each owes his character to his own mother.'[8] *Taijiao* was of no avail to the lower strata of society, sons of 'tigers and wolves'.

In his *True notes on praying for a descendant* (1590), Yuan Huang emphasized the notion of blood. Pure blood had always been a concern of the higher classes; it was a symbol of noble descent, vital in a country repeatedly invaded by 'barbarians'. Yuan correlated the quality of blood to the physical health of the baby. The *jing*, or vital substance animating all creatures, was produced by blood. 'When the eyes are tired of looking, the blood is dissipated by looking; when the ears are tired of listening, the blood is dissipated by listening; when the mind is tired of thinking, the blood is dissipated by thinking.'[9] Abuse of alcohol and incorrect dietary habits also affected the blood; its solidity or fragility (*jiancui*) influenced the baby's constitution.

The lore of *taijiao* rapidly penetrated popular culture. Strange stories and tales about the influence of external impressions on the character of the foetus abound in Chinese literature. Belief in the efficacy of pre-natal education, still widespread at the beginning of the twentieth century, was often associated with eugenics. One popular treatise typically deplored the lowering of the 'racial strength' of the nation; another underlined how the 'intelligence or stupidity of the race' could be influenced by *taijiao*.[10] Some of these treatises were reprinted almost every year, thus reaching a much larger readership. Chen Jianshan, the popular evolutionist, attacked pre-natal education in a short study published as part of a popular science series for young people.[11]

The first direct references to eugenics in China date from the

8 Wu Shenyuan, *Zhongguo renkou sixiang shigao* (Draft on the history of Chinese population thought), Chongqing: Zhongguo shehui kexue chu-banshe, 1986, p. 70.

9 Ibid., p. 199.

10 Song Jiazhao, *Taijiao* (Prenatal education), Shanghai: Zhonghua shuju, 1914, p. 1. Song Mingzhi, *Taijiao* (Prenatal education), Shanghai: Zhonghua shuju, 1914, p. 5.

11 Chen Jianshan, *Taijiao* (Prenatal education), Shanghai: Shangwu yin-shuguan, 1926.

turn of the century. Race improvement was an integral part of the discourse of race as lineage. The reformer Tan Sitong, for instance, referred briefly to the 'science of race advancement' in his *Study of humanity (Renxue)*:

> Nowadays, electricity is able to transmit heat and power without a wire and to take a photograph of the liver and lungs. It can also test the material activity of the brain: in the course of time, it will be possible to eliminate its heavy nature and preserve its lightness, to decrease the body and increase the mind. If we also pay attention to the science of race advancement [*jinzhong zhi xue*], each generation will be superior to the other; through endless transformations, it will give birth to another race, which uses solely its intelligence and not its strength, having only a spirit and no body.[12]

Tan incorporated race improvement into his own cosmological philosophy, which was derived mainly from Confucian and Daoist teachings. Eugenics was a means of realizing an ideal spiritual wholeness. Controlling the evolution of the race would permit the body to be dissolved and the mind transcended; spiritual unity with the cosmos would then be achieved.

Kang Youwei's eugenic thought was more realistic. He considered the 'amelioration of the race' to be the prerequisite for an ideal society. The government should build pleasure hostels, situated in agreeable surroundings, where young people could meet. Pregnant women should then be led to a pre-natal education hospital (*taijiaoyuan*), where qualified doctors would prescribe food and supervise their activities. The disabled, the mentally diseased and the mentally deficient would be sterilized.[13] Like most of the Chinese reformers, Liang Qichao admired the Spartans, who used to cast out babies considered unfit.[14]

12 Tan Sitong, *Tan Sitong quanji* (Collected writings of Tan Sitong), Beijing: Zhonghua shuju, 1981, p. 366.
13 Liang Qichao, 'Nanhai Kang xiansheng zhuan' (Biography of Kang Youwei) in *Yinbingshi wenji* (Complete works of Liang Qichao), Shanghai: Zhonghua shuju, 1941, 3, 6: 78.
14 Liang Qichao, 'Sibada xiaoshi' (Short history of the Spartans) in *Yinbingshi zhuanji* (Complete works of Liang Qichao), Shanghai: Zhonghua shuju, 1941,

Eugenics also caught the fancy of the revolutionaries. Zhang
Binglin boldly claimed that 'the superiority or inferiority inherent
in heredity is responsible for intelligence or stupidity; the purity or
impurity of the blood is responsible for strength or weakness.' He
believed that people of poor racial stock could be improved by
interbreeding with a 'superior strain' of blood: 'After eight generations, the inferior blood will be no more than 1/128th, which
corresponds almost to a superior race.'[15] Within the discourse of
race as nation, eugenics became an instrument for national revival.
An article published in the *Eastern Miscellany* in 1905, for example,
promoted medicine as the only science capable of improving the
biological quality of the population in times of racial war.[16]

EXPANSION

During the New Culture Movement, there was a growth of
interest in eugenics. This pseudo-science, together with genetics,[17]
was briefly introduced to the reading public in 1918 by Professor
Chen Yinghuang. He described eugenics as a science capable of
curing society by expelling diseased elements, a process called
renzhong gailiang, 'improvement of the race', or *youshengxue*,
'science of superior birth'.[18] A textbook devoted exclusively to
eugenics appeared in 1919: *The science of race improvement* was a
compilation of translated American works, mainly on heredity

4, 15: 1–19. Liang also admired Kaiser Wilhelm II for his concern about the
health of the 'German race'; see ibid., 3, 4: 117.
15 Zhang Binglin, *Qiushu* (Book of raillery), Shanghai: Gudian wenxue chubanshe, 1958, p. 40.
16 Hai Huo, 'Yixue yu shehui zhi guanxi' (The relationship between medicine and society), *Dongfang zazhi*, 2, no. 4 (April 1905), p. 8.
17 On the development of non-human genetics in Republican China, see L.A.
Schneider, 'Genetics in Republican China' in J.Z. Bowers, J.W. Hess and N.
Sivin (eds), *Science and medicine in twentieth-century China: Research and education*,
Ann Arbor, University of Michigan Center for Chinese Studies, 1988,
pp. 3–30.
18 Chen Yinghuang, *Renleixue* (Anthropology), Shanghai: Shangwu yinshuguan, 1928 (1st edn 1918), p. 242.

and genetics, but also on eugenics.[19] It was a highly technical work, one which did not prescribe the application of eugenic principles in China.

A call for the emulation of the Western concern with race appeared first in the reputable journal *New Education* in 1919, edited by Jiang Menglin. Xia Yuzhong, the editor of Beijing Normal University's textbooks and a professor of Chinese literature, regretted that the material progress of modern civilization had not been accompanied by racial improvement. 'Society is still crammed with all the evil, the ugly, the false, the wicked, the scrambling, the base, the stupid, the brutish and the vexing elements of the human race, filled with all the bad phenomena that could lead a superior person to commit suicide.' Eugenists would differentiate between those elements that should be preserved and those that should be eliminated. Xia advocated the founding of eugenic laboratories at the provincial level and the establishment of a special village where people with perfect brains and ideal bodies could be bred in order to generate the future 'model race'.[20] Such early writings on eugenics were dominated by the discourse of the reformers: the world was interpreted in terms of racial war. The very term 'eugenics' (*youshengxue*) was reminiscent of 'struggle for survival' (*youshengliebai*, literally 'the superior win, the inferior lose'), and was homophonous with 'science of how the superior win'. Hu Zongyuan's opening sentence in his article on the fundamental reform of the race was characteristic: 'Some ethnologists claim that the intelligent races rule, the stupid [*yu*] races serve, the strong flourish, the weak perish.'[21] Because heredity determined the intelligence or stupidity of a race, explained Hu, a thorough reform of the nation's genetic resources was imperative for China's revival.

---

19 Chen Shoufan, *Renzhong gailiangxue* (Race improvement), Shanghai: Shangwu yinshuguan, 1928 (1st edn 1919).
20 Xia Yuzhong, 'Shuzhongxue yu jiaoyu' (Eugenics and education), *Xinjiaoyu*, 2, no. 4 (Dec. 1919), p. 395.
21 Hu Zongyuan, 'Genben gaizao renzhong zhi wenti' (The problem of fundamentally reforming the race), *Funü zazhi*, 5, no. 3 (March 1919), p. 1.

Some social thinkers also turned to eugenics at the beginning of the 1920s. *The Ladies Journal*, for instance, introduced its readership to the mainline eugenics of Charles Davenport at the end of 1919,[22] and cited the Eugenics Laboratory of Sir Francis Galton as well as the Eugenics Education Society of Leonard Darwin.[23] Ding Wenjiang, to take a more notorious example, argued that science, especially eugenics and ecology, could help to solve China's population problems by 'rational means'.[24]

In 1923, the respected periodical *Eastern Miscellany* initiated the publication of the first comprehensive exposition of eugenic principles. The slim volume was co-authored by Zhou Jianren,[25] the science editor of the Commercial Press in Shanghai and brother of the famous writer Lu Xun, together with Chen Changheng,[26] a specialist in population problems. *Evolution and eugenics* rapidly became a best-seller.

Chen Changheng established a correlation between the idea of progress and eugenics.[27] The unfolding of progress had always been hampered by racial degeneration. Great civilizations such as Babylon, Greece, Rome, Spain and Turkey had collapsed as a

22 Dong Zhuli, 'Renzhong gailiangxue zhi yanjiu fangfa' (C.B. Davenport, *The research methods of the science of race improvement*), *Funü zazhi*, 5, no. 12 (Dec. 1919), pp. 1–8; 6, no. 1 (Jan. 1920), pp. 6–10.
23 San Wu, 'Bi ren wo guan' (My point of view on contraception), *Funü zazhi*, 6, no. 12 (Dec. 1920), pp. 1–7.
24 Ding Wenjiang, 'Zhesixue yu pudie' (Eugenics and clan records), *Gaizao*, 3 (1920–21), no. 4, pp. 37–44, no. 6, pp. 7–16; see also D.W.Y. Kwok, *Scientism in Chinese thought, 1900–1950*, Yale University Press, 1965, p. 114.
25 Zhou had already published an article on the principles of eugenics in *Eastern Miscellany*. This article was later integrated in his *Evolution and eugenics*; see Zhou Jianren, 'Shanzhongxue de lilun yu shishi' (The theory of eugenics and its implementation), *Dongfang zazhi*, 18, no. 2 (Jan. 1921), pp. 56–64.
26 Chen Changheng, a pioneer in the field of population theories, would later erect birth control and eugenics as the cornerstones of his 'child-bearing revolution' (*shengyu geming*); see chapter 3 of his *Sanminzhuyi yu renkou zhengce* (The Three Principles of the People and population policies), Shanghai: Shangwu yinshuguan, 1930. Chen was also a committee member of the legislative yuan.
27 Chen Changheng and Zhou Jianren, *Jinhualun yu shanzhongxue* (Evolution and eugenics), Shanghai: Shangwu yinshuguan, 1925 (1st edn 1923), pp. 5–10.

consequence of racial decrepitude, and China would soon go the same way. Eugenics would empower man to direct the course of societal evolution. Following the reformers, Chen harped on the theme of racial extinction. He described how Western states were actively engaged in eugenic policies and how they had succeeded in progressively raising the vitality of the 'race'.[28] Whereas the 'races' of the West were becoming increasingly strong and vibrant, 'national subjugation and racial extinction' (*wangguomiezhong*, a concise and frequently used epigram) were thought to pose a threat to a Middle Kingdom in decay.

Zhou Jianren explained the principles of evolution and the mechanisms of heredity. Statistics proved that not only physical characteristics, but also mental traits could be inherited: idiots could not produce intelligent children.[29] As was explained in chapter 4, the belief in the inheritance of mental characteristics was essentially non-Darwinian, and was related to the Lamarckian paradigm of unilinear evolution. Belief in biological determinism gained further influence with the rediscovery of hereditary principles by Mendel at the turn of the century. 'Science' demonstrated how one's character was determined by Mendelian factors. The Mendelian revolution, by claiming that nature could not be overcome by nurture, led to the belief that the spread of unfit characters should be prevented for the sake of 'progress'. In Republican China, many popular writers exploited the Mendelian idea that genetic factors determined the character of an individual. Zhou Jianren asserted that the proliferation of 'unfit' elements drained the race's resources and endangered society. He went on to advocate the speedy limitation of their reproduction: 'If one wants to restrict the reproduction of the unfit, one can only segregate them. An active method would be to attempt to remove their reproductive capacity, and only after that can they be released.'[30]

A year after the appearance of *Evolution and eugenics*, the Commercial Press published a study of heredity written by Liu Xiong.

28 Ibid., pp. 13–16.
29 Ibid., p. 68.
30 Ibid., p. 75.

Like Zhou Jianren, Liu represented the worst current of eugenics. He accepted the inheritance of intellectual capacity, the dichotomy between inferior and superior people and the ruthless application of negative eugenics to the 'unfit'. Liu maintained that it was the responsibility of eugenics to eliminate 'inferior elements' in order to preserve the race's superior strain.[31] Two themes of Liu's work in particular should be noted, since they would recur in the discourse of race improvement in China:

First, there was the concept of *class*. In Liu Xiong's view, eugenics should be directed toward specifically defined classes. The racial health of the lower strata of society should be raised in order to dissolve the class system that had prevailed in the past: only then could social harmony be achieved. Intellectuals were defined as a 'class' (*jieji*), opposed to elements 'without intelligence' that propagated at the bottom of society. Whereas Chen Changheng's theories were still dominated by the idea of racial extinction (*baozhong*), characteristic of the reformers' discourse of race, Liu advanced a different vision: the lower classes had to be elevated to the level of the superior class. Racial uniformity within the nation, instead of racial superiority among nations, would ensure the survival of the country. The focus was shifted from racial differences between nations to racial differences between classes. By translocating the myth of superiority from race to class, the intellectuals set themselves up as a privileged social group, the repository of racial purity.

Secondly, there was the concept of *individualism*. 'The limit of individual liberty is that it should not infringe upon others and that it should not harm the development of the race.' In the special paragraph that Liu devoted to the interaction of individual and race, it was explained that individualism had to be restricted when it threatened the racial welfare of society. The foremost duty of the citizen was to contribute actively to the race: 'When one assumes the task of protecting the race's superior characteristics, one

31 The following is based on Liu Xiong, *Yichuan yu yousheng* (Heredity and eugenics), Shanghai: Shangwu yinshuguan, part of the popular science series 'Universal Library', 1926 (1st edn 1924), pp. 74–83.

cannot consider only individual liberty and comfort.' The subordination of the individual to the group was a concern that often emerged in eugenic writings.

Until the mid-1920s, however, the idea of race improvement remained confined to a narrow group of intellectuals. It was only with Pan Guangdan (1898–1967) that eugenics would become a household word in China.[32] He enrolled at Dartmouth College in 1922 to study zoology and in 1924 proceeded from there to Columbia University to read for a higher degree. Although Pan had had one leg amputated after an athletic injury,[33] he was to become China's most popular eugenist.

Pan Guangdan became interested in eugenics as a student at Qinghua University. On graduation from Dartmouth, he and several fellow-students founded the first eugenic organization in China, 'The Chinese Eugenics Institute' (Zhongguo yousheng xuehui), which put forward proposals for the enactment of eugenic laws. The following year, Pan wrote an introduction to the worldwide eugenic movement. It described the general principles of eugenics and listed the name, address, date of founding and principal publications of each of the most important institutions.[34] In

32 Pan Guangdan has recently been recognized as China's 'pioneer' in the field of eugenics; see Li Chonggao, 'Youshengxue de youlai yu fazhan' (The future and development of eugenics) in Xing jiaoyu yu yousheng (Sexual education and eugenics), Shanghai: Shanghai kexue jishu chubanshe, 1987, vol. 2, p. 200. Some of his work was reprinted in the 1980s. It is beyond the scope of this chapter to examine his entire output, and here we will attempt only to outline his eugenic discourse on the basis of his most influential writings.

33 H.L. Boorman (ed.), Biographical dictionary of Republican China, New York: Columbia University Press, 1971, p. 61. See also Ying Zi, Zhongguo xin xueshu renwu zhi (Bibliographies of Chinese famous modern scientists), Hong Kong: Zhiming shuju, 1956, pp. 79–82. Pan appears to have been a rather bookish person, oblivious to the outside world and often engrossed in the study of Chinese family genealogies.

34 Pan's introduction was originally published in the Dongfang zazhi, 22, no. 22 (Nov. 1925), 'Ershi nianlai shijie zhi yousheng yundong' (The eugenics movement in the world during the last twenty years), pp. 60–83, and was reprinted in Pan Guangdan, Youshengxue (Eugenics), Shanghai: Shangwu yinshuguan, 1933. The following discussion refers to this edition.

his article, Pan called for the 'citizenization' (*gongminhua*) of the movement, as eugenics could not be considered the responsibility of scientists alone:[35] race improvement was closely related to the politics of the state. The emergence of the nation coalesced with the rise of the race.

Pan also tackled the problem of race improvement in China. In *The eugenic question in China*,[36] he described two mutually exclusive processes of selection: natural selection (*tianran xuanze* or *tianze*), which was the evolutionists' object of investigation, and cultural selection (*wenhua xuanze* or *huaze*), the concern of the eugenists. The recent intrusion of Western culture had interfered dramatically with the process of natural selection in China. The purpose of Pan's short study was to analyze the effects of this new cultural influence on the 'Chinese race'. The first section focused on different aspects of cultural selection in China prior to the country's opening to the West:[37]

(1) Familism (*jiazuzhuyi*), as opposed to Western individualism (*gerenzhuyi*), was viewed as a positive factor in the preservation of the race's vitality. The Chinese family stressed the duties of its members more than their rights. 'Individual liberty and happiness have to recede into the background or be sacrificed entirely in the struggle for survival of the race.'

(2) Chinese religions had never really opposed marriage. The Confucian emphasis on filial piety and procreation was compatible with 'racial order' (*zhongzu zhian*).

(3) The traditional matrimonial system had never interfered with 'racial hygiene' (*zhongzu weisheng*), as the individual's role was minimized to ensure collective harmony. Arranged marriages and low rates of divorce were valued positively by Pan. Bigamy was not necessarily negative, since it was practised only by noble and rich families, whose blood was generally superior to that of the

35 Ibid., p. 44.
36 Pan Guangdan, 'Zhongguo zhi yousheng wenti' (China's eugenic problem), *Dongfang zazhi*, 21, no. 22 (Nov. 1924), pp. 15–32, reprinted in Pan, *Youshengxue*.
37 Ibid., pp. 71–85.

common people. Although he admitted that the concubinage system had a negative influence on the race's health, Pan Guangdan judged that traditional Chinese marriage customs were altogether sound.

(4) Population growth had so far remained free from any kind of cultural interference. The reproduction rate was high, but it had always been counterbalanced by a high mortality.

(5) Rural life maintained the race's vitality. The urban style of life only stimulated a decadent individualism that contributed nothing to the race.

Pan concluded that the negative influence of cultural selection had never been significant in China. Westernization, however, had already begun to affect social organization in a number of ways. First, medical hygiene had wiped out the process of natural selection, allowing inferior people to proliferate; secondly, Western matrimonial practices emphasized romanticism, advocated a late marriage age, espoused ideals unattainable for many young Chinese and put undue emphasis on the financial independence of the female partner; thirdly, the upper classes, motivated by individualism, tended to limit their offspring; and finally, the expansion of urbanization led to the dissemination of evil practices throughout the country.[38] Pan Guangdan called for a critical re-evaluation of Western civilization. Foreign cultural penetration had upset the country's social organization and undermined its racial health; cultural selection had disturbed a delicate balance that could be redressed only by eugenics.

In this early article, Pan Guangdan had laid out what were to become the dominant themes of his thought, namely faith in the inherent superiority of the intellectual class, distrust of Western individualism, and confidence in the family as the basic unit of the nation-race. Pan spent much of his time teaching and writing on the concepts of eugenics that he had elaborated during this early period. His ideal family, for instance, was conceptualized in his *Chinese family problems* (1928). This study presented the results of a survey of readers of the magazine *Xuedeng* concerning marriage

38 Ibid., pp. 93–103.

and family status. The introduction equated family with *xuetong*, 'stock', 'breed' or 'strain':[39] this constituted the biological unit of the race. The genetic inheritance of the family should be improved, for only then could it become an 'instrument for struggle and survival'.[40] Pan was opposed to birth control, late marriage and female independence, pointing instead to the positive aspects of the traditional marriage system. His faith in the racial superiority of intellectuals, shared by many eugenists, was expressed in his work on blood kinship among Chinese stage actors. Inspired by such outdated works as Galton's *Hereditary genius* (1869) and Havelock Ellis' *A study of British genius*, it studied the clan records of famous acting families in order to demonstrate that the assortative mating intuitively practised by certain families had produced a large number of famous actors. Actor families had succeeded in preserving the desirable genetic qualities: theatrical talent, Pan believed, had been transmitted by the genes.[41]

APOGEE

Pan was an outspoken advocate of eugenics and for many years crusaded for its adoption. Together with the Chinese Committee for Racial Hygiene, he initiated the publication of a *Eugenics Monthly*, which contained essays, short stories and reviews.[42] The spread of a eugenic discourse, however, cannot be ascribed to the activity of one scholar. Many intellectuals in the late 1920s were actively engaged in the promotion of racial betterment. Pan's concern with the family converged with the preoccupations of Yi Jiayue, one of the most respected writers on family problems. Yi believed that the family could strengthen the country's 'racial

39 Pan Guangdan, *Zhongguo zhi jiating wenti* (Problems of the Chinese family), Shanghai: Xinyue shudian, 1940 (1st edn 1928), p. 2.
40 Ibid., p. 111.
41 Pan Guangdan, *Zhongguo lingren xueyuan zhi yanjiu* (Research on the blood relationship of Chinese actors), Shanghai: Shangwu yinshuguan, 1941.
42 The *Yousheng yuekan* (Eugenics monthly) appeared from May 1931 to Feb. 1932.

organization' and was beneficial to the 'struggle for survival'.[43] Popular textbooks on heredity explained the principles of eugenics and the dangers of racial degeneration on the strength of Mendelian genetics.[44] A doctrinaire *ABC of eugenics* was published in 1929,[45] and an *Introduction to the science of race improvement* in 1932.[46] The *Student's Magazine* urged university students to undertake research in eugenics for the advancement of the race, the state, and the individual.[47]

After 1930, the casual use of eugenic arguments became increasingly common in scholarly circles. 'Race improvement' and 'racial hygiene' became the catchwords of the day. Medical journals initiated the study of 'racial biology'.[48] In his *Racial hygiene*, Dr Jin Zizhi, for instance, explained how the future of the nation was dependent on the physical condition of the race.[49] One eugenist even warned that masturbation would endanger the racial health of the nation.[50] Eugenic discourse also pervaded lower levels of culture. Marriage guides anticipated that beautiful, superior men and women would marry one another to 'regenerate' the race.[51] A popular guide for women emphasized how the 'superiority' or

43 Yi Jiayue, *Jiating wenti* (Problems of the family), Shanghai: Shangwu yinshuguan, 1920, p. 149.

44 See for instance Chen Jianshan, *Yichuanxue qianshuo* (Elementary introduction to heredity), Shanghai: Zhonghua shuju, 1926, pp. 145–51, and Wang Qishu, *Yichuanxue gailun* (Introduction to heredity), Shanghai: Shangwu yinshuguan, 1926, last chapter.

45 Hua Rucheng, *Youshengxue ABC* (ABC of eugenics), Shanghai: Shijie shuju, 1929.

46 Qian Xiaoqiu, *Renzhong gailiangxue gailun* (Introduction to the science of race improvement), Shanghai: Shenzhou guoguangshe, 1932.

47 Wu Zhenzi, 'Women wei shenme yao yanjiu youshengxue' (Why we should study eugenics), *Xuesheng zazhi*, 15, no. 9 (Sept. 1928), pp. 31–6.

48 'Minzu shengwuxue xulun' (Introduction to racial biology), *Yixue* (Medicine), 1, no. 1 (July 1931).

49 Jin Zizhi, *Minzu weisheng* (Racial hygiene), Shanghai: Shangwu yinshuguan, 1930, p. 1.

50 Review in *Yousheng yuekan*, 2, no. 2 (Feb. 1932), p. 5.

51 Ma Chonggan, *Jiehun zhidao* (Marriage guide), Shanghai: Qinfen shuju, 1931, pp. 11–12.

'inferiority' of children depended on their parents; it described hereditary diseases as the 'germs of race betterment' which menaced the race with degeneration and final extinction.[52] Physical education was exalted; strength and fitness replaced Confucian values of delicacy and frailty. The profound sense of threat which pervaded Republican China led to an obsession with physical prowess and military power. Versions of pastoral also intruded into the discourse of race: rural life was thought to invigorate the individual and maintain biological vitality.

By the mid-1930s, discussions on race improvement began to appear regularly in daily newspapers. In 1935, a Hong Kong daily heralded the imminent breeding of 'scientific babies' by eugenic methods.[53] The same year, eugenic laws were explained in the *Xinwenbao* by Yan Duhe, a popular author of 'mandarin ducks and butterfly' literature.[54] The *Central Daily* devoted two pages to the 'Question of race improvement',[55] while the *New China Times* introduced heredity and eugenics to its readers.[56] Pan Guangdan wrote on 'Eugenics and racial health' in the *Beijing Morning*,[57] which a month later published a paper analyzing the eugenic content of Chinese proverbs[58] and an article urging philanthropists to pay more attention to questions of race improvement.[59] Similar developments were taking place in the West, documented in the

---

52 Zhang Jixiu, *Funü zhuance* (Special handbook for women), Shanghai: Shangwu yinshuguan, 1937, pp. 52–61.
53 'Renzhong gailiang xiansheng jiang you kexue yinghai chuxian' (First signs of race improvement: Imminent appearance of scientific babies), *Xianggang gongshang*, 18 Jan. 1935.
54 Yan Duhe, 'Youshenglü' (Eugenic laws), *Xinwenbao*, 12 May 1935.
55 'Minzu gaizao wenti' (The problem of race reform), *Zhongyang ribao*, 20 Aug. 1935.
56 'Yichuan yu yousheng' (Heredity and eugenics), *Shishi xinbao*, 11 Jan. 1935.
57 Pan Guangdan, 'Yousheng yu minjianzukang' (Eugenics and racial health), *Beiping chenbao*, 3 March 1935.
58 'Zhongguo yanyu zhong de yousheng jianjie' (Eugenic views in Chinese proverbs), *Beiping chenbao*, 7 April 1935.
59 Shen Songnian, 'Zhenzheng cishanjia ying zhuyi youshengxue' (Real philanthropists should pay attention to eugenics), *Beiping chenbao*, 19 April 1935.

enormous secondary literature which has been produced in recent years. The principal difference with developments in China is that eugenics in Germany and in the United States often achieved legislative expression. Many states passed eugenic sterilization laws and limited marriage selection. Racist policies towards those who were considered 'inferior' culminated in Nazism.

Not everybody in China believed in the regenerating virtues of eugenics. Most opponents of the pseudo-science were population specialists. In 1928, a heated debate was pursued by Sun Benwen, who had obtained a Ph.D. at New York University and was professor of sociology at Fudan University, and Pan Guangdan. Sun stood entirely on the side of nurture,[60] and refuted Pan's biological determinism. Four arguments emerged from his scathing criticism: first, man could not be considered an animal; secondly, cultural influence could not be reduced to a biological characteristic; thirdly, IQ tests were not indicative of inherited intelligence; and fourthly, wealth and position did not reflect one's inherent abilities.[61] Sun found it difficult to gauge 'intelligence', and doubted whether qualities such as 'superiority' and 'inferiority' existed at birth.[62] As eugenics had proved capable only of eliminating the so-called 'unfit' elements of society, Sun drily referred to it as a 'science of inferior birth' (*lieshengxue*, as opposed to *youshengxue*, or 'science of superior birth'). Despite his critical attitude, Sun Benwen still professed a belief in the future possibility of breeding people like cattle.[63]

Chen Tianbiao, another researcher in population problems, judged that nature and nurture played equally important roles, and frowned on the idea of a dominant heredity.[64] Chen was neverthe-

60 Sun Benwen, 'Zai lun wenhua yu youshengxue' (Culture and eugenics again), *Shehui xuejie*, 1, no. 2 (Feb. 1927), pp. 1–8.
61 Ru Song, 'Ping youshengxue yu huanjinglun de lunzheng' (Reviewing the controversy between eugenics and environment), *Ershi shiji*, 1, no. 1 (Feb. 1931), p. 60.
62 Sun Benwen, *Renkoulun ABC* (ABC of population theories), Shanghai: Shijie shuju, 1928, pp. 109–11.
63 Ibid., p. 112.
64 Chen Tianbiao, *Renkou wenti yanjiu* (Research on population problems), Shanghai: Liming shuju, 1930, pp. 33–4.

less eager to subscribe to the idea of a marriage ban for people with contagious diseases, the mentally disturbed, the feeble-minded and the maimed (*sic*); he also advocated increased eugenic activities in China.[65] Xu Shilian, a specialist in population theories, contrasted euthenics (*youyexue*), the science of environmental improvement, to eugenics (*youshengxue*).[66] Xu was critical of the scientific basis of eugenics, and disputed the idea that a relationship existed between social position and intellectual capacity.[67] His rebuttal of the latter was based mainly on Herbert Jennings' *Biological basis of human nature* (1930), a study that had exposed the fallacies of eugenics. On the other hand, Chen Da, one of the most respected sociologists of the Republican era,[68] drew imperturbably upon Goddard's *Feeblemindedness* and Tredgold's *Mental deficiency*,[69] the epitome of eugenic bigotry. These works had been discredited in the West by a growing body of anti-eugenic research, but were still used by the author to validate his vision of race improvement. Chen Da invited Pan Guangdan to lecture at Qinghua University in eugenics and sociology. Incidentally, both Chen Da and Pan Guangdan were closely related to Liang Qichao, who was also based at Qinghua.

In the West, academic attacks on eugenics had proliferated since the First World War. Leading scientists like J.B.S. Haldane, Julian Huxley, Lancelot Hogben and Herbert Jennings turned against eugenics and denounced the race and class prejudice it cultivated. G.K. Chesterton's collection of essays from the early 1920s, *Eugenics and other evils*, became a 'staple of the anti-eugenic

65 Ibid., p. 143.
66 Xu Shilian, *Renkoulun gangyao* (Essentials of population theory), Shanghai: Zhonghua shuju, 1934, p. 267.
67 Ibid., pp. 273–5.
68 See Yuan Fang and Quan Weitian, 'Sociologist Chen Da', *Chinese Sociology and Anthropology*, 13, no. 3 (Spring 1981), pp. 59–74; the *Eugenics Monthly* published a letter from Chen in support of the spread of eugenics and the foundation of eugenic journals; see *Yousheng yuekan* (Eugenics monthly), 2, no. 1 (Jan. 1932), p. 28.
69 Chen Da, *Renkou wenti* (Population problems), Shanghai: Shangwu yinshuguan, 1934, pp. 201–2.

arsenal on both sides of the Atlantic'.[70] Apart from some isolated specialists active in the social sciences, this trend found few echoes among Chinese scientists. In his *Race improvement* (1936), Yu Jingrang voiced his concern about the declining birth-rate of the higher classes,[71] while distancing himself from eugenic policies. It was only in the revised edition of the work (1947), however, that the author publicly denounced Nazi eugenics, sterilization policies, and marriage restrictions on the so-called lower classes.[72]

Only a few authors were openly opposed to eugenics. Indeed, many gave free rein to their class prejudices in expounding the most utopian visions of race improvement. Zhang Junjun's *Reform of the Chinese race*, first published in 1935, was an exercise in race dissection. The original superior Han bloodstream had been submerged by successive strains of worthless barbarian blood; intermarriage and migration had led to the progressive degeneration of the Chinese race. Zhang diagnosed the race's illness by analyzing its height, weight, infant mortality, life expectancy, vitality, feeding patterns, character and spiritual defects. When compared to other countries situated between the 20th and 33th parallels (Burma, for instance, was inhabited by small, black, treacherous and lazy people),[73] it appeared that the Chinese were quite superior in intelligence, though not in physical strength. Statistics revealed that at least 50 per cent of the 13,485 students tested were in poor physical shape.[74] To remedy the feebleness of the race, the author prescribed a stable nation with a strong central government.[75] Eugenics was central to the reform of the race: dysgenic marriages had to be proscribed, whereas selective mating with 'superior elements' of other races should be encouraged. A 'Draft for the

---

70 D.J. Kevles, *In the name of eugenics: Genetics and the use of human heredity*, New York: Alfred Knopf, 1985, p. 120.
71 Yu Jingrang, *Renzhong gailiang* (Improvement of the race), Shanghai: Zhengzhong shuju, 1947 (1st edn 1936), p. 44.
72 Ibid., preface.
73 Zhang Junjun, *Zhongguo minzu zhi gaizao* (The reform of the Chinese race), Shanghai: Zhonghua shuju, 1937 (1st edn 1935), p. 169.
74 Ibid., p. 195.
75 Ibid., p. 226 ff.

Implementation of Shenxi's Race Reform' was appended to
Zhang's study. It included a plan for an Institute of Race Reform,
in which the eugenics department would be responsible for enact-
ing eugenic laws. It would have to register and investigate marriages, including family pedigrees, and could be consulted on
matrimonial matters. It would reward spiritually and physically
'healthy' marriages and encouraged 'superior births'. Finally, it
would be responsible for preventing 'unhealthy' marriages. These
were unions in which one of the partners was feebleminded,
mentally disordered, afflicted with a communicable disease, physically weak, tubercular or 'criminally inclined'. The department
in charge of IQ tests was expected to classify citizens as 'intelligent'
(*shangzhi*) or 'stupid' (*xiayu*), an absurd dualization characteristic
of the author's rigid and categoric approach to heredity. The very
terminology Zhang applied revealed the direct influence of the
classics: 'superior intelligence (*shangzhi*) and inferior stupidity
(*xiayu*) cannot be changed,' said the *Analects*.[76]

Zhang Junjun's list of genetically defective elements matched
the worst of Western eugenic theories in vagueness. The term
'feeble-minded' (*dineng*) was used indiscriminately for almost any
type of mental deficiency. 'Mentally disordered' (*shenjingbing*), a
favourite term of abuse to this day, was left undefined, whereas
'physically weak' (*shenti xuruo*) was nothing more than a conven-
ient term to apply to any type of person judged deleterious to
society. The perception of criminality as a biological flaw reflected
the popular belief in the inheritance of behavioural traits: social
pathology was rooted in the genes, not in society. In imperial
China, families with a psychotic member were often excluded from
the marital pool, as society emphasized the hereditary basis of
mental disease.[77]

In the West, the gradual reification of the spiritual sphere of life
had transformed intelligence into an entity that was thought to be

76 *Lunyu* (Analects), *Yanghuo*, 17: 3.
77 Keh-ming Lin, 'Traditional Chinese medical beliefs and their relevance for
mental illness and psychiatry' in A. Kleinman and Liu Tsung-Yi, *Normal and
abnormal behaviour in Chinese culture*, Dordrecht: D. Reidel, 1981, pp. 106-7.

measurable. Belief in the measurement of intelligence was translated into the use of a strict terminology for all the 'levels' of
intelligence that researchers were thought to have discerned.
Chinese eugenics, in comparison, remained vague. Drawing upon
the traditional distinction between the uneducated masses and
the cultured élite, the dichotomy between 'stupidity' and
'intelligence' was often sufficient. Those who made the effort to
distinguish various levels of intellectual deficiency were rare. Ke
Xiangfeng, for instance, classified the 'unfit' into morons (benzi),
imbeciles (daizi) and idiots (chizi), each corresponding to a different IQ level. Ke was an exception: he advocated the 'rational-
ization' of all population problems, and wanted 'rational' criteria
for the classification of inferior elements.[78]

Zhang Junjun championed drastic measures – segregation, exile
and castration – to prevent the procreation of people he had so
vaguely classified as 'unfit'. Exile was a long-standing traditional means of isolating criminals by sending them to the edges
of the empire, far from the civilized centre. Castration was the
cruellest form of sterilization. The majority of eugenists who
eventually came to find virtue in sterilization prescribed vasectomy,
which left the patient sterile but did not affect his sexuality.
Zhang's study concluded with extracts from correspondence
expressing admiration and support for his eugenic project. Shao
Lizi, governor of Shenxi province from 1933–6, endorsed Zhang's
'Draft for the Implementation of Shenxi's Race Reform'. Other
enthusiastic supporters included Zhang Xueliang, once the most
powerful warlord in the north of China, then deputy commander-
in-chief of operations against the communists in the north-west;
Pan Gongzhan, an influential journalist and publisher, member of
the Central Executive Committee of the Guomindang and future
vice-minister of information; Cai Yuanpei, founder and president
of the prestigious Academia Sinica; Chen Lifu, head of the organization department of the Guomindang, and other high-ranking
officials. Eugenic ideas were of course fostered by the Guomindang,

78 Ke Xiangfeng, *Xiandai renkou wenti* (Modern population problems), Shanghai: Zhengzhong shuju, 1934, p. 381.

whose own New Life Movement was partly inspired by a preoccupation with a 'strong race and a strong nation'.[79] Pan Guangdan also planned a book on the New Life Movement and eugenics (*Xinshenghuo yu youshengxue*). It never appeared, presumably because of the outbreak of the Sino-Japanese War in 1937. The Japanese invasion plunged the country into a prolonged war that pushed plans for race reform into the background. The Second World War, followed by the civil war between the Communist Party and the Guomindang from 1945 to 1949, was the main reason why eugenic ideas did not achieve institutional form. The Committee for the Study of Population Policies, organized by the Ministry of Social Affairs in 1941, was the first official attempt to approach population problems in a systematic way. It recommended the segregation of physically and mentally handicapped persons from the normal population for what was called 'cultural advancement and racial rejuvenation'. As people were recognized to be unequally endowed, the report advocated a differential birthrate: 'Thus viewed', said the report, 'some individuals may have children, others not.'[80] The committee – whose members included Chen Changheng, Chen Da and Pan Guangdan – also encouraged the use of sterilization for the racial rejuvenation of the country.

Zhang Junjun and other eugenists cited Hitler and Nazi eugenic policies as a positive example for China, a country much more backward than Germany.[81] Wei Juxian, a respected scholar and author of a substantial article on the origins of the Han people, claimed that if eugenic policies were not adopted immediately,

79 Jiang Zhongzheng (Jiang Jieshi), *Xinshenghuo yundong* (The New Life Movement), Shanghai: Zhengzhong shuju, 1935, pp. 27, 41.
80 Chen Ta, *Population in modern China*, New York: Octagon Books, 1974, pp. 76–7.
81 Zhang Junjun, *Zhongguo minzu*, p. 266. Three separate translations of Hitler's *Mein Kampf* had been published in China by 1935. Many biographies of Hitler and books on National Socialism were published until the 1940s. The reception and interpretation of German Nazism and Italian Fascism in China from the 1930s onwards would undoubtedly be a fruitful and revealing research topic.

then the race was doomed to imminent extinction.[82] A eugenic laboratory (*renzhong gailiangsuo*) would have to be established in every county. Young men and women reaching marriageable age would be selected by a qualified doctor who would allow the strong and the healthy to have sexual intercourse. Expectant mothers would remain under medical control until parturition, at which stage 'weak' offspring would be eliminated. Superior babies would be called 'model person' (*mofanren*); on the other hand, products bred without supervision would be labelled 'elimination person' (*taotairen*): reproduction by such individuals would be strictly prohibited as soon as model persons made up two-thirds of the population. Wei Juxian's eugenic discourse was inspired by the Nazi experience.[83] His article explained in detail how eugenic laws in Germany decreed the 'forceful elimination' of entire categories of people judged deficient, such as sex criminals, the incurably sick, the feebleminded and those afflicted with hereditary diseases. Wei regretted only the Nazis' lack of determination, for their laws were not always carried out in a 'thoroughgoing way'. Although such wavering could be tolerated in the German case, a much firmer hand would be required in China to resist the cultural, economic and military invasions of other nations.

82 The following is based on Wei Juxian, 'Zhongguo minzu qiantu zhi shi de kaocha' (Study on the future of the Chinese race), *Qiantu*, 1, no. 10 (Oct. 1933), pp. 17–18.

83 Many newspapers, including specialized medical periodicals, regularly reported on German eugenic matters. The *Zhonghua yixue zazhi* (Chinese medical journal), for instance, published a detailed account of the 1935 Nuremberg Laws, forbidding any kind of union between a Jew and an Aryan (*Zhonghua yixue zazhi*, 21, no. 10 (1935), pp. 1176–7). These reports were obviously filtered by the journal's own interests. Two months later it published a proposal by the Association of German Doctors on the establishment of Matchmaking Centres (*hunyin jieshaosuo*). These would guide young people in their search for partners, celibacy being viewed as harmful to the race (ibid., no. 12, p. 1474). Such proposals reflected the journal's concern about marital matters and celibacy in China.

For Japanese reactions to Nazi racial policies, see J.P. Fox, 'Japanese reactions to Nazi Germany's racial legislation', *Wiener Library Bulletin*, 23, nos. 2–3 (1969), pp. 46–50, based on German sources.

According to William Kirby, who has studied the relations between Republican China and Germany, most Chinese admirers of National Socialism actually had few reservations about Nazi racism.[84] Anti-semitism received relatively little attention, whereas the German preoccupation with race was hailed as an example worthy of emulation. In the West, Nazi eugenics drew little criticism until the mid-1930s. It was the cruelty of German policies that eventually led to a strong reaction, supported by a long-standing and influential anti-eugenic coalition among people of both secular and religious backgrounds.[85] Paul Popenoe, then a leading eugenist, later admitted that Hitlerism had been the major factor accounting for the decline of interest in race and eugenics from the mid-1930s onwards.[86] In China, however, the fortune of eugenics suffered less from the Nazi example. After 1945, Chinese eugenists continued to toy with outdated genetic concepts such as the inheritance of behavioural traits. Hao Qinming, for instance, concluded his university textbook on heredity with a paragraph entitled 'The urge for race improvement'.[87] Idiots (chiyu), demented people (kuangdian), epileptics, those afflicted with 'loathsome' diseases, the malformed and those suffering from hereditary diseases would not be allowed to marry. Intervention of a coercive nature was not imperative for people with minor infirmities like deafness, dumbness, blindness or baldness: education would convince them of the necessity of voluntary sterilization. Moral principles also guided the idea of rewarding 'superior' parents who bred 'intelligent' children.

84 W.C. Kirby, Germany and Republican China, Stanford University Press, 1984, p. 167. An analysis of the Nazi press in China, along with the translation of an anti-semitic pamphlet, appears in F. Kreissler, L'action culturelle allemande en Chine. De la fin du XIXᵉ siècle à la seconde guerre mondiale, Paris: Editions de la Maison des Sciences de l'Homme, 1989, pp. 98–112, 269. Kreissler's study, however, concerns only the German community in China; there is no attempt to explore Chinese reactions to German racial theories.

85 Kevles, In the name of eugenics, p. 118.

86 D.K. Pickens, Eugenics and the progressives, Nashville: Vanderbilt University Press, 1968, p. 99, n. 44.

87 The following is based on Hao Qinming, Yichuanxue (Genetics), Shanghai: Zhengzhong shuju, 1948, pp. 207–9.

In Europe, works like Lionel Penrose's pioneering study on the mentally deficient of Colchester (1938) had taken the field far beyond the naiveties of eugenics. The simplistic belief in the inheritance of intellectual and behavioural characteristics could no longer be held by any serious scientist writing after the Second World War. Hao Qinming's compilation of undesirable elements included many ill-defined and archaic terms like 'idiots', 'demented' or 'people with loathsome diseases'. The author also expounded a theory on the differential birth-rates of 'idiots' and 'intellectuals'; idiots proliferated rapidly and threatened to outbreed the intellectuals, thereby upsetting the fragile balance of society. Only mass sterilization could ward off the menace of racial cretinism. As an exercise, Hao's students were asked to draft a plan for the implementation of eugenic policies on the provincial level. They were also required to produce a letter advising the legislative court to legalize sterilization.[88]

A final example is Hu Buchan's widely-read *Eugenics and human heredity*, first published in 1936 and reprinted several times until 1959 without textual alterations. Hu gave a succinct description of the various methods of race improvement.[89] The Spartan method of physically eliminating unfit infants was cruel and contradicted the spirit of eugenics. Both neo-Malthusianism and *laissez-faire* policies were categorically rejected by the author. Education of the population and marriage restrictions were invaluable methods of improving the nation's racial stock, but could have only a limited impact. Polygamy was effective with farm animals, but was immoral and illegal when applied to human society. This left segregation and sterilization as the only reliable eugenic techniques. Hu Buchan, whose textbook provided a balanced account of the intricate mechanisms of human heredity, resisted the temptation of defining those he referred to as 'unhealthy'. His class bias, however, emerged in a chapter concerning birth control. Hu deplored

---

88 Ibid., p. 227.
89 This section is based on Hu Buchan, *Youshengxue yu renlei yichuanxue* (Eugenics and human genetics), Taipei: Zhengzhong shuju, 1959 (1st edn 1936), pp. 175-8.

the declining birth rates of intellectuals. Although he admitted that there was no definite criterion for determining the superiority of the higher classes and the inferiority of the lower, he argued that most statistics had clearly demonstrated a higher IQ among the former. Hu's class bias rested on social anxiety. His encounters with the lower classes filled him with apprehension: 'The streets are full of beggars, carrying each other on their backs, tramping around hand in hand; for it is true that the poorer people are, the higher their rate of reproduction.'[90] Hu carried the contrast between China's social classes a step further by comparing them to Rome: the ancient city had declined because the pure-blooded Romans had voluntarily limited their births, whereas slaves and foreigners had multiplied without restriction. The author thus explicitly equated the intellectuals with pure-blooded nobles, downgrading other classes to the status of brutish slaves.[91]

We have seen how social perceptions of skin colour and physical characteristics existed in traditional China and how racial stereotypes emerged gradually during the nineteenth century. At the turn of the century, the reformers rationalized these stereotypes and forged a discourse of race which depicted the Chinese as a distinct biological group. During the first decade of the twentieth century, the revolutionaries constructed the concept of nation by portraying the Han Chinese as the descendants of the mythical Yellow Emperor. After the overthrow of the Manchu dynasty and the foundation of the Republic in 1911, however, the fear of racial extinction continued to preoccupy many social thinkers. Some rejected the idea of a united Han nation and instead focused upon differences within the 'race': intellectuals were designated as 'superior', the lower classes as 'inferior'. The popularity of eugenics among the educated classes reflected both a concern with national revival and a search for group identity. The adoption of the pseudo-science was facilitated by a distrust of individualism,

90 Ibid., p. 204.
91 Elsewhere, the author generously extended the notion of pure blood (*chunxue*) to the entire Chinese 'race', regardless of class. Westerners and Japanese, on the other hand, were all of 'mixed blood' (*hunxue*); ibid., p. 118.

disbelief in democracy, and the absence of a religion which disregarded bodily attributes in favour of a paramount spirit. The traditional hierarchy, which distinguished sharply between educated scholars and uneducated peasants, also contributed to the emergence of eugenics during the 1920s and '30s. Eugenics, however, remained narrowly confined to the realm of ideas. It achieved organizational expression only rarely; nor did it affect practical policies. Its defenders, as well as its critics, were ideologues, not scientists. Eugenics also came under attack in the communist era, briefly discussed in the epilogue.

7

EPILOGUE

RACE AS CLASS (1949–?)

The discourse of race was officially abolished following the communist takeover of China in 1949.[1] Anthropology departments had been suspended by the end of 1949, and 'bourgeois' social sciences like anthropology and sociology were proscribed in 1952.[2] Propaganda campaigns under the supervision of reformed anthropologists were launched with the aim of eradicating racial discourse,[3] and anthropologists came under bitter attack in the wake of the anti-rightist campaign of 1957. They were accused of having used disrespectful anthropometric methods that insulted the national minorities. It was also suspected that many of their studies were meant to prove racist ideas of minority inferiority.[4] Although the idea of racial exclusiveness became taboo, the underlying notions that had caused it to be expressed did not disappear. The messianic idea of unification (the *datong*, or 'One World' ideal) was now expressed in a phraseology based on the concept of class struggle, whereas the artificial dichotomization between Chinese and Westerners in biological terms of 'race' was merely reformulated in social terms of 'class'. Eugenic theories were increasingly applied to the individual's social origins: the best

1 Ubukata Naokichi, 'Chūgoku ni okeru jinshu sabetsu no kinshi' (On the prohibition of racial discrimination in China), *Hikakuhō kenkyū*, 6 (April 1953), pp. 40–6.
2 See R.K. Wu and C.H. Liu, 'The history of physical anthropology in China', *Homo*, 35 (1984), pp. 127–34; Wu Rukang, 'Antropologiia v Kitae', *Sovietskaia Antropologiia*, 3, no. 1 (1959), pp. 107–12.
3 See, for instance, Zhou Jianren, *Lun youshengxue yu zhongzu qishi* (About eugenics and racial discrimination), Beijing: Sanlian shudian, 1950.
4 G.E. Guldin, 'Chinese anthropologies', *Chinese Sociology and Anthropology*, 20, no. 4 (Summer 1988), p. 9. On the relationship between anthropology and the minorities, see also G. Gjessing, 'Chinese anthropology and New China's policy toward her minorities', *Acta Sociologica*, 2, no. 1 (1956), pp. 45–68.

people were 'born red'. During the Cultural Revolution, blood-lineage theories surfaced to prove the biological inheritance of class attitudes.[5] Traditional proverbs that had often been invoked in eugenic circles during the 1920s and '30s resurfaced: 'a phoenix begets phoenixes, a wolf begets wolves.'[6]

Although there is nothing in Mao's writings which deals directly with the idea of race, it is clear that his sense of nationalism was based on a strong racial consciousness and a sense of biological continuity. Like most politicians who grew to maturity in Republican China, he perceived the Chinese 'nation' (*minzu*) as a biologically distinct group: being Chinese was a matter of 'culture' as well as 'race'. As a student of Li Dazhao, it is also likely that he coalesced the notions of 'class' and 'race' into a vision of the struggle of the 'coloured people' against 'white imperialism'. Stuart Schram writes that 'Mao's appeal is not merely to a union based upon revolutionary principles, but to the visceral solidarity of peoples long oppressed and humiliated by the white powers of Europe and America.'[7] In an often quoted speech, delivered in 1963, Mao claimed that 'in Africa, in Asia, in every part of the world there is racism; in reality, racial problems are class problems.'[8] The race problem had become a class problem.

Official propaganda fostered the idea that only Westerners could indulge in racism, the Chinese having become the leaders of the victimized 'coloured' people in the historical struggle against 'white imperialism'. It was an important ingredient of anti-imperialist propaganda, which reached almost hysterical propor-

5 On theories of 'natural redness', see Gordon White, *The politics of class and class origin: The case of the Cultural Revolution*, Canberra: Australian National University, 1976, and Richard Curt Krauss, 'Class conflict and the vocabulary of social analysis', *The China Quarterly*, 69 (March 1977), pp. 54–74.

6 See for instance Gao Yuan, *Born red: A chronicle of the Cultural Revolution*, Stanford University Press, 1987, pp. 84, 113, 119, 122, 209.

7 S.R. Schram, *The political thought of Mao Tse-tung*, New York: Praeger, 1969, p. 374.

8 'Mao zhuxi jiejian Feizhou pengyou fabiao zhichi Meiguo heiren douzheng de shengming' (Chairman Mao meets our African friends and issues a statement in support of the American blacks' struggle), *Renmin ribao* (People's Daily), 9 Aug. 1963, p. 1.

tions during the Korean War[9] and the Cultural Revolution. Louis Barcata met some Chinese intellectuals in 1967 and was particularly struck by a professor from Shanghai:

> Whatever his views on domestic issues, in foreign policy the professor stood by Mao unconditionally. He hated the Russians who, he claimed, behaved more like opponents than comrades. He regarded the Vietnam conflict as a 'holy war', and as the prelude to an inevitable conflict between the races. For this professor, who had done some traveling in the world, and who had once gone to South Africa to study apartheid, the white man is the only creature on earth whose behavior is fundamentally warped, whose being suffers from a mechanical flaw; the white man is the 'greatest source of discord in all creation'. The others who took part in the discussion agreed with him completely. I was taken aback by the very vehemence of their posture. These seven men saw the history of mankind as nothing but a sequence of brutal injustices inflicted by the white man on the colored peoples of the world. These Chinese intellectuals were convinced that the coming world conflict would be ignited not solely by an ideological confrontation but by racial antagonism. It would be an epic struggle between the races – an Armageddon in which China would lead the exploited colored peoples in their battle against the powers of white reaction.[10]

In Africa, the Chinese initially tried to capitalize on a common racial identity, urging that 'we blacks stick together' against the 'white race',[11] an idea which was met with scepticism on the African side. Acting troupes endeavoured to propagate the idea of

9 For example *Choushi Meidi, bishi Meidi, mieshi Meidi* (Hate American imperialism, disdain American imperialism, despise American imperialism), Shanghai: Wenhuibao, 1950, p. 39, reviewing racism against Blacks, Jews, Mexicans, Indians, Japanese, Chinese, Puerto Ricans, Filipinos, and others.

10 L. Barcata, *China in the throes of the Cultural Revolution*, New York: Hart Publishing Co., 1968, pp. 193–4.

11 A. Hutchison, *China's African revolution*, London: Hutchinson, 1975, p. 179.

racial solidarity, as was exemplified by a play performed in Rwanda in the early 1960s:

> A tableau depicted a black man sitting on a throne; a Chinese actor with a white mask then entered and knocked him off [groans from crowd]. A Chinese with no mask entered, knocks the 'white man' in turn off the throne, picks up the African from the ground and helps him back on to the throne [cheers from crowd].'[12]

Despite the communist imagery of racial harmony and unity with the underdog, the Chinese adopted an aloof and exclusive attitude during their stay in Africa. Blacks studying in China also complained about racial prejudice. To take one example among many, Emmanuel Hevi, a Ghanaian studying in China in the early 1960s, testified to the continuous discrimination blacks had to endure in China. He perceived paternalism as an important form of prejudice: 'In all their dealings with us the Chinese behaved as if they were dealing with people from whom normal intelligence could not be expected.'[13] Friction between African students and Chinese has increased since the reform program launched by Deng Xiaoping at the beginning of the 1980s, sometimes leading to violent clashes involving casualties on both sides.

Racial discourse has tended to reappear in periods of internal and external tension. At the height of the Sino-Soviet rift, the Chinese Communist Party increasingly harped on the theme of racial differences between Russians and Chinese.[14] Racial hatred

---

12 Ibid., p. 192, n. 3.

13 E.J. Hevi, *An African student in China*, London: Pall Mall Press, 1963, p. 187. Many incidents, such as a doctor asking why his skin was still so black if he washed regularly, led Hevi to the conclusion that the Chinese people were either supremely ignorant or supremely ill-intentioned; ibid., p. 187.

14 'Her insistence that the Soviet Union is not an Asian country and is thus unqualified for Afro-Asian leadership stops just short of open racism', noted Ishwer Ojha; I.C. Ojha, *Chinese foreign policy in an age of transition*, Boston: Beacon Press, 1969, p. 214. See also W.J. Parente, 'Communism and the problem of race: From propaganda theme to polycentric factor', unpubl. doctoral thesis, Washington, DC: Georgetown University, 1970.

reached a peak during the Third Afro-Asian Solidarity Conference in February 1963, when the Chinese delegates vehemently insisted that the 'white' Russians would never commit themselves whole-heartedly to the anti-imperialist struggle.[15] When the Soviet Union later signed an atomic test-ban treaty with the United States and Britain, the Chinese interpreted it as an affront to the 'coloured people' of the world. With the gradual rapprochement of the two superpowers since the accession to power of Mikhail Gorbachev, the idea of racial identity again proved tempting to some Chinese. Signs of an elemental form of racial nationalism, together with some form of re-Confucianization, are already reappearing in the post-Tiananmen era.

The myth of race is still widespread in the modern world. The discernible physical differences between population groups have led all too easily to sterile theories of biological determinism. Although the discourse of race is situated on the periphery of the Chinese symbolic universe, it has shown singular resilience throughout recent history and has tended to drift towards the centre in periods of instability. Moreover, as was pointed out at the beginning of this study, racial prejudice is hardly peculiar to the Chinese: it was certainly more virulent and widespread in the West. Yet if it is true that this discourse has never been trans-lated into practice with the gruesome efficiency characteristic of certain Western countries, it would be wrong to underestimate its pervasiveness and tenacity. The myth of race has vitiated the ideals of harmony and equality present in all civilizations, impeding societies from breaking free from prejudice and transcending their insularity. It has reinforced fear and ignorance. As Yang Lien-sheng wrote, racism should be 'spelled out in order to be dispelled'.[16]

15 H. Brahm, 'Pekings Spiel mit der Rassenfrage', *Osteuropa*, 15 (Nov.–Dec. 1965), p. 816.
16 Yang Lien-sheng, 'Historical notes on the Chinese world order' in J.K. Fairbank (ed.), *The Chinese world order: Traditional China's foreign relations*, Cam-bridge, Mass.: Harvard University Press, 1968, p. 27.

BIBLIOGRAPHY
PRIMARY SOURCES

Abbreviations

DFZZ   *Dongfang zazhi*
FNZZ   *Funü zazhi*
XDPL   *Xiandai pinglun*
YBSWJ   Liang Qichao, *Yinbingshi wenji*
YBSZJ   Liang Qichao, *Yinbingshi zhuanji*
YPZZ   A Ying, *Yapian zhanzheng wenxue*

Anonymous, 'Bu pingdeng lü' 不平等律 (Laws on inequality), *XDPL*, 1, no. 38 (Aug. 1925), pp. 6–10.

——, *Renzhongxue* 人種學 (Anthropology), n.d., end of the Qing; copy consulted at the Capital Library, Beijing.

A Ying 阿英, comp., *Yapian zhanzheng wenxue ji* 鴉片戰爭文學集 (Collection of literary writings on the Opium War), Beijing: Guji chubanshe, 1957.

'Ai tongbao zhi jiangwang' 哀同胞之將亡 (Grieving for the perishing of overseas Chinese), *DFZZ*, 1, no. 12 (Dec. 1904), p. 88.

Anti-foreign teachings in text-books of China, supplement to the *International Gleanings from Japan*, no. 16 (Oct. 1932), Tokyo: Sokokusha.

Barcata, L., *China in the throes of the Cultural Revolution*, New York: Hart Publishing Company, 1968.

Barnes, G.G., *Enter China! A study in race contacts*, London: Edinburgh House Press, 1928.

'Bianzheng rengui lun' 辨正人鬼論 (About properly distinguishing men from devils), *Wanguo gongbao*, 15 (2 Dec. 1882), pp. 146–7.

Binchun 斌椿, *Chengcha biji* 乘槎筆記 (Travels abroad), Beijing: Yuelu shushe, 1985.

Bolin 伯林, 'Tiyu' 體育 (Physical education), *Yunnan*, 1 (Aug. 1906), pp. 37–44.

Cao Bohan 曹伯韓, *Shijie dili chubu* 世界地理初步 (Elementary world geography), Shanghai: Shenghuo shudian, 1948.

——, *Shijie dili gangyao* 世界地理網要 (Essentials of world geography), Shanghai: Dongnan chubanshe, 1943.

Changyanbao 昌言報 (The Verax), Aug. 1898–Nov. 1898, photolithograph, Taipei: Zhonghua shuju, 1967.

Chen Anren 陳安仁, *Renlei jinhuaguan* 人類進化觀 (The concept of human evolution), Shanghai: Taidong tushuju, 1929.

Chen Changheng 陳長衡, *Sanminzhuyi yu renkou zhengce* 三民主義與人口政策 (The Three Principles of the People and population policies), Shanghai: Shangwu yinshuguan, 1930.

Chen Changheng and Zhou Jianren 周建人, *Jinhualun yu shanzhongxue* 進化論與善種學 (Evolution and eugenics), Shanghai: Shangwu yinshuguan, 1925 (1st edn 1923).

Chen Da 陳達, *Renkou wenti* 人口問題 (Population problems), Shanghai: Shangwu yinshuguan, 1934.

Chen Darong 陳大榕, *Dongwu yu rensheng* 動物與人生 (Animals and life), Shanghai: Shangwu yinshuguan, 1928 (1st edn 1916).

Chen Duxiu 陳獨秀, 'Dong Xi minzu genben sixiang zhi chayi' 東西民族根本思想之差異 (Fundamental differences in thought between the peoples of the East and the West) in *Chen Duxiu wenji*, 陳獨秀文集 Shanghai: Yadong tushuguan, 1922, pp. 57–62.

Chen Duo 陳鐸 *et al.* (eds), *Riyong baike quanshu* 日用百科全書 (Daily encyclopedia), Shanghai: Shangwu yinshuguan, 1919.

Chen Jianshan 陳兼善, *Jinhualun qianshuo* 進化論淺說 (Elementary introduction to the theory of evolution), Shanghai: Zhonghua shuju, 1932.

——, *Renlei naosui zhi jinhua* 人類腦髓之進化 (The evolution of the human brain), Shanghai: Zhengzhong shuju, 1947.

——, 'Shi renlei' 釋人類 (Explaining mankind), *Minduo zazhi*, 5, no. 1 (March 1924), pp. 1 ff.

——, *Taijiao* 胎教 (Prenatal education), Shanghai: Shangwu yinshuguan, 1926.

——, *Yichuanxue qianshuo* 遺傳學淺說 (Elementary introduction to heredity), Shanghai: Zhonghua shuju, 1926.

Chen Lunjiong 陳倫炯, *Haiguo wenjian lu* 海國聞見錄 (Record of things seen and heard about the maritime countries), Zhengzhou: Zhongzhou guji chubanshe, 1985.

Chen Shoufan 陳壽凡, *Renzhong gailiangxue* 人種改良學 (Race improvement), Shanghai: Shangwu yinshuguan, 1928 (1st edn 1919).

Chen Ta, *Population in modern China*, New York: Octagon Books, 1974.

Chen Tianbiao 陳天表, *Renkou wenti yanjiu* 人口問題研究 (Research on population problems), Shanghai: Liming shuju, 1930.

Chen Tianhua 陳天華, *Chen Tianhua ji* 陳天華集 (Collected works of Chen Tianhua), Changsha: Hunan renmin chubanshe, 1982.

Chen Yinghuang 陳映璜, *Renleixue* 人類學 (Anthropology), Shanghai: Shangwu yinshuguan, 1928 (1st edn 1918); repr. Taipei: Xueren yuekan zazhi she, 1971.

Chen Yucang 陳雨蒼, *Renti de yanjiu* 人體的研究 (Research on the human body), Shanghai: Zhengzhong shuju, 1937.

Cheo, E.Y., *Black Country girl in red China*, London: Hutchinson, 1980.

Chinese history, Beijing: Foreign Languages Press, 1987.

Choushi Meidi, bishi Meidi, mieshi Meidi, 仇視美帝, 鄙視美帝, 蔑視美帝 (Hate American imperialism, disdain American imperialism, despise American imperialism), Shanghai: Wenhuibao, 1950.

Cui Guoyin 崔國因, *Chushi Mei Ri Bi riji* 出使美日秘日記 (Mission to America, Japan and Peru), Beijing: Huangshan shushe, 1988.

Darwin, C.R., *On the origin of species* (repr. of the 1st edn), with a foreword by C.D. Darlington, London: Watts, 1950.

Ding Wenjiang 丁文江, 'Zhesixue yu pudie' 哲嗣學與譜牒 (Eugenics and clan records), *Gaizao*, 3 (1920–1), no. 4, pp. 37–44, no. 6, pp. 7–16.

Dong Zhuli 董祝鳌, 'Renzhong gailiangxue zhi yanjiu fangfa' 人種改良學之研究方法 (C.B. Davenport, *The research methods of the science of race improvement*), *FNZZ*, 5, no. 12 (Dec. 1919), pp. 1–8, 6, no. 1 (Jan. 1920), pp. 6–10.

Downing, C.T., *The fan-qui in China in 1836–1837*, London: Henry Colburn, 1838.

Du Yaquan 杜亞泉 *et al.* (eds), *Dongwuxue da cidian* 動物學大詞典 (Great dictionary of zoology), Shanghai: Shangwu yinshuguan, 1927 (1st edn 1923).

Feisheng 飛生, 'Eren zhi xingzhi' 俄人之性質 (The Russians' nature), *Zhejiangchao*, 1 (Feb. 1903), pp. 4–5, 2 (March 1903), pp. 77–9.

Fryer, J., *Gezhi congshu* 格致叢書 (Scientific series), 1901.

Fu Yunsen 傅運森, *Renwen dili* 人文地理 (Human geography), Shanghai: Shangwu yinshuguan, 1914.

Gao Yuan, *Born red: A chronicle of the Cultural Revolution*, Stanford University Press, 1987.

'Geguo renzhong leikao' 各國人種類考 (Study of the types of human races), *Hunan tongsu yanshuobao* (Hunan journal of popular speeches), 12 (Sept. 1903).

Gong Tingzhang 宮廷璋, *Renlei yu wenhua jinbu shi* 人類與文化

進步史 (History of the progress of culture and mankind), Shanghai: Shangwu yinshuguan, 1926.

Graves, R.H., *Forty years in China, or China in transition*, Wilmington: Scholarly Resources, 1972 (1st edn 1895).

Gu Jiegang 顧頡剛, 'Huangdi' 黃帝 (Yellow Emperor) in *Shilin zashi* 史林雜事 (Miscellaneous historical studies), Beijing: Zhonghua shuju, 1963, pp. 176–84.

Gu Shi 顧實, *Rensheng erbainian* 人生二百年 (Man may live two hundred years), Shanghai: Shangwu yinshuguan, 1929.

Gu Shoubai 顧壽白, *Renleixue* 人類學 (Anthropology), Shanghai: Shangwu yinshuguan, 1924.

——, *Renleixue dayi* 人類學大意 (Main points of anthropology), Shanghai: Shangwu yinshuguan, 1924.

Guoli tushuguan 國立圖書館, *Jin bainian lai Zhong yi xishu mulu* 近百年來中譯西書目錄 (Catalogue of Western works translated into Chinese during the last hundred years), Taipei: Zhonghua wenhua chuban shiye weiyuanhui, 1958.

Guo Yaogen 過耀根, *Renlei jinhua zhi yanjiu* 人類進化之研究 (Research on the evolution of mankind), Shanghai: Shangwu yinshuguan, 1916.

Hai Huo 海蠖, 'Yixue yu shehui zhi guanxi' 醫學與社會之關係 (The relationship between medicine and society), *DFZZ*, 2, no. 4 (April 1905), pp. 7–10.

Hao Qinming 郝欽銘, *Yichuanxue* 遺傳學 (Genetics), Shanghai: Zhengzhong shuju, 1948.

Hardy, E.J., *John Chinaman at home*, London: Fisher Unwin, 1907.

'Heinu xuexiao' 黑奴學校 (Schools for the black slaves), *Jiangsu*, 7 (Oct. 1903), p. 168.

'Heinu yi yu qi wo huaren ye' 黑奴亦慾欺我華人耶 (The black slave also wants to humiliate the Chinese), *DFZZ*, 1, no. 11 (Nov. 1904), p. 80.

'Heiren zhi baifen' 黑人之白粉 (The black's white powder), *Zhejiangchao*, 7 (Sept. 1903), p. 172.

'Hengbin Huashang ru Ribenjizhe sishi yu ren!' 橫濱華商入日本籍者四十餘人 (More than forty Chinese merchants in Yokohama enter the Japanese nationality!), *Jiangsu*, 7 (Oct. 1903), pp. 152–7.

Hevi, E.J., *An African student in China*, London: Pall Mall Press, 1963.

Holcombe, C., *The real Chinaman*, New York: Dodd and Mead, 1895.

Hu Bingxiong 胡炳熊, 'Lun Zhongguo zhongzu' 論中國種族 (About the Chinese race), *DFZZ*, 4, no. 8 (Aug. 1908), pp. 361–85.

Hu Buchan 胡步蟾, *Youshengxue yu renlei yichuanxue* 優生學與人類遺傳學 (Eugenics and human genetics), Shanghai: Zhengzhong shuju, 1959 (1st edn 1936).

Hu Huanyong 胡煥庸, *Shijie dili* 世界地理 (World geography), Shanghai: Zhengzhong shuju, 6th edn 1947 (1st edn 1942).

Hu Jia 胡嘉, 'Hekeer duiyu jinhualun zhi gongxian' 赫克爾對於進化論之貢獻 (Haeckel's contribution to the theory of evolution), *Minduo*, 3, no. 4 (April 1922).

——, 'Hekeer zhi zhushu yu Hekeer yanjiu zhi cankaoshu' 赫克爾之著書與赫克爾研究之參考書 (The work of Haeckel and reference material on Haeckel), *Xuedeng*, 10 Aug. 1922.

——, 'Hekeerzhuyi yu Zhongguo' 赫克爾主義與中國 (Haeckelism and China), *Xuedeng*, 9–10 Aug. 1922.

Hu Zongyuan 胡宗瑗, 'Genben gaizao renzhong zhi wenti' 根本改造人種的問題 (The problem of fundamentally reforming the race), *FNZZ*, 5, no. 3 (March 1919), pp. 1–5.

Hua Rucheng 華汝成, *Youshengxue ABC* 優生學 ABC (ABC of eugenics), Shanghai: Shijie shuju, 1929.

'Huanghuo yuce' 黃禍預測 (Forecast of the yellow peril), *Jiangsu*, 1 (April 1903), pp. 103–7.

Huang Shaoxu 黃紹緒 *et al.* (eds), *Riyong baike quanshu* 日用百科全書 (Daily encyclopedia), Shanghai: Shangwu yinshuguan, 1934.

Huang Wenshan 黃文山, 'Fuxing Zhonghua minzu de jiben yuanze' 復興中華民族的基本原則 (Fundamental principles for reviving the Chinese nation), *Minzu zhi shang lun* 民族之上論 (About the nation going up), Hankou: Duli chubanshe, 1938.

——, 'Zhongzuzhuyi lun' 種族主義論 (About racism), in *Huang Wenshan xueshu luncong* 黃文山學術論叢 (Collected studies on society), Taipei: Zhonghua shuju, 1959, pp. 225–54.

Huang Zhenxia 黃震遐, 'Huangren zhi xue' 黃人之血 (Blood of the yellow race), *Qianfeng yuekan* (Vanguard monthly), 1, no. 7 (July 1931), pp. 1–166.

Huang Zunxian 黃遵憲, *Renjinglu shicao qianzhu* 人境廬詩草淺注 (Collection of annotated poems by Huang Zunxian), Shanghai: Guji chubanshe, 1981.

Hung, F., (Hong Yuan), 'Racial superiority and inferiority complex', *The China Critic*, 9 Jan. 1930, p. 29.

Hunter, W.C., *The 'fan kwae' at Canton before the treaty days, 1825–1844*, Shanghai: Kelly and Walsh, 1911.

Huxley, T.H., and J. Huxley, *Evolution and ethics*, London: Pilot Press, 1947.

Jian Bozan 翦伯贊 *et al.* (eds), *Wuxu bianfa* 戊戌變法 (The Hundred Days), Shanghai: Shenzhou guoguang she, 1953.

Jiang Guanyun 蔣觀雲, 'Zhongguo renzhong kao' 中國人種考 (Inquiry into the Chinese race), *Xinmin congbao*, 38-9 (Oct. 1903) to 60 (Jan. 1905).

Jiang Xiangqing 蔣湘青, *Renti celiangxue* 人體測量學 (The science of body measurements), Shanghai: Qinfen shuju, 1935.

Jiang Zhiyou 蔣智由, *Zhongguo renzhong kao* 中國人種考 (Inquiry into the Chinese race), Shanghai: Huatong shuju, 1929 (1st edn 1910).

Jiang Zhongzheng 蔣中正 (Jiang Jieshi), *Xinshenghuo yundong* 新生活運動 (The New Life Movement), Shanghai: Zhengzhong shuju, 1935.

Jin He 金和, 'Shuo gui' 説鬼 (About ghosts) in *YPZZ*, pp. 44-5.

Jin Zizhi 金子直, *Minzu weisheng* 民族衛生 (Racial hygiene), Shanghai: Shangwu yinshuguan, 1930.

Kang Youwei 康有為, *Datongshu* 大同書 (One World), Beijing: Guji chubanshe, 1956.

Ke Xiangfeng 柯象峯, *Xiandai renkou wenti* 現代人口問題 (Modern population problems), Shanghai: Zhengzhong shuju, 1934.

Legge, J., *The Chinese classics*, London: Henry Frowde, 1860-72.

——, *The Li Chi*, Hong Kong University Press, 1967.

Li Chi, *The formation of the Chinese people: An anthropological inquiry*, Cambridge, Mass.: Harvard University Press, 1928.

Li Chonggao 李崇高, 'Youshengxue de youlai yu fazhan' 優生學的由來與發展 (The future and development of eugenics) in *Xing jiaoyu yu yousheng* 性教育與優生 (Sexual education and eugenics), Shanghai: Shanghai kexue jishu chubanshe, 1987, vol. 2, pp. 198-201.

Li Chunsheng 李春生, *Tianyanlun shuhou* 天演論書后 (Postscript on the theory of evolution), Fuzhou: Meihua shuju, 1907.

Li Da 李達, *Minzu wenti* 民族問題 (Problems of nationalities), Shanghai: Nanqiang shuju, 1929.

Li Gui 李圭, *Huanyou diqiu xinlu* 環遊地球新錄 (New records on my travels around the world), Beijing: Yuelu shushe, 1985.

Li Meizheng 李梅徵, *Shijie ruoxiao minzu wenti* 世界弱小民族問題 (Problems of the world's weak nations), Shanghai: Guomin gemingjun disi jituanjun dishiqi jun zhengzhi xunlianbu, 1928.

Li Xuezeng 李學曾, *Yazhou zhongzu dili* 亞洲種族地理 (Racial geography of Asia), Shanghai: Zhengzhong shuju, 1947.

Li Zhongkui 李仲揆 'Huangren hai you shengcun de yudi ma?' 黃人還有生存的餘地嗎 (Is there still a territory where the yellow race can subsist?), *XDPL*, 3, no. 60 (Jan. 1926), pp. 144–8.

Li Zongwu 李宗武, *Renwen dili ABC* 人文地理 *ABC* (ABC of human geography), Shanghai: Shijie shuju, 1929.

Liang Boqiang 梁伯強, 'Yixueshang Zhongguo minzu zhi yanjiu' 醫學上中國民族之研究 (Medical research on the Chinese race), *DFZZ*, 23, no. 13 (July 1926), pp. 87–100.

Liang Qichao 梁啓超, 'Dili yu wenming zhi guanxi' 地理與文明之關係 (The relation between geography and civilization) in *YBSWJ*, 4, 10: 106–16.

——, 'Lun Hunan ying ban zhi shi' 論湖南應辦之事 (About the affairs Hunan should handle) in *YBSWJ*, 2, 3: 40–8.

——, 'Lun Mei Fei Ying Du zhi zhanshi guanxi yu Zhongguo' 論美菲英杜之戰事關係與中國 (About the effects of international conflicts on China) in *YBSWJ*, 4, 11: 1–3.

——, 'Lun minzu jingzheng zhi dashi' 論民族競爭之大勢 (About the general trend of racial struggles) in *YBSWJ*, 4, 10: 10–35.

——, 'Lun xue Ribenwen zhi yi' 論學日本文之益 (About the advantage of learning Japanese) in *YBSWJ*, 2, 4: 80–2.

——, 'Lun Zhongguo guomin zhi pinge' 論中國國民之品格 (About China's national quality) in *YBSWJ*, 5, 14: 1–5.

——, 'Lun Zhongguo renzhong zhi jianglai' 論中國人種之將來 (About the future of the Chinese race) in *YBSWJ*, 2, 3: 48–54.

——, 'Lun Zhongguo xueshu sixiang bianqian zhi dashi' 論中國學術思想變遷之大勢 (About the general trend of the changes in Chinese scientific thought) in *YBSWJ*, 3, 7: 1–104.

——, 'Lun Zhongguo zhi jiangqiang' 論中國之將強 (About the future power of China) in *YBSWJ*, 2, 2: 11–17.

——, 'Mieguo xinfa lun' 滅國新法論 (About a new way of exterminating a country) in *YBSWJ*, 3, 6: 32–47.

——, 'Nanhai Kang xiansheng zhuan' 南海康先生傳 (Biography of Kang Youwei) in *YBSWJ*, 3, 6: 78.

——, 'Ouzhou dili dashi lun' 歐洲地理大勢論 (About the general trend of European geography) in *YBSWJ*, 4, 10: 101–6.

——, '*Qingyibao* zhi xingzhi' 清議報之性質 (The nature of the *Qingyibao*) in *YBSWJ*, 3, 6: 54.

——, 'Shengjixue xueshuo yange xiaoshi' 生計學學說沿革小史 (Short history of the evolution of the science of livelihood) in *YBSWJ*, 5, 12: 1–60.

——, 'Sibada xiaoshi' 斯巴達小史 (Short history of the Spartans) in
YBSZJ, 4, 15: 1–19.

——, 'Xixue shu mubiao (zhaize)' 西學書目標摘擇 (A choice of
books to study the West) in Jian Bozan *et al.* (eds), *Wuxu bianfa* (The
Hundred Days), Shanghai: Shenzhou guoguang she, 1953, vol. 1,
pp. 447–62.

——, 'Xiaweiyi youji' 夏威夷遊記 (Travel notes on Hawaii) in
YBSZJ, 5, 22: 185–96.

——, 'Xin dalu youji' 新大陸遊記 (Travel notes on America) in
YBSZJ, 5, 22: 1–147.

——, 'Xinminshuo' 新民說 (About renewing the people) in *YBSZJ*,
3, 4: 1–162.

——, 'Xin shixue' 新史學 (New historiography) in *YBSWJ*, 4,
9: 1–32.

——, 'Yazhou dili dashi lun' 亞洲地理大勢論 (About the general
trend in Asian geography) in *YBSWJ*, 4, 10: 69–77.

——, 'Yuenan zhi wangguo shi' 越南之亡國史 (The history of
Vietnam's national subjugation) in *YBSZJ*, 4, 19: 1–28.

——, 'Zhengzhixue dajia Bolunzhili zhi xueshuo' 政治學大家伯倫
知理之學說 (The doctrine of the great political scientist
Bluntschli) in *YBSWJ*, 5, 13: 67–89.

——, 'Zhongguoshi xulun' 中國史敘論 (About Chinese history) in
YBSWJ, 3, 6: 1–12.

——, *Yinbingshi quanji* 飲冰室全集 (Complete works of Liang
Qichao), Shanghai: Zhonghua shuju, 1941.

Lincang 霖蒼, 'Tiexuezhuyi zhi jiaoyu' 鐵血主義之教育 (Iron-
blooded education), *Zhejiangchao*, 10 (Dec. 1903), pp. 63–70.

Lin Huixiang 林惠祥, *Wenhua renleixue* 文化人類學 (Cultural
anthropology), Shanghai: Shangwu yinshuguan, 1934.

——, *Shijie renzhong zhi* 世界人種誌 (Records on the races of the
world), Shanghai: Shangwu yinshuguan, 1933 (1st edn 1932).

Lin Shu 林紓, transl., *Heinu hutian lu* 黑奴呼天錄 (Record of the
black slave who laments to heaven), Beijing: Shangwu yinshuguan,
1981.

Lin Yan 林炎, *Zhongguo minzu de youlai* 中國民族的由來 (Origins of the Chinese race), Shanghai: Yongxiang yinshuguan, 1947.

Lin Yutang, *My country and my people*, New York: John Ray, 1935.

Linzhen 林針, *Xihai jiyou cao* 西海記遊草 (Draft travel notes on the
Western seas), Beijing: Yuelu shushe, 1985.

Liu Huru 劉虎如, *Rensheng dili gaiyao* 人生地理概要 (General

principles of human geography), Shanghai: Shangwu yinshuguan, 1931.

Liu Jiyuan 劉紀元, *Tiyu weisheng* 體育衛生 (Hygiene in physical education), Changsha: Shangwu yinshuguan, 1939.

Liu Min 劉敏, *Renleixue tixi* 人類學體系 (Anthropological systems), Shanghai: Xinken shudian, 1932.

Liu Shipei 劉師培, 'Huangdi jinian shuo' 黃帝紀年説 (About a calendar based on the Yellow Emperor) in *Huangdi hun* 黃帝魂 (The soul of the Yellow Emperor), 1904, repr. Taipei: Zhonghua minguo shiliao congbian, 1968, pp. 1–4.

Liu Xiong 劉雄, *Yichuan yu yousheng* 遺傳與優生 (Heredity and eugenics), Shanghai: Shangwu yinshuguan, 1926 (1st edn 1924).

Lou Tseng-Tsiang, *Souvenirs et pensées*, Bruges: Desclée de Brouwer, 1945.

Lu Song 陸嵩, 'Jiangzhou shugan' 江州述感 (Relating impressions from Jiangzhou) in *YPZZ*, p. 143.

Lu Xinqiu 陸新球, *Jinhua yichuan yu yousheng* 進化遺傳與優生 (Evolutionary heredity and eugenics), Shanghai: Zhongguo kexue tushu yiqi gongsi, 1949.

Lu Xun, *Selected writings*, Yang Xianyi and Gladys Yang, transl., Beijing: Foreign Languages Press, 1980.

Ma Chonggan 馬崇淦, *Jiehun zhidao* 結婚指導 (Marriage guide), Shanghai: Qinfen shuju, 1931.

Ma Huan 馬歡, *Yingya shenglan jiaozhu* 瀛涯勝覽校註 (Annotated overall survey of the ocean shores), edited, with notes, by Feng Chengjun, Beijing: Zhonghua shuju, 1955.

Ma Junwu 馬君武, *Shehuixue yinlun* 社會學引論 (A guide to sociology), Shanghai: Xijiang ouhuashe, 1903.

——, transl., *Wuzhong yuanshi* 物種原始 (C.R. Darwin, *The origin of species*), Shanghai: Zhonghua shuju, 1919.

Mackenzie, R., *The nineteenth century: A history*, London: T. Nelson and Sons, 1889.

Mao Qixun 毛起鷂 and Liu Honghuan 劉鴻煥, *Women de zuguo* 我們的祖國 (Our fatherland), Shanghai: Duli chubanshe, 1945.

'Mao zhuxi jiejian Feizhou pengyou fabiao zhichi Meiguo heiren douzheng de shengming' 毛主席接見非洲朋友發表支持美國黑人鬥爭的聲明 (Chairman Mao meets our African friends and issues a statement in support of the American blacks' struggle), *Renmin ribao* (People's Daily), 9 Aug. 1963.

Milne, W.C., *Life in China*, London: G. Routledge, 1857.

'Minzu gaizao wenti' 民族改造問題 (The problem of race reform), *Zhongyang ribao*, 20 Aug. 1935.

'Minzu shengwuxue xulun' 民族生物學叙論 (Introduction to racial biology), *Yixue* (Medicine), 1, no. 1 (July 1931).

Nieuhof, J., *Het gezantschap der Neerlandtsche Oost-Indische Compagnie aan den Grooten Tartarischen Cham den tegenwoordigen Keizer van China*, Amsterdam: Jacob van Meurs, 1665.

Pan Guangdan 潘光旦, 'Ershi nianlai shijie zhi yousheng yundong' 二十年來世界之優生運動 (The eugenics movement in the world during the last twenty years), *DFZZ*, 22, no. 22 (Nov. 1925), pp. 60–83.

——, review of Donald Young (ed.), *The American negro*, 1928, in *The China Critic*, 28 Aug. 1930, p. 838.

——, *Youshengxue* 優生學 (Eugenics), Shanghai: Shangwu yinshuguan, 1933.

——, *Yousheng yu kangzhan* 優生與抗戰 (Eugenics and war of resistance), Shanghai: Shangwu yinshuguan, 1943.

——, 'Yousheng yu minjianzukang' 優生與民健族康 (Eugenics and racial health), *Beiping chenbao*, 3 March 1935.

——, *Zhongguo lingren xueyuan zhi yanjiu* 中國伶人血緣之研究 (Research on the blood relationship of Chinese actors), Shanghai: Shangwu yinshuguan, 1941 (2nd imp. 1987).

——, *Zhongguo zhi jiating wenti* 中國之家庭問題 (Problems of the Chinese family), Shanghai: Xinyue shuju, 1940 (1st edn 1928).

——, 'Zhongguo zhi yousheng wenti' 中國之優生問題 (China's eugenic problem), *DFZZ*, 21, no. 22 (Nov. 1924), pp. 15–32.

——, *Ziran taotai yu Zhonghua minzuxing* 自然淘汰與中華民族性 (Natural selection and the character of the Chinese race), Shanghai: Xinyue shudian, 1928.

—— (ed.), *Yousheng yuekan* 優生月刊 (Eugenics monthly), May 1931–Feb. 1932.

Pan Yan 潘彦, 'Huangzhong wuhai yu baizhong lun' 黃種無害於白種論 (The debate about the harmlessness of the yellow race to the white race), *Changyanbao*, 7 (Sept. 1898), pp. 21–2.

Parker, E.H., *Chinese account of the Opium War*, Wilmington: Scholarly Resources, 1972.

Price, F.W., *San min chu i: The Three Principles of the People*, Shanghai: China Committee, Institute of Pacific Relations, 1927.

Qi Sihe 齊思和, 'Zhongzu yu minzu' 種族與民族 (Race and nationality), *Yugong*, 7, nos. 1-2-3 (April 1937), pp. 25-34.

'Qiguai renzhong' 奇怪人種 (A strange race of men), *Zhejiangchao*, 9 (Nov. 1903), p. 113.

Qi Zhaoxi 祁兆熙, *You Meizhou riji* 遊美洲日記 (Diary on my travels in America), Beijing: Yuelu shushe, 1985.

Qian Mu 錢穆, *Huangdi* 黃帝 (The Yellow Emperor), Taipei: Dongda tushu youxian gongsi, 1944.

Qian Xiaoqiu 錢嘯秋, *Renzhong gailiangxue gailun* 人種改良學概論 (Introduction to the science of race improvement), Shanghai: Shenzhou guoguangshe, 1932.

'Ren fen wulei shuo' 人分五類説 (The theory of dividing mankind into five races), *Gezhi huibian*, 7, no. 2 (1892).

'Rengui bian' 人鬼辨 (Distinguishing between man and devil), *Wanguo gongbao*, 14 (8 July 1882), pp. 421-2.

Rensheng dilixue 人生地理學 (Human geography), Shanghai: Qunyi shuju, 1907.

'Renzhong' 人種 (Human races), 'Huangdi zhuan' 黃帝傳 (Biography of the Yellow Emperor), 'Pangu yilai zhongzu jingzheng de dashi' 盤古以來種族競爭的大勢 General trend of racial struggles since Pangu), *Zhongguo baihuabao* (The China vernacular), no. 1 (Dec. 1903) onwards.

'Renzhong gailiang xiansheng jiang you kexue yinghai chuxian' 人種改良先聲將有科學嬰孩出現 (First signs of race improvement: Imminent appearance of scientific babies), *Xianggang gongshang*, 18 Jan. 1935.

'Renzu' 人祖 (Ancestors of mankind), *Jiangsu*, 3 (June 1903), pp. 141-3.

Review of *Tiyuxue* 體育學 (Physical education), *Zhejiangchao*, 4 (May 1903), p. 18a.

Rodes, J., *Scènes de la vie révolutionnaire en Chine (1911-1914)*, Paris: Plon, 1917.

Ru Chunpu 茹春浦, 'Zhonghua minzu zhi you yige chulu' 中華民族只有一個出路 (There is only one way out for the Chinese race), *Qiantu*, 2, no. 3 (March 1934).

Ru Song 如松, 'Ping youshengxue yu huanjinglun de lunzheng' 評優生學與環境論的論爭 (Review of the controversy between eugenics and environment), *Ershi shiji*, 1, no. 1 (Feb. 1931), pp. 57-124.

San Wu 三無, 'Bi ren wo guan' 避姙我觀 (My point of view on contraception), *FNZZ*, 6, no. 12 (Dec. 1920), pp. 1–7.

Shangwu yinshuguan tushu mulu (1897–1949) 商務印書館圖書目錄 (Catalogue of books edited by the Commercial Press, 1897–1949), Beijing: Shangwu yinshuguan, 1981.

Shen Songnian 沈松年, 'Zhenzheng cishanjia ying zhuyi youshengxue' 眞正慈善家應注意優生學 (Real philanthropists should pay attention to eugenics), *Beiping chenbao*, 19 April 1935.

'Shijie geguo bingshi shenti zhi changduan' 世界各國兵士身體之長短 (Comparative height of soldiers from different countries of the world), *Youxue yibian*, 3 (Jan. 1903), pp. 276–7.

Shi Lu 史廬, *Yichuanxue dayi* 遺傳學大意 (Outline of heredity), Shanghai: Shenzhou guoguangshe, 1931.

Shiwubao 時務報 (Current affairs), Aug. 1896–March 1898, repr. Taipei: Zhonghua shuju, 1967.

Shulou 書樓, 'Jiaoyuhui wei mintuan zhi jichu' 教育會爲民團之基礎 (Education associations as a foundation for civil corps), *Jiangsu*, 1 (April 1903), pp. 13–19.

Song Mingzhi 宋銘之, *Taijiao* 胎教 (Prenatal education), Shanghai: Zhonghua shuju, 1914.

Song Jiazhao 宋嘉釗, *Taijiao* 胎教 (Prenatal education), Shanghai: Zhonghua shuju, 1914 (11th edn 1923).

Spencer, H., *The study of sociology*, London: Williams and Norgate, 1907.

Sun Benwen 孫本文, *Renkoulun ABC* 人口論 *ABC* (ABC of population theories), Shanghai: Shijie shuju, 1928.

——, 'Zai lun wenhua yu youshengxue' 再論文化與優生學 (Culture and eugenics again), *Shehui xuejie*, 1, no. 2 (Feb. 1927), pp. 1–8.

Sun Wen 孫文, *Sanminzhuyi* 三民主義 (The three principles), Shanghai: Shangwu yinshuguan, 1927.

Taiping yulan 太平御覽 (Song encyclopaedia), Taipei: Xinxing shuju, 1959.

Tan Sitong 覃嗣同, *Tan Sitong quanji* 覃嗣同全集 (Collected writings of Tan Sitong), Beijing: Zhonghua shuju, 1981.

Tang Caichang 唐才常, *Juedianmingzhai neiyan* 覺顚冥齋內言 (Essays on political and historical matters), Taipei: Wenhai chubanshe, 1968.

——, *Tang Caichang ji* 唐才常集 (Works of Tang Caichang), Beijing: Zhonghua shuju, 1980.

Tang Zhijun 湯志鈞 (ed.), *Zhang Taiyan zhenglun xuanji* 章太炎政

論選集 (Selected political writings of Zhang Binglin), Beijing: Zhonghua shuju, 1977.

Tao Menghe 陶孟和, 'Zhang Bolun de zhongzushuo' 張伯倫的種族説 (The race theories of Chamberlain), *XDPL*, 5, no. 114 (Feb. 1927), pp. 184–9.

——, 'Zhongzu wenti' 種族問題 (Racial problems), *XDPL*, 3, no. 61 (Feb. 1926), pp. 167–70; no. 63 (Feb. 1926), pp. 206–9.

Taosheng 韜生, 'Haishang de Meiren' 海上的美人 (The Americans on the sea), *Zhejiangchao*, 6 (Aug. 1903), pp. 1–11.

Terrien de Lacouperie, A.E.J.B., *Western origin of the early Chinese civilisation from 2300 B.C. to 200 A.D.*, London: Asher, 1894.

'Tong ding tong' 痛定痛 (Sorrow calms the sorrow), *Jiangsu*, 3 (June 1903), p. 124.

Tong Runzhi 童潤之, 'Zhongguo minzu de zhili' 中國民族的智力 (The intelligence of the Chinese race), *DFZZ*, 26, no. 3 (Feb. 1929), pp. 67–76.

Tsou Jung, *The revolutionary army: A Chinese nationalist tract of 1903*, intro. and transl. by J. Lust, Paris: Mouton and Co., 1968.

Turner, J.A., *Kwang Tung, or five years in south China*, Hong Kong: Oxford University Press, 1988 (1st edn 1894).

'Waiguo yangren tan shi sheng' 外國洋人嘆十聲 (The foreigner sighs ten times) in *YPZZ*, pp. 253–4.

Wanguo gongbao 萬國公報 (The globe magazine), vol. 14, 8 July 1882.

'Wanguo zhongzu yuanshi biao' 萬國種族原始表 (Table of the origins of the various nations' races), *Hunan tongsu yanshuobao* (Hunan journal of popular speeches), 12 (Sept. 1903).

Wang Boping 王伯平, 'Zai lun Zhongguo minzu qiyuan wenti' 再論中國民族起源問題 (Again about the question of the origins of the Chinese race), *Qiantu*, 2, no. 3 (March 1934), pp. 1–9.

Wang Chong, *Lun-heng*, transl. by A. Forke, New York: Paragon Book Gallery, 1962.

Wang Hualong 王華隆, *Xinzhu renwen dilixue* 新著人文地理學 (Newly written human geography), Shanghai: Shangwu yinshuguan, 1928 (1st edn 1925).

Wang Qishu 王其澍, *Yichuanxue gailun* 遺傳學概論 (Introduction to heredity), Shanghai: Shangwu yinshuguan, 1926.

Wang Wentai 汪文臺 and Huang Pengnian 黃彭年, *Hongmaofan Yingjili kaolüe* 紅毛番英吉利考略 (A short study of the English red-haired barbarians) in *YPZZ*, pp. 756–63.

Wang Xiangze 王亨澤, 'Shengwu yizu lun' 生物一祖論 (About one origin for all species), *Xinyijie*, 3 (Dec. 1906), pp. 103–9.

Wang Zhi 王芝, *Haike ritan* 海客日譚 (Notebooks of a journey to England), Taipei: Wenhai chubanshe, 1969.

Wang Zhongyang 汪仲洋, 'Gengzi liuyue wenzhou shanjing' 庚子六月聞舟山警 (Alarm at hearing the foreign ships beyond the mountains in the sixth month of 1840) in *YPZZ*, p. 191.

Wei Juxian 衛聚賢, 'Zhongguo minzu qiantu zhi shi de kaocha' 中國民族前途之史的考察 (Study on the future of the Chinese race), *Qiantu*, 1, no. 10 (Oct. 1933), pp. 1–18.

Wen Yiduo 聞一多, *Wen Yiduo quanji* 聞一多全集 (Complete works of Wen Yiduo), Hong Kong: Yuandong tushu gongsi, 1968.

——, 'Wo shi Zhongguoren' 我是中國人 (I am Chinese), *XDPL*, 2, no. 33 (July 1925), pp. 136–7.

Wheaton, H., *Elements of international law*, London: Stevens, 1889.

Wieger, L., *Moralisme officiel des écoles, en 1920*, Imprimerie de Hienhien, 1921.

Wu Dingliang, 'On metopism of Chinese skulls and its relation to the size of cranial measurements', *Renleixue jikan* (Collected papers on anthropology), Zhongyang yanjiuyuan lishi yuyan yanjiusuo, 1941, vol. 2, pp. 83–9.

'Wuhu youtai' 嗚呼猶太 (Alas the Jew), *Zhejiangchao*, 7 (Aug. 1903), p. 165.

Wu Jianchang 吳建常, *Shehuixue tigang* 社會學提綱 (An outline of sociology), Shanghai, 1903.

Wu Jinding 吳金鼎, *Shandongren tizhi zhi yanjiu* 山東人體質之研究 (Research on the physical constitution of the Shandong people), Beijing: Guoli zhongyang yanjiuyuan lishi yuyan yanjiusuo, 1931.

Wu Jingheng 吳敬恆 (Wu Zhihui 吳稚暉), *Tianyanxue tujie* 天演學圖解 (Illustrated explanation of evolutionism), Shanghai: Wenming shuju, 1911.

Wu Tingfang, *America through the spectacles of an Oriental diplomat*, New York: Stokes, 1914.

Wu Zelin 吳澤霖, *Xiandai zhongzu* 現代種族 (Contemporary races), Shanghai: Xinyue shudian, 1932.

Wu Zelin and Ye Shaochun 葉紹純, *Shijie renkou wenti* 世界人口問題 (Problems of the world population), Shanghai: Shangwu yinshuguan, 1938.

Wu Zhenzi 吳振茲, 'Women wei shenme yao yanjiu youshengxue'

我們爲什麼要研究優生學 (Why we should study eugenics), *Xuesheng zazhi*, 15, no. 9 (Sept. 1928), pp. 31-6.

Wu Zhihui 吳稚暉, 'Renlei yuanshi shuo' 人類原始説 (About the origins of mankind) in *Wu Zhihui xiansheng quanji* 吳稚暉先生全集 (Collected works of Wu Zhihui), vol. 1, pp. 145-55, Taipei: Zhongyang wenwu gongying she, 1969; first published in *Xinshiji*, 39 (1907).

Xixue gezhi daquan 西學格致大全 (Compendium of Western science), Hong Kong: Xianggang shuju, 1897.

Xia Yuzhong 夏宇衆, 'Shuzhongxue yu jiaoyu' 淑種學與教育 (Eugenics and education), *Xinjiaoyu*, 2, no. 4 (Dec. 1919), pp. 395-8.

Xiangbao leicuan 湘報類纂 (Classified compilation of articles from the *Xiangbao*), Feb. 1898-April 1898, Taipei: Datong shuju, 1968.

Xiangxue xinbao 湘學新報 (The Hunan news), 1897-8, repr. Taipei: Zhonghua shuju, 1966.

'Xing yixue tong' 興醫學通 (On promoting medicine), *Hubei xueshengjie*, 2 (Feb. 1903), pp. 61-72.

Xu Jiyu 徐繼畬, *Yinghuan zhilüe* 瀛環志略 (A brief survey of the maritime circuit), Osaka: Kanbun, 1861.

Xu Shidong 徐時棟, *Toutouji* 偷頭記 (Notes on stealing a head) in *YPZZ*, pp. 835-7.

Xu Shilian 許仕廉, *Renkoulun gangyao* 人口論綱要 (Essentials of population theory), Shanghai: Zhonghua shuju, 1934.

Xue Deyu 薛德煜, *Renti shengli weishengxue tiyao* 人體生理衛生學提要 (Précis of human physiological health science), Shanghai: Shangwu yinshuguan, 1921.

Xue Fucheng 薛富成, *Chushi siguo riji* 出使四國日記 (Diary in four countries), Changsha: Hunan renmin chubanshe, 1981.

——, *Chushi Ying, Fa, Yi, Bi siguo riji* 出使英法意比四國日記 (Diary in four countries), Taipei: Wenhai chubanshe, 1966-7.

Yalu 亞盧, 'Zheng Chenggong zhuan' 鄭成功傳 (A biography of Zheng Chenggong), *Jiangsu*, 4 (July 1903), pp. 61-71.

Yan Duhe 顏獨鶴, 'Youshenglü' 優生律 (Eugenic laws), *Xinwenbao*, 12 May 1935.

Yan Fu 顏復, *Qunxue siyan* 羣學肆言 (H. Spencer, *The study of sociology*), Beijing: Shangwu yinshuguan, 1981.

——, *Tianyanlun* 天演論 (T.H. Huxley and J. Huxley, *Evolution and ethics*), Beijing: Shangwu yinshuguan, 1981.

——, *Yan Fu shiwen xuan* 顏復詩文選 (Selected poems and writings of Yan Fu), Beijing: Renmin wenxue chubanshe, 1959.

Yan Yi 顏一, *Jinhua yaolun* 進化要論 (Essentials of evolution), Tokyo: Kaiming shudian, 1903.

Ye Dehui 葉德輝 (ed.), *Yijiao congbian* 異教叢編 (Documents of the campaign against the 1898 reform movement), Taipei: Wenhai chubanshe, 1970.

Ye Weidan 葉爲耽, *Zhendanren yu Zhoukoudian wenhua* 震旦人與周口店文化 (The Zhendan man and the culture of Zhoukoudian), Shanghai: Shangwu yinshuguan, 1936.

Ye Xuesheng 葉血生, 'Zhongguo kaifang lun' 中國開放論 (About the opening of China), *Zhejiangchao*, 6 (Aug. 1903), pp. 1–12.

Yen, W.W., *East-West kaleidoscope 1877–1946: An autobiography*, New York: St John's University, 1974.

'Yichuan yu yousheng' 遺傳與優生 (Heredity and eugenics), *Shishi xinbao*, 11 Jan. 1935.

Yi Jiayue 易家鉞, *Jiating wenti* 家庭問題 (Problems of the family), Shanghai: Shangwu yinshuguan, 1920.

Yi Nai 易鼐, 'Zhongguo yi yi ruo wei qiang shuo' 中國宜以弱爲强説 (China should take its weakness for strength), *Xiangbao leicuan*, vol. 1, pp. 18–24.

'Yindu miewang zhi yuanyin' 印度滅亡之原因 (The reasons for the extinction of India), *Zhejiangchao*, 1 (Feb. 1903), pp. 1–9.

'Yindu zhi huaqiao' 印度之華僑 (India's overseas Chinese), *Qiantu*, 2, no. 11 (Nov. 1934), pp. 2–3.

Yin Guangren 印光任 and Zhang Rulin 張汝霖, *Aomen jilüe* 澳門紀略 (Notes on Macao), 1751 edn.

You Jiade 游嘉德, *Renlei qiyuan* 人類起源 (Origins of mankind), Shanghai: Shijie shuju, 1929.

Yu Jingrang 于景讓, *Renzhong gailiang* 人種改良 (Improvement of the race), Shanghai: Zhengzhong shuju, 1947 (1st edn 1936).

Yuyi 余一, 'Minzuzhuyi lun' 民族主義論 (On nationalism), *Zhejiangchao*, 1 (Feb. 1903), pp. 1–6.

Yuan Shunda 袁舜達, 'Renlei shehui fan taotai zhi xianxiang ji qi jiujifa' 人類社會反淘汰之現象及其救濟法 (The phenomenon of reversed selection in human society and the method of relieving it), *DFZZ*, 18, no. 24 (Dec. 1921), pp. 34–43.

Yuanyun 願雲, 'Sike zhenglun' 四客政論 (Four political views), *Zhejiangchao*, 7 (Sept. 1903), pp. 41–50.

Zhang Binglin 章炳麟, 'Lun xuehui you yi yu huangren ji yi baohu' 論學會有益於黃人及宜保護 (About the benefit of study societies for the yellows and that they should urgently be protected), *Shiwubao*, 19 (March 1897).

——, 'Menggu shengshuai lun' 蒙古盛衰論 (About the rise and fall of the Mongols), *Changyanbao*, 9 (Sept. 1898).

——, *Qiushu* 訄書 (Book of raillery), Shanghai: Gudian wenxue chubanshe, 1958.

Zhang Deyi, 張德彝, *Hanghai shuqi* 航海述奇 (Travels abroad), Beijing: Yuelu shushe, 1985.

——, *Ou Mei huanyouji* 歐美環遊記 (Notes on travelling around Europe and America), Beijing: Yuclu shushe, 1985.

——, *Suishi Faguo ji* 隨使法國記 (Notes on following the mission to France), Beijing: Yuelu shushe, 1985.

——, *Suishi Ying E ji* 隨使英俄記 (Notes on following the mission to England and Russia), Beijing: Yuelu shushe, 1985.

Zhang Jixiu 張寄岫, *Funü zhuance* 婦女專冊 (Special handbook for women), Shanghai: Shangwu yinshuguan, 1937.

Zhang Junjun 張君俊, *Minzu suzhi zhi gaizao* 民族素質之改造 (The reform of the race's quality), Shanghai: Shangwu yinshuguan, 1943.

——, *Zhongguo minzu zhi gaizao* 中國民族之改造 (The reform of the Chinese race), Shanghai: Zhonghua shuju, 1937 (1st edn 1935).

——, *Zhongguo minzu zhi gaizao, xubian* 中國民族之改造續編 (Sequel to the reform of the Chinese race), Shanghai: Zhonghua shuju, 1936.

Zhang Junli 張君勱, *Minzu fuxing zhi xueshu jichu* 民族復興之學術基礎 (The scientific foundation for national revival), Beijing: Zaishengshe, 1935.

Zhang Liyuan 張栗原, *Renleixue dayi* 人類學大意 (Main points of anthropology), Shanghai: Shenzhou guoguangshe, 1931.

Zhang Nan 張楠 and Wang Renzhi 王忍之 (eds), *Xinhai geming qian shinian jian shilun xuanji* 辛亥革命前十年間史論選集 (Selected material on debates of the ten years preceding the 1911 Revolution), Beijing: Sanlian shudian, 1963.

Zhang Qiyun 張其昀, 'Huangdi zisun' 黃帝子孫 (Sons of the Yellow Emperor, speech held during the National Festival of Grave Sweeping, 5 April 1941) in *Minzu sixiang* 民族思想 (Nationalist thought), Taipei: Zhengzhong shuju, 1951, pp. 1–7.

Zhang Weizong 張慰宗, *Jinhualun ABC* 進化論 ABC (ABC of evolution), Shanghai: Shijie shuju, 1928.

Zhang Xichen 章錫琛, 'Baihuo shi' 白禍史 (History of the white peril), *DFZZ*, 10, no. 3 (Sept. 1913), pp. 13–23.

Zhang Xie 張燮, *Dong Xi yang kao* 東西洋考 (Geography of southeast Asia), Beijing: Zhonghua shuju, 1981.

Zhang Xinglang 張星烺, 'Tangshi Feizhou heinu shuru Zhongguo kao' 唐時非洲黑奴輸入中國考 (The importation of black African slaves into China during the Tang), *Furen xuezhi*, 1, 1928, pp. 101–19.

——, 'Zhongguo renzhong Yindu-Riermanzhong fenzi' 中國人種印度日爾曼種分子 (Indo-Germanic elements in the Chinese race), *Furen xuezhi*, 1, 1928, pp. 179–94.

Zhang Yuanruo 章淵若, *Zhongguo minzu zhi gaizao yu zijiu* 中國民族之改造與自救 (Reform and salvation of the Chinese race), Shanghai: Shangwu yinshuguan, 1934.

Zhang Zhaotong 張肇桐, review of *Weilai shijie lun* 未來世界論 (About the future world), *Jiangsu*, 3 (June 1903), p. 20a.

Zhang Zhidong 張之洞, *Zhang Wenxiang gong quanji* 張文襄公全集 (The complete papers of Zhang Zhidong), Beijing, 1937.

Zhang Ziping 張資平, *Hekeer* 赫克爾 (Haeckel), Shanghai: Kaiming shudian, 1934.

——, *Renlei jinhualun* 人類進化論 (The theory of human evolution), Shanghai: Shangwu yinshuguan, 1930.

——, *Renwen dilixue* 人文地理學 (Human geography), Shanghai: Shangwu yinshuguan, 1926 (1st edn 1924).

Zhang Zuoren 張作人, *Renlei tianyan shi* 人類天演史 (History of human evolution), Shanghai: Shangwu yinshuguan, 1930.

Zhang Zuoren and Zhu Xi 朱洸, *Dongwuxue* 動物學 (Zoology), Shanghai: Shangwu yinshuguan, 1947.

Zhao Rugua 趙汝适, *Zhufanzhi* 諸蕃誌 (Records on the various barbarians), Beijing: Zhonghua shuju, 1956.

Zheng Chang 鄭昶, *Shijie ruoxiao minzu wenti* 世界弱小民族問題 (Problems of the feeble and weak races of the world), Shanghai: Zhonghua shuju, 1936.

Zhigang 志剛, *Chushi Taixiji* 初使泰西記 (Notes on the first mission to the West), Beijing: Yuelu shushe, 1985.

Zhong Guang 重光, 'Renzhongshi' 人種史 (History of human races), *Juemin* (Awake the people), 8 (July 1904).

'Zhongguo yanyu zhong de yousheng jianjie' 中國諺語中的優生見解 (Eugenic views in Chinese proverbs), *Beiping chenbao*, 7 April 1935.

Zhonghua yixue zazhi 中華醫學雜誌 (China medical journal), 20–2 (1934–6).

Zhongkan 重堪, 'Zizhipian' 自治篇 (On self-government), *Zhejiang-chao*, 6 (Aug. 1903), pp. 1–10.

Zhou Jianren 周建人, *Lun youshengxue yu zhongzu qishi* 論優生學與種族歧視 (About eugenics and racial discrimination), Beijing: Sanlian shudian, 1950.

——, 'Renzhong qiyuan shuo' 人種起源説 (Legends about the origins of human races), *DFZZ*, 16, no. 11 (June 1919), pp. 93–100.

——, 'Shanzhongxue de lilun yu shishi' 善種學的理論與實施 (The theory of eugenics and its implementation), *DFZZ*, 18, no. 2 (Jan. 1921), pp. 56–64.

——, 'Shanzhongxue yu qi jianlizhe' 善種學與其建立者 (Eugenics and its founders), *DFZZ*, 17, no. 18 (Sept. 1920), pp. 69–75.

Zhou Qichang 周其昌, *Renlei de qiyuan he fenbu* 人類的起源和分佈 (Origins and distribution of mankind), Shanghai: Dadong shuju, 1927.

Zhou Qinghua 周青樺, *Taiwan Kejia suwenxue* 臺灣客家俗文學 (Folk literature of the Hakka in Taiwan), Taipei: Dongfang wenhua shuju, 1971.

Zhu Weiji 朱維基, *Shengwu de jinhua* 生物的進化 (Evolution of organisms), Shanghai: Yongxiang yinshuguan, 1948 (1st edn 1945).

Zhu Xi 朱洗, *Women de zuxian* 我們的祖先 (Our ancestors), Shanghai: Wenhua shenghuo chubanshe, 1940.

Zhu Yu 朱彧, *Pingzhou ketan* 萍洲可談 (Anecdotes and stories), Changsha: Shangwu yinshuguan, 1935–6.

SECONDARY SOURCES

A Ying 阿英, *Zhongguo lianhuan tuhua shihua* 中國連環圖畫史話 (History of the picture-story book), Beijing: Renmin meishu chubanshe, 1984.

Allport, G.W., *The nature of prejudice*, Reading, Mass.: Addison Wesley, 1989.

Andreski, S., *Herbert Spencer: Structure, function and evolution*, London: Nelson, 1971.

Ariès, P., *Essais sur l'histoire de la mort en Occident*, Paris: Seuil, 1975.

Arkush, R.D., *Fei Xiaotong and sociology in revolutionary China*, Cambridge, Mass.: Harvard University Press, 1981.

Bakhtin, M., *Rabelais and his world*, Cambridge, Mass.: Harvard University Press, 1968.

Banton, M., *Racial consciousness*, New York: Longman, 1988.

——, *Racial theories*, Cambridge University Press, 1987.

——, *The idea of race*, Boulder: Westview Press, 1978.

Barrett, T.H., 'History writing and spirit writing in seventeenth-century China', *Modern Asian Studies*, 23, no. 3 (1989), pp. 597–622.

Barth, F. (ed.), *Ethnic groups and boundaries: The social organization of cultural difference*, Bergen: Universitctsförlaget, 1969.

Bastid, M., 'Currents of social change' in D. Twitchett and J.K. Fairbank (eds), *The Cambridge history of China*, Cambridge University Press, 1980, vol. 11, part 2, pp. 535–602.

Berger, P.L., and T. Luckmann, *The social construction of reality: A treatise in the sociology of knowledge*, New York: Doubleday, 1966.

Bergère, M.-C., *The golden age of the Chinese bourgeoisie, 1911–1937*, Cambridge University Press, 1989.

Bernal, M., 'Liu Shih-p'ei and National Essence' in C. Furth (ed.), *The limits of change: Essays on conservative alternatives in Republican China*, Cambridge, Mass.: Harvard University Press, 1976, pp. 90–112.

Blackburn, J., *The white men: The first response of aboriginal peoples to the white man*, London: Orbis, 1979.

Bo Yang 柏楊, *Choulou de Zhongguoren* 醜陋的中國人 (The ugly Chinese), Taipei: Linbai chubanshe, 1985.

Bodde, D., 'Types of Chinese categorical thinking' in *Essays on Chinese civilization*, Princeton University Press, 1981, pp. 141–60.

Bond, M., *The psychology of the Chinese people*, Hong Kong: Oxford University Press, 1984.

Boorman, H.L. (ed.), *Biographical dictionary of Republican China*, New York: Columbia University Press, 1971.

Bornstein, M.H., 'The influence of visual perception on culture', *American Anthropologist*, 77, no. 4 (Dec. 1975), pp. 774–98.

Bowler, P.J., *Evolution: The history of an idea*, Berkeley: University of California Press, 1984.

——, *The non-Darwinian revolution: Reinterpreting a historical myth*, Baltimore: Johns Hopkins University Press, 1988.

Boxer, C.R., 'Macao as a religious and commercial entrepot in the 16th and 17th centuries', *Acta Asiatica*, 26 (1974), pp. 64–90.

——, *Portuguese society in the tropics: The municipal councils of Goa, Macao, Bahia and Luanda, 1510–1800*, Madison: University of Wisconsin Press, 1965.

Brahm, H., 'Pekings Spiel mit der Rassenfrage', *Osteuropa*, 15 (Nov.–Dec. 1965), pp. 813–22.

Bray, F., 'Essence et utilité. La classification des plantes cultivées en Chine', *Extrême-Orient – Extrême-Occident*, 10 (1988), pp. 13–27.

Britton, R.S., *The Chinese periodical press, 1800–1912*, Shanghai: Kelly and Walsh, 1933.

Burov, V.G., *Mirovozzrenie Kitaiskogo myslitelya XVII veka Van Chuan'-shanya*, Moscow: Izdatel'stvo Nauka, 1976.

Cassinelli, C.W., *Total revolution: A comparative study of Germany under Hitler, the Soviet Union under Stalin and China under Mao*, Santa Barbara: Clio Books, 1976.

Chan Hok-lam, *Legitimation in imperial China: Discussions under the Jurchen-Chin dynasty, 1115–1234*, Seattle: University of Washington Press, 1984.

Chang Hao, *Liang Ch'i-ch'ao and intellectual transition in China, 1890–1907*, Cambridge, Mass.: Harvard University Press, 1971.

——, *Chinese intellectuals in crisis: Search for order and meaning 1890–1911*, Berkeley: University of California Press, 1987.

Chen Chang-fang, 'Barbarian paradise: Chinese views of the United States, 1784–1911', unpubl. doctoral thesis, Bloomington: Indiana University, 1985.

Chen Chi-Yun, 'Liang Ch'i-ch'ao's missionary education: A case study of missionary influence on the reform', *Papers on China*, 16 (1962), pp. 66–125.

Ch'en, J., *China and the West: Society and culture, 1815–1937*, London: Hutchinson, 1979.

——, 'Yiguo, "yihua": liangci dazhan jian Yingyu guojia Zhongguo liuxuesheng taidu he xingwei de bianqian' 異國異化 :兩次大戰間英語國家中國留學生態度和行爲的變遷 (Estrangement in strange lands: Attitudinal and behavioural changes of Chinese students in English-speaking countries between the two world wars), ms. presented at the Institute of Modern History, Beijing, Summer 1990.

Ch'en, K., 'Anti-Buddhist propaganda during the Nan-Ch'ao', *Harvard Journal of Asiatic Studies*, 15 (1952), pp. 166–92.

——, *Buddhism in China: An historical survey*, Princeton University Press, 1964.

Chih, A., *L'Occident 'Chrétien' vu par les Chinois vers la fin du XIXᵉ siècle, 1870–1900*, Paris: Presses Universitaires de France, 1962.

Chu, S.C., 'China's attitudes toward Japan at the time of the Sino-Japanese War' in A. Iriye (ed.), *The Chinese and the Japanese: Essays in political and cultural interactions*, Princeton University Press, 1980, pp. 74–95.

Ch'u T'ung-tsu, *Law and society in traditional China*, Paris: Mouton, 1965.

Clark, L.L., *Social Darwinism in France*, Tuscaloosa: University of Alabama Press, 1984.

Coates, A., *A Macao narrative*, Hong Kong: Heinemann, 1978.

Cohen, P.A., *China and Christianity: The missionary movement and the growth of Chinese antiforeignism, 1860–1870*, Cambridge, Mass.: Harvard University Press, 1963.

——, 'Christian missions and their impact to 1900' in D. Twitchett and J.K. Fairbank (eds), *The Cambridge history of China*, Cambridge University Press, 1978, vol. 10, part 1, pp. 543–90.

——, *Discovering history in China: American historical writing on the recent Chinese past*, New York: Columbia University Press, 1984.

Cohen, W.B., *The French encounter with Africans: White response to blacks, 1530–1880*, Bloomington: Indiana University Press, 1980.

Cole, J.H., 'Social discrimination in traditional China: The To-min of Shaohsing', *Journal of the Economic and Social History of the Orient*, 25, part 1 (1982), pp. 100–11.

Crossley, P.K., 'The Qianlong retrospect on the Chinese-martial (*hanjun*) banners', *Late Imperial China*, 10, no. 1 (June 1989), pp. 63–107.

——, 'Thinking about ethnicity in early modern China', *Late Imperial China*, 11, no. 1 (June 1990), pp. 1–35.

——, *Orphan warriors: Three Manchu generations and the end of the Qing world*, Princeton University Press, 1990.

——, 'The rhetoric of difference: Emergence of racial discourse in Qing China', paper presented at The Johns Hopkins University, Baltimore, 25 Feb. 1991.

——, 'Ming ethnology' (forthcoming).

Curtin, P.D., *The image of Africa: British ideas and action, 1780–1850*, Madison: University of Wisconsin Press, 1964.

Dardess, J.W., *Confucianism and autocracy: Professional elites in the foundation of the Ming dynasty*, Berkeley: University of California Press, 1983.

Davis, N.Z., *Society and culture in early modern France*, Stanford University Press, 1987.

Devisse, J., and S. Labib, 'Africa in inter-continental relations' in D.T. Niane (ed.), *Unesco general history of Africa*, Berkeley: University of California Press, 1984, vol. 4, pp. 635–72.

Dikötter, F., 'La représentation du Japon et des Japonais dans la caricature chinoise (1923–1937)', unpubl. MA thesis, University of Geneva, 1985.

——, 'Eugenics in Republican China', *Republican China*, 15, no. 1 (Nov. 1989), pp. 1–18.

——, 'Group definition and the idea of "race" in modern China (1793–1949)', *Ethnic and Racial Studies*, 13, no. 3 (July 1990), pp. 421–32.

——, review of Wong Young-tsu, *Search for modern nationalism*, *Bulletin of the School of Oriental and African Studies*, 53, part 3 (Oct. 1990), pp. 559–60.

——, 'The yolk and the ticks', *Republican China*, 17, no. 1 (Nov. 1991).

——, 'The limits of benevolence: Wang Shiduo (1802–1889) and population control', *Bulletin of the School of Oriental and African Studies*, 55, part 1 (Feb. 1992).

——, 'The discourse of race and the medicalization of public and private space in modern China (1895–1949)', *History of Science* (forthcoming).

——, 'The yolk and the ticks: Birth, sex and death in modern China (1895–1949)' (forthcoming).

Ding Wenjiang 丁文江, *Liang Rengong xiansheng nianpu changbian chugao* 梁任公先生年譜長編初稿 (A first draft chronological biography of Liang Qichao), Taipei: Shijie shuju, 1959.

Drake, F.W., *China charts the world: Hsu Chi-yü and his geography of 1848*, Cambridge, Mass.: Harvard University Press, 1975.

Drège, J.-P., *La Commercial Press de Shanghai, 1897–1949*, Paris: Presses Universitaires de France, 1978.

Dreyer, J.T., *China's forty millions: Minority nationalities and national integration in the People's Republic of China*, Cambridge, Mass.: Harvard University Press, 1976.

Duyvendak, J.J.L., *China's discovery of Africa*, London: Arthur Probsthain, 1949.

Eastman, L.E., 'Political reformism in China before the Sino-Japanese War', *Journal of Asian Studies*, 27, no. 4 (Aug. 1968), pp. 695–710.

Eberhard, W., *A dictionary of Chinese symbols: Hidden symbols in Chinese life and thought*, London: Routledge and Kegan Paul, 1986.

Elisseeff, D., *La femme au temps des empereurs de Chine*, Paris: Stock, 1988.

Elliott, M., 'Bannerman and townsman: Ethnic tension in nineteenth century Jiangnan', *Late Imperial China*, 11, no. 1 (June 1990), pp. 36–74.

Elman, B.A., *Classicism, politics, and kinship: The Ch'ang-chou school of*

New Text Confucianism in late imperial China, Berkeley: University of California Press, 1990.

——, *From philosophy to philology: Intellectual and social aspects of change in late imperial China*, Cambridge, Mass.: Harvard University Press, 1984.

Endicott-West, E., *Mongolian rule in China: Local administration in the Yuan dynasty*, Cambridge, Mass.: Harvard University Press, 1989.

Epstein, A.L., *Ethos and identity: Three studies in ethnicity*, London: Tavistock, 1978.

Essien-Udom, E.U., *Black nationalism: The rise of the black Muslims in the U.S.A.*, Harmondsworth: Penguin, 1966.

Fairbank, J.K. (ed.), *The Chinese world order: Traditional China's foreign relations*, Cambridge, Mass.: Harvard University Press, 1968.

Fairbank, J.K., E.O. Reischauer and A.M. Craig, *East Asia: The modern transformation*, Boston: Houghton Mifflin, 1965.

Farrar, N.E., *The Chinese in El Paso*, El Paso: Texas Western Press, 1972.

Fincher, J., 'China as a race, culture and nation: Notes on Fang Hsiao-ju's discussion of dynastic legitimacy' in D.C. Buxbaum and F.W. Mote (eds), *Transition and permanence: Chinese history and culture. A festschrift in honour of Dr Hsiao Kung-ch'üan*, Hong Kong: Cathay Press, 1972, pp. 59–69.

Fisher, T.S., 'Accommodation and loyalism: The life of Lü Liu-liang (1629–1683)', *Papers on Far Eastern History*, 15 (March 1977), pp. 97–104.

Fletcher, J., 'The heyday of the Ch'ing order in Mongolia, Sinkiang and Tibet' in D. Twitchett and J.K. Fairbank (eds), *The Cambridge history of China*, Cambridge University Press, 1978, vol. 10, part 1, pp. 375–85.

Flohr, H., 'Biological bases of social prejudices' in V. Reynolds, V. Falgar and I. Vine (eds), *The sociobiology of ethnocentrism: Evolutionary dimensions of xenophobia, discrimination, racism and nationalism*, London: Croom Helm, 1987.

Fogel, J.A., *Politics and sinology: The case of Naito Konan (1866–1934)*, Cambridge, Mass.: Harvard University Press, 1984.

——, 'Race and class in Chinese historiography', *Modern China*, 3 (July 1977), pp. 346–75.

Forke, A., *The world conception of the Chinese: Their astronomical, cosmological and physico-philosophical speculations*, London: Arthur Probsthain, 1925.

Fox, J.P., 'Japanese reactions to Nazi Germany's racial legislation', *Wiener Library Bulletin*, 23, nos. 2–3 (1969), pp. 46–50.

Franke, H., 'Sung embassies: Some general observations' in M. Rossabi (ed.), *China among equals: The Middle Kingdom and its neighbors, 10th–14th centuries*, Berkeley: University of California Press, 1983, pp. 116–48.

Freeman, R.B., 'Darwin in Chinese', *Archives of Natural History*, 13, no. 1 (1986), pp. 19–24.

Fu Lo-shu, 'Teng Mu, a forgotten Chinese philosopher', *T'oung Pao*, 52 (1965), pp. 35–96.

Furth, C., 'Blood, body and gender: Medical images of the female condition in China, 1600–1850', *Chinese Science*, 7 (Dec. 1986), pp. 43–66.

——, 'Concepts of pregnancy, childbirth, and infancy in Ch'ing dynasty China', *Journal of Asian Studies*, 46, no. 1 (Feb. 1987), pp. 7–35.

——, 'The sage as rebel: The inner world of Chang Ping-lin' in C. Furth (ed.), *The limits of change: Essays on conservative alternatives in Republican China*, Cambridge, Mass.: Harvard University Press, 1976, pp. 113–50.

——, (ed.), *The limits of change: Essays on conservative alternatives in Republican China*, Cambridge, Mass.: Harvard University Press, 1976.

Gasster, M., *Chinese intellectuals and the revolution of 1911: The birth of modern Chinese radicalism*, Seattle: University of Washington Press, 1969.

——, 'The Republican revolutionary movement' in D. Twitchett and J.K. Fairbank (eds), *The Cambridge history of China*, Cambridge University Press, 1980, vol. 11, part 2, pp. 463–534.

Gellner, E., *Nations and nationalism*, Oxford: Basil Blackwell, 1983.

Gernet, J., *China and the Christian impact: A conflict of cultures*, Cambridge University Press, 1985.

Gjessing, G., 'Chinese anthropology and New China's policy toward her minorities', *Acta Sociologica*, 2, no. 1 (1956), pp. 45–68.

Glick, T.F. (ed.), *The comparative reception of Darwinism*, Austin: University of Texas Press, 1974.

Gollwitzer, H., *Die gelbe Gefahr. Geschichte eines Schlagworts*, Göttingen: Vandenhoeck and Ruprecht, 1962.

Görög, V., *Noirs et blancs. Leur image dans la littérature orale africaine*, Paris: SELAF, 1976.

Greene, J.C., *The death of Adam: Evolution and its impact on Western thought*, Ames: Iowa State University Press, 1959.

Gregor, A.J., 'Nazional-fascismo and the revolutionary nationalism of Sun Yat-sen', *Journal of Asian Studies*, 39, no. 1 (Nov. 1979), pp. 21–37.

Grieder, J.B., *Intellectuals and the state in modern China: A narrative history*, New York: Free Press, 1981.

Guldin, G.E., 'Chinese anthropologies', *Chinese Sociology and Anthropology*, 20, no. 4 (Summer 1988), pp. 3–32.

Haas, W., review of J.R. Pusey, *China and Charles Darwin*, *Journal of the History of Biology*, 17 (1984), pp. 435–6.

Han Jinchun 韓錦春 and Li Yifu 李毅夫, 'Hanwen "minzu" yici de chuxian ji qi zaoqi shiyong qingkuang' 漢文 " 民族 " 一詞的 出現及其早期實用情況 (The first appearance of the term *minzu* in Chinese and the circumstances of its early use), *Minzu yanjiu* 民族研究, 2 (1984), pp. 36–43.

Hansson, H.A., 'Regional outcast groups in late imperial China', unpubl. doctoral thesis, Cambridge, Mass.: Harvard University, 1988.

Hao Xiang 郝翔, 'Lun Zhongguo jindai zichan jieji zhexue dui jinhualun xueshuo de gaizao' 論中國近代資產階級哲學對進化論學說的改造 (The transformation of the theory of evolution by bourgeois philosophy in modern China), *Zhongguo zhexue shi yanjiu* 中國哲學史研究, 1 (1988), pp. 79–84.

Hao Yen-p'ing, *The comprador in nineteenth century China: Bridge between East and West*, Cambridge, Mass.: Harvard University Press, 1970.

Hao Yen-p'ing and Wang Erh-min, 'Changing Chinese views of Western relations, 1840–1895' in D. Twitchett and J.K. Fairbank (eds), *The Cambridge history of China*, Cambridge University Press, 1980, vol. 11, part. 2, pp. 142–201.

Hayford, C.W., *To the people: James Yen and village China*, New York: Columbia University Press, 1990.

He Liankui 何聯奎, 'Sishi nianlai zhi Zhongguo minzuxue' 四十年 來之中國民族學 (Forty years of Chinese ethnology) in Li Ximou 李熙謀 (ed.), *Zhonghua minguo kexue zhi* 中華民國科學誌 (Records on science in the Republic of China), Taipei: Zhonghua wenhua chuban shiye weiyuanhui, 1955, pp. 1–21.

Heberer, T., *China and its national minorities*, Armonk, N.Y.: M.E. Sharpe, 1989.

——, 'Probleme der Nationalitätentheorie und des Nationsbegriffs in China', *Internationales Asienforum*, 16, nos. 1–2 (May 1985), pp. 109–24.

Henderson, J.B., *The development and decline of Chinese cosmology*, New York: Columbia University Press, 1984.

Hevia, James L., 'A multitude of lords: Qing court ritual and the Macartney embassy of 1793', *Late Imperial China*, 10, no. 2 (Dec. 1989), pp. 72–105.

Hinsch, B., *Passions of the cut sleeve: The male homosexual tradition in China*, Berkeley: University of California Press, 1990.

Hirth, F., *China and the Roman Orient: Researches into their ancient and medieval relations as represented in old Chinese records*, Hong Kong: Kelly and Walsh, 1885.

Hirth, F., and W.W. Rockhill, *Chau Ju-kua: His work on the Chinese and Arab trade in the 12th and 13th centuries, entitled Chu-fan-chi*, St. Petersburg: Printing Office of the Imperial Academy of Sciences, 1911.

Hourani, A., *Arabic thought in the liberal age, 1798–1939*, Cambridge University Press, 1983.

Hsiao Kung-chuan, *A history of Chinese political thought*, Princeton University Press, 1979.

Hsien Rin, 'The synthesizing mind in Chinese ethno-cultural adjustment' in G. de Vos and L. Romanucci-Ross, *Ethnic identity: Cultural continuities and change*, Palo Alto: Mayfield, 1975.

Hsu Kai-yu, *Wen I-to*, Boston: Twayne Publishers, 1980.

Hu Hsien Chin, *The common descent group in China and its functions*, New York: Viking Fund Publications in Anthropology, 1948.

Huang, P., *Liang Ch'i-ch'ao and modern Chinese liberalism*, Seattle: University of Washington Press, 1972.

Huard, P., 'Depuis quand avons-nous la notion d'une race jaune?', *Institut Indochinois pour l'Etude de l'Homme*, 4 (1942), pp. 40–1.

Hummel, A.W. (ed.), *Eminent Chinese of the Ch'ing period (1644–1912)*, Washington, DC: US Govt. Printing Office, 1944.

Hutchison, A., *China's African revolution*, London: Hutchinson, 1975.

Isaacs, H.R., 'Group identity and political change: The role of color and physical characteristics', *Daedalus*, Spring 1967, pp. 353–75.

Jahoda, G., *White man: A study of the attitudes of Africans to Europeans in Ghana before independence*, London: Oxford University Press, 1961.

Jansen, M.B., *Japan and its world: Two centuries of change*, Princeton University Press, 1980.

——, 'Japan and the Chinese Revolution of 1911' in D. Twitchett and J.K. Fairbank (eds), *The Cambridge history of China*, Cambridge University Press, 1980, vol. 11, part 2, pp. 339–74.

Jay, J.W., 'Memoirs and official accounts: The historiography of the Song loyalists', *Harvard Journal of Asiatic Studies*, 50, no. 2 (Dec. 1990), pp. 589–612.

Jing Junjian, 'Hierarchy in the Qing dynasty', *Social Sciences in China* (1982), 1, pp. 156–92.

Joachim, C., 'Flowers, fruit, and incense only: Elite versus popular in Taiwan's religion of the Yellow Emperor', *Modern China*, 16, no. 1 (Jan. 1990), pp. 3–38.

Kamachi Noriko, *Reform in China: Huang Tsun-hsien and the Japanese model*, Cambridge, Mass.: Harvard University Press, 1981.

Keene, D., *The Japanese discovery of Europe, 1720–1830*, rev. edn, Stanford University Press, 1969.

Kevles, D.J., *In the name of eugenics: Genetics and the use of human heredity*, New York: Alfred Knopf, 1985.

Kimble, G.H.T., *Geography in the Middle Ages*, London: Methuen, 1938.

Kirby, W.C., *Germany and Republican China*, Stanford University Press, 1984.

Kobayashi Toshihiko, 'Sun Yatsen and Asianism: A positivist approach' in J.Y. Wong (ed.), *Sun Yatsen: His international ideas and international connections, with special emphasis on their relevance today*, Sydney: Wild Peony, 1987, pp. 15–37.

Kondō Kuniyasu 近藤邦康, ' "Kindaika" to minzoku' ' 近代化' と民族 ('Modernization' and nationality), *Shisō* 思想, 454 (April 1962), pp. 10–19.

——, 'Shō Heirin ni okeru kakumei shisō no keisei' 章炳麟於ける革命思想の成形 (On the formation of Zhang Binglin's revolutionary thought), *Tōyō bunka kenkyūjo kiyō* 東洋文化研究所紀要, 28 (March 1962), pp. 207–24.

Krauss, R.C., 'Class conflict and the vocabulary of social analysis', *The China Quarterly*, 69 (March 1977), pp. 54–74.

Kreissler, F., *L'action culturelle allemande en Chine. De la fin du XIXᵉ siècle à la seconde guerre mondiale*, Paris: Editions de la Maison des Sciences de l'Homme, 1989.

Kung, S.W., *Chinese in American life: Some aspects of their history, status, problems, and contributions*, Seattle: University of Washington Press, 1962.

Kwok, D.W.Y., *Scientism in Chinese thought, 1900–1950*, New Haven: Yale University Press, 1965.

Laitinen, K., *Chinese nationalism in the late Qing dynasty: Zhang Binglin as an anti-Manchu propagandist*, London: Curzon Press, 1990.

Lamley, H.J., 'Hsieh-tou: The pathology of violence in south-eastern China', *Ch'ing-shih Wen-t'i*, 3, no. 7 (Nov. 1977), pp. 1–39.

Lanciotti, L., ' "Barbaren" in altchinesischer Sicht', *Antaios*, 6 (March 1968), pp. 570–81.

Langlois, J.D. (ed.), *China under Mongol rule*, Princeton University Press, 1981.

Lee, F.R., and J.B. Saunders, *The Manchu anatomy and its historical origin*, Taipei: Li Ming Cultural Enterprise Co., 1981.

Lee, L.O., and A.J. Nathan, 'The beginnings of mass culture: Journalism and fiction in the late Ch'ing and beyond' in D. Johnson, A.J. Nathan and E.S. Rawski (eds), *Popular culture in late imperial China*, Berkeley: University of California, 1985, pp. 360–95.

Leonard, J.K., *Wei Yuan and China's rediscovery of the maritime world*, Cambridge, Mass.: Harvard University Press, 1984.

Leslie, D., 'Early Chinese ideas on heredity', *Asiatische Studien*, 7 (1953), pp. 26–46.

Lessa, W.A., *Chinese body divination, its forms, affinities and functions*, Los Angeles: United World, 1968.

Leung, A.K., 'Autour de la naissance: La mère et l'enfant en Chine aux XVIᵉ et XVIIᵉ siècles', *Cahiers Internationaux de Sociologie*, 76 (Jan.–June 1984), pp. 51–70.

Levenson, J.R., *Liang Ch'i-ch'ao and the mind of modern China*, Cambridge, Mass.: Harvard University Press, 1953.

Lévi-Strauss, C., *Race et histoire*, Paris: Unesco, 1952.

——, *La pensée sauvage*, Paris: Plon, 1962.

——, *Mythologiques: Le cru et le cuit*, Paris: Plon, 1964.

Lewis, C.M., *Prologue to the Chinese revolution: The transformation of ideas and institutions in Hunan province, 1891–1907*, Cambridge, Mass.: Harvard University Press, 1976.

Li Ao 李敖, *Dubai xiade chuantong* 獨白下的傳統 (Tradition descended as a monologue), Taipei: Wenxing shudian, 1988.

Li Liangyu 李良玉, 'Xinhai geming shiqi de paiman sixiang' 辛亥革命時期的派滿思想 (Anti-Manchuism during the period of the 1911 Revolution), *Nanjing daxue xuebao* 南京大學學報, 2 (1989), pp. 67–77.

Lin Keh-ming, 'Traditional Chinese medical beliefs and their relevance for mental illness and psychiatry' in A. Kleinman and Liu Tsung-Yi,

Normal and abnormal behaviour in Chinese culture, Dordrecht: D. Reidel, 1981.

Lin Yaohua 林耀華, 'Guanyu "minzu" yici de shiyong he yiming de wenti' 關於 " 民族 " 一詞的實用和異名的問題 (About the problems of the synonyms and the use of the term *minzu*), *Lishi yanjiu* 歷史研究, 2 (Feb. 1963), pp. 171–90.

Lin Yutang, *A history of the press and public opinion in China*, London: Oxford University Press, 1933.

Linck, G., *Frau und Familie in China*, Munich: C.H. Beck, 1988.

Lipman, J.N., 'Ethnicity and politics in Republican China', *Modern China*, 10, no. 3 (July 1984), pp. 285–316.

Lo Jung-p'ang, 'The emergence of China as a sea power during the late Sung and early Yüan periods', *Far Eastern Quarterly*, 14, no. 4 (1955), pp. 489–503.

Lo, W.W., *The life and thought of Yeh Shih*, Hong Kong: The Chinese University Press, 1974.

Ma Kanwen 馬堪溫, 'Zuguo Qingdai jiechu de yixuejia Wang Qingren' 祖國清代傑出的醫學家王清任 (Wang Qingren, outstanding medical scientist of the Qing dynasty), *Kexueshi jikan* 科學史緝刊, 6 (1963), pp. 66–74.

MacGaffey, W., 'The West in Congolese experience' in P.D. Curtin, *Africa and the West: Intellectual responses to European culture*, Madison: University of Wisconsin Press, 1972, pp. 49–74.

McMahon, K., 'A case for Confucian sexuality: The eighteenth-century novel, *Yesou puyan*', *Late Imperial China*, 9, no. 2 (Dec. 1988), pp. 32–55.

McMorran, I., 'Wang Fu-chih and the Neo-Confucian tradition' in W.T. De Bary, *The unfolding of Neo-Confucianism*, New York: Columbia University Press, 1975, pp. 413–68.

——, 'The patriot and the partisans: Wang Fu-chih's involvement in the politics of the Yung-li court' in J.D. Spence and J.E. Wills (eds), *From Ming to Ch'ing: Conquest, region, and continuity in seventeenth-century China*, New Haven: Yale University Press, 1979, pp. 133–66.

McMullen, D., 'Views of the state in Du You and Liu Zongyuan' in S. Schram (ed.), *Foundations and limits of state power in China*, London: School of Oriental and African Studies, 1987, pp. 59–86.

Mahler, J.G., *The Westerners among the figurines of the T'ang dynasty of China*, Rome: Istituto Italiano per il Medio ed Estremo Oriente, 1959.

Martel, P. (ed.), *L'invention du Midi. Représentation du Sud pendant la période révolutionnaire*, Aix-en-Provence: Edisud, *Amiras: Repères Occitans*, nos. 15–16, 1987.

Maspero, H., *La Chine antique*, Paris: Imprimerie Nationale, 1955.

Mathieu, R., *Etude sur la mythologie et l'ethnologie de la Chine ancienne. Traduction annotée du Shanhai jing*, Paris: Institut des Hautes Etudes Chinoises, 1983.

Médeiros, F. de, 'Recherches sur l'image des noirs dans l'Occident médiéval, 13ᵉ–15ᵉ siècles', unpubl. doctoral thesis, University of Paris, 1973.

Meisner, M., *Li Ta-chao and the origins of Chinese Marxism*, New York: Atheneum, 1970.

Meissner, W., *Philosophy and politics in China: The controversy over dialectical materialism in the 1930s*, London: C. Hurst, and Stanford: Stanford University Press, 1990.

Meserve, R.I., 'The inhospitable land of the barbarian', *Journal of Asian History*, 16 (1982), pp. 51–89.

Mi Chu Wiens, 'Anti-Manchu thought during the early Ch'ing', *Papers on China*, 22A (1969), pp. 1–24.

Mills, J.V.G., *Ying-yai sheng-lan: The overall survey of the ocean shores*, Cambridge University Press, 1970.

Moseley, G., 'China's fresh approach to the national minority question', *The China Quarterly*, 24 (Dec. 1965), pp. 15–27.

Mosse, G.L., *Toward the final solution: A history of European racism*, New York: Howard Fertig, 1978.

Mote, F.W., 'Confucian eremitism in the Yüan period' in A.F. Wright (ed.), *The Confucian persuasion*, Stanford University Press, 1960, pp. 202–40.

Müller, C.C., 'Die Herausbildung der Gegensätze: Chinesen und Barbaren in der frühen Zeit' in W. Bauer (ed.), *China und die Fremden. 3000 Jahre Auseinandersetzung in Krieg und Frieden*, Munich: C.H. Beck, 1980, pp. 43–76.

Muramatsu, Y., 'Some themes in Chinese rebel ideologies' in A.F. Wright (ed.), *The Confucian persuasion*, Stanford University Press, 1960, pp. 241–68.

Murphey, R., *The outsiders: The Western experience in India and China*, Ann Arbor: University of Michigan Press, 1977.

Nagata, S., *Untersuchungen zum Konservatismus im China des späten 19. Jahrhunderts*, Wiesbaden: Otto Harrassowitz, 1978.

Netolitzky, A., *Das Ling-wai tai-ta von Chou Ch'ü-fei. Eine Landeskunde*

Südchinas aus dem 12. Jahrhundert, Wiesbaden: Franz Steiner Verlag, 1977.

Ojha, I.C., *Chinese foreign policy in an age of transition*, Boston: Beacon Press, 1969.

Onogawa Hidemi 小野川秀美, 'Zhang Binglin de paiman sixiang' 章炳麟的派滿思想 (Zhang Binglin's anti-Manchu thought), *Dalu zazhi* 大陸雜誌, 44, no. 3 (March 1972), pp. 39–60.

Paradis, J.G., *T.H. Huxley: Man's place in nature*, Lincoln: University of Nebraska Press, 1978.

Parente, W.J., 'Communism and the problem of race: From propaganda theme to polycentric factor', unpubl. doctoral thesis, Washington, DC: Georgetown University, 1970.

Paul, D.B., 'The selection of the "survival of the fittest" ', *Journal of the History of Biology*, 21, no. 3 (Fall 1988), pp. 411–24.

Peel, J.D.Y., *Herbert Spencer: The evolution of a sociologist*, London: Heinemann, 1971.

Peng Yingming 彭英明, 'Guanyu woguo minzu gainian lishi de chubu kaocha' 關於我國民族概念歷史的初步考查 (Preliminary investigation with respect to the history of the concept of nation in our country), *Minzu yanjiu* 民族研究, 1985, 2, pp. 5–11.

Pick, D., *Faces of degeneration: A European disorder, c. 1848–c. 1918*, Cambridge University Press, 1989.

Pickens, D.K., *Eugenics and the progressives*, Nashville: Vanderbilt University Press, 1968.

Poliakov, L., *Le mythe aryen. Essai sur les sources du racisme et des nationalismes*, Bruxelles: Editions Complexe, 1987.

Porkert, M., *Die chinesische Medizin*, Düsseldorf: ECON Verlag, 1982.

Pusey, J.R., *China and Charles Darwin*, Cambridge, Mass.: Harvard University Press, 1983.

Qi Sihe 齊思和 et al. (ed.), *Yapian zhanzheng* 鴉片戰爭 (The Opium War), Shanghai: Shenzhou guoguangshe, 1954.

Rankin, M.B., *Early Chinese revolutionaries: Radical intellectuals in Shanghai and Chekiang, 1902–1911*, Cambridge, Mass.: Harvard University Press, 1971.

Rawski, E.S., *Education and popular literacy in Ch'ing China*, Ann Arbor: University of Michigan Press, 1979.

Reynolds, V., V. Falgar and I. Vine (eds), *The sociobiology of ethnocentrism: Evolutionary dimensions of xenophobia, discrimination, racism and nationalism*, London: Croom Helm, 1987.

Rogers, J.A., 'Darwinism and social Darwinism', *Journal of the History of Ideas*, 33, no. 2 (1972), pp. 265–80.

Rosenblatt, P.C., 'Origins and effects of group ethnocentrism and nationalism', *The Journal of Conflict Resolution*, 8, no. 2 (1964), pp. 131–46.

Rowe, W.T., 'The public sphere in modern China', *Modern China*, 3 (July 1990), pp. 309–29.

Rui Yifu 芮逸夫, 'Minzuxue zai Zhongguo' 民族學在中國 (Anthropology in China), *Dalu zazhi* 大陸雜誌, 3, no. 7 (Oct. 1951), pp. 1–4, and 3, no. 8 (Oct. 1951), pp. 17–21.

Sakai Tadai 酒井忠夫, 'Mindai no nichiyō ruishu to shomin kyōiku' 明代の日用類書と庶民教育 (Ming popular encyclopedias and popular education) in Hayashi Tomoharu 林友春, *Kinsei Chūgoku kyōiku shi kenkyū* 近世中國教育史研究 (History of modern Chinese education), Tokyo: Kokudosha, 1958.

Santangelo, P., ' "Chinese and barbarians" in Gu Yanwu's thought' in *Collected papers of the XXXIXth Congress of Chinese Studies*, Tübingen, 1988, pp. 183–99.

Scalapino, R.A., 'Prelude to Marxism: The Chinese student movement in Japan, 1900–1910' in A. Feuerwerker *et al.* (eds), *Approaches to modern Chinese history*, Berkeley: University of California Press, 1967, pp. 190–215.

Scalapino, R.A., and G.T. Yu, *Modern China and its revolutionary process: Recurrent challenges to the traditional order, 1850–1920*, Berkeley: University of California Press, 1985.

Schafer, E.H., *The vermilion bird: T'ang images of the south*, Berkeley, University of California Press, 1967.

Schiffrin, H.Z., *Sun Yat-sen and the origins of the Chinese revolution*, Berkeley: University of California Press, 1970.

Schmidt, S.J. (ed.), *Der Diskurs des radikalen Konstruktivismus*, Frankfurt: Suhrkamp, 1990.

Schmotzer, J.S., 'The graphic portrayal of "all under heaven" (*t'ien-hsia*): A short study of Chinese world views through pictorial representations', unpubl. doctoral thesis, Washington, DC: Georgetown University, 1973.

Schneider, L.A., *Ku Chieh-kang and China's new history*, Berkeley: University of California Press, 1971.

——, 'National Essence and the new intelligentsia' in C. Furth (ed.), *The limits of change: Essays on conservative alternatives in Republican*

China, Cambridge, Mass.: Harvard University Press, 1976, pp. 57–89.

——, 'Genetics in Republican China' in J.Z. Bowers, J.W. Hess and N. Sivin (eds), *Science and medicine in twentieth century China: Research and education*, Ann Arbor: Center for Chinese Studies, 1988, pp. 3–30.

Schram, S.R., *The political thought of Mao Tse-tung*, New York: Praeger, 1969.

Schwartz, B.I., *In search of wealth and power: Yen Fu and the West*, Cambridge, Mass.: Harvard University Press, 1964.

Shapiro, S., *Jews in old China: Studies by Chinese scholars*, New York: Hippocrene Books, 1984.

Sharabi, H.B., *Arab intellectuals and the West: The formative years, 1875–1914*, Baltimore: Johns Hopkins University Press, 1970.

Sharman, L., *Sun Yat-sen: His life and its meaning*, Stanford University Press, 1968.

Shih Lun, 'The black-headed people' in Li Yu-ning (ed.), *First emperor of China: The politics of historiography*, New York: International Arts and Sciences Press, 1975, pp. 242–58.

Shih, V.Y.C., 'The ideology of the T'ai-p'ing t'ien-kuo', *Sinologica*, 3 (1953), pp. 1–15.

——, 'Some Chinese rebel ideologies', *T'oung Pao*, 44 (1956), pp. 150–226.

Shimada Kenji, *Pioneer of the Chinese revolution: Zhang Binglin and Confucianism*, Stanford University Press, 1990.

Shimao, E., 'Darwinism in Japan', *Annals of Science*, 38 (1981), pp. 93–102.

Shu Xincheng 舒新城, *Jindai Zhongguo liuxue shi* 近代中國留學史 (A history of Chinese students abroad in recent times), Shanghai: Zhonghua shuju, 1933.

Simon, W.M., 'Herbert Spencer and the social organism', *Journal of the History of Ideas*, 21, no. 2 (April–June 1960), pp. 294–9.

Sivin, N., 'Science and medicine in imperial China – the state of the field', *Journal of Asian Studies*, 47, no. 1 (Feb. 1988), pp. 41–90.

Snowden, F.M., *Before colour prejudice: The ancient view of Blacks*, Cambridge, Mass.: Harvard University Press, 1983.

Spence, J.D., *The memory palace of Matteo Ricci*, London: Faber and Faber, 1985.

Stepan, N., *The idea of race in science: Great Britain, 1800–1960*, London: Macmillan, 1982.

Sugimoto Masayoshi and D.L. Swain, *Science and culture in traditional Japan, A.D. 600–1854*, Cambridge, Mass.: MIT Press, 1978.

Sun, E.Z., 'The growth of the academic community 1912–1949' in J.K. Fairbank and A. Feuerwerker (eds), *The Cambridge history of China*, vol. 13, part 2, Cambridge University Press, 1986, pp. 361–420.

Takakusu, J., 'Le voyage de Kanshin en Orient (742–754)', *Bulletin de l'Ecole Française d'Extrême-Orient*, 28 (1928), pp. 441–72.

Tang Zhijun 湯志鈞, *Wuxu bianfa renwu zhuangao* 戊戌變法人物傳稿 (Draft biographies of leading figures of the reform movement), Beijing: Zhonghua shuju, 1982.

——, Zhang Taiyan de shehuixue' 章太炎的社會學 (Zhang Binglin's study of sociology) in Zhang Nianchi 章念馳 (ed.), *Zhang Taiyan shengping yu xueshu* 章太炎生平與學術 (The life and work of Zhang Binglin), Beijing: Sanlian shudian, 1988, pp. 532–42.

Tao Jing-shen, 'Barbarians or Northerners: Northern Sung images of the Khitans' in M. Rossabi (ed.), *China among equals: The Middle Kingdom and its neighbors, 10th–14th centuries*, Berkeley: University of California Press, 1983, pp. 66–88.

——, *Two sons of heaven: Studies in Sung-Liao relations*, Tucson: University of Arizona Press, 1988.

Teng, S.Y., and J.K. Fairbank, *China's response to the West: A documentary survey 1839–1923*, Cambridge, Mass.: Harvard University Press, 1954.

Thapar, R., 'The image of the barbarian in early India', *Comparative Studies in Society and History*, 13 (1971), pp. 408–36.

Thomas, K., *Man and the natural world: Changing attitudes in England, 1500–1800*, Harmondsworth: Penguin Books, 1984.

Thompson, L.G., *Ta t'ung shu: The one world philosophy of K'ang Yu-wei*, London: Geo. Allen and Unwin, 1958.

T'ien Ju-k'ang, 'Traditional Chinese beliefs and attitudes toward mental illness' in W.S. Tseng and D.Y.H. Wu (eds), *Chinese culture and mental health*, Orlando: Academic Press, 1983, pp. 67–81.

Tillman, H.C., 'Proto-nationalism in twelfth-century China?', *Harvard Journal of Asiatic Studies*, 39, no. 2 (Dec. 1979), pp. 403–28.

Ubukata Naokichi 幼方直言, 'Chūgoku ni okeru jinshu sabetsu no kinshi'中國に於ける人種差別の禁止(On the prohibition of racial discrimination in China), *Hikakuhō kenkyū* 比法研究, 6 (April 1953), pp. 40–6.

Verlinden, C., 'Esclavage noir en France méridionale et courants de traite en Afrique', *Annales du Midi*, 128 (1966), pp. 335–443.

Vernon, M.D., *The psychology of perception*, Harmondsworth: Penguin Books, 1971.

Vierheller, E., *Nation und Elite im Denken von Wang Fu-chih (1619–1692)*, Hamburg: Gesellschaft für Natur- und Völkerkunde Ostasiens, 1968.

Vine, I., 'Inclusive fitness and the self-system: The roles of human nature and sociocultural processes in intergroup discrimination' in V. Reynolds, V. Falgar and I. Vine (eds), *The sociobiology of ethnocentrism: Evolutionary dimensions of xenophobia, discrimination, racism and nationalism*, London: Croom Helm, 1987.

Wagatsuma, H., 'Problems of cultural identity in modern Japan' in G. de Vos and L. Romanucci-Ross (eds), *Ethnic identity: Cultural continuities and change*, Palo Alto: Mayfield, 1975, pp. 307–34.

——, 'The social perception of skin color in Japan', *Daedalus*, Spring 1967, pp. 407–43.

Wakeman, F., *Strangers at the gate: Social disorder in south China, 1839–1861*, Berkeley: University of California Press, 1966.

Waley, A., *The Opium War through Chinese eyes*, London: Geo. Allen and Unwin, 1958.

Waltham, C., *Shu ching, book of history: A modernized edition of the translation of James Legge*, London: Geo. Allen and Unwin, 1971.

Wang, E., 'The k'un-lun slave: A legend', *Asia*, 41 (1941), pp. 134–5.

Wang Ermin 王泛森, 'Shangzhan guannian yu zhongshang sixiang' 商戰觀念與重商思想 (The idea of commercial warfare and the importance attached to commerce), *Zhongyang yanjiuyuan jindaishi yanjiusuo jikan* 中央研究院近代史研究所緝刊, 5 (June 1966), pp. 1–91.

Wang Fansen 王泛森, *Zhang Taiyan de sixiang (1868–1919) ji qi dui ruxue chuantong de chongji* 章太炎的思想及其對儒學傳統的衝擊 (Zhang Binglin's thought from 1868 to 1919 and his attack on the Confucian tradition), Taipei: Shibao wenhua chuban shiye youxian gongsi, 1985.

Wang Gungwu, 'The Nanhai trade: A study of the early history of Chinese trade in the South China Sea', *Journal of the Malayan Branch of the Royal Asiatic Society*, 31, no. 182 (1958), pp. 1–135.

Wang Lei, 'The definition of "nation" and the formation of the Han nationality', *Social Sciences in China*, 4, no. 2 (June 1983), pp. 167–88.

Wang Yu 王煜, 'Zhang Taiyan jinhuaguan pingxi' 章太炎進化

觀評析 (An appraisal of Zhang Binglin's view of evolution) in Zhang Nianchi 章念馳 (ed.), *Zhang Taiyan shengping yu xueshu* 章太炎生平與學術 (The life and work of Zhang Binglin), Beijing: Sanlian shudian, 1988, pp. 232–99.

Weber, J., *Revolution und Tradition. Politik im Leben des Gelehrten Chang Ping-lin (1869–1936) bis zum Jahre 1906*, Hamburg: MOAG Mitteilungen, 1986.

Wheatley, P., 'Geographical notes on some commodities involved in Sung maritime trade', *Journal of the Malayan Branch of the Royal Asiatic Society*, 32, no. 186 (1959), pp. 5–140.

White, G., *The politics of class and class origin: The case of the Cultural Revolution*, Canberra: Australian National University, 1976.

Whitehead, P.J.P., 'Darwin in Chinese: Some additions', *Archives of Natural History*, 15, no. 1 (1988), pp. 61–2.

Wilhelm, R., 'Chinesische Frauenschönheit', *Chinesisch-Deutscher Almanach*, 1931, pp. 19–32.

Wong, Chimin K., and Wu Lien-teh, *History of Chinese medicine*, Tianjin: The Tientsin Press, 1932.

Wong Young-tsu, *Search for modern nationalism: Zhang Binglin and revolutionary China, 1869–1936*, Hong Kong: Oxford University Press, 1989.

Wright, A.F., *Buddhism in Chinese history*, Stanford University Press, 1959.

Wu Rukang, 'Antropologiia v Kitae', *Sovietskaia Antropologiia*, 3, no. 1 (1959), pp. 107–12.

Wu, R.K., and C.H. Liu, 'The history of physical anthropology in China', *Homo*, 35 (1984), pp. 127–34.

Wu Shenyuan 吳申元, *Zhongguo renkou sixiang shigao* 中國人口思想史稿 (Draft on the history of Chinese population thought), Chongqing: Zhongguo shehui kexue chubanshe, 1986.

Yang Lien-sheng, 'Historical notes on the Chinese world order' in J.K. Fairbank (ed.), *The Chinese world order: Traditional China's foreign relations*, Cambridge, Mass.: Harvard University Press, 1968, pp. 20–34.

Yen Chung-nien, 'A Chinese anatomist of the nineteenth century', *Eastern Horizon*, 15, no. 5 (1976), pp. 49–51.

Ying Zi 穎子, *Zhongguo xin xueshu renwu zhi* 中國新學術人物誌 (Bibliographies of Chinese famous modern scientists), Hong Kong: Zhiming shuju, 1956.

Young, E.P., 'Ch'en T'ien-hua (1875–1905): A Chinese nationalist',

Papers on China, 13 (1959), pp. 113–62.

Young Lung-chang, 'Regional stereotypes in China', *Chinese Studies in History*, 21, no. 45 (Summer 1988), pp. 32–57.

Yuan Fang and Quan Weitian, 'Sociologist Chen Da', *Chinese Sociology and Anthropology*, 13, no. 3 (Spring 1981), pp. 59–74.

Zhang Binglun, 'Researches in heredity and breeding' in *Ancient China's technology and science*, edited by the Institute of the History of Natural Sciences, Beijing: Foreign Languages Press, 1983, pp. 281–91.

Zhang Lu 章魯, 'Guanyu "minzu" yici de shiyong he fanyi qing-kuang' 關於 " 民族 " 一詞的實用和翻譯情況 (About the situation of the use and translation of the term *minzu*), *Minzu tuanjie* 民族團結, 7 (July 1962), pp. 34–9.

Zhang Minru 張敏如, *Zhongguo renkou sixiang jianshi* 中國人口思想簡史 (Brief history of Chinese population thought), Beijing: Zhongguo renmin daxue chubanshe, 1982.

Ziadat, A.A., *Western science in the Arab world: The impact of Darwinism*, Basingstoke: Macmillan, 1986.

Zürcher, E., *The Buddhist conquest of China: The spread and adaptation of Buddhism in early medieval China*, Leiden: E.J. Brill, 1959.

CHARACTER LIST

airenzhong 矮人種
aizhongaiguo 愛種愛國

baigui 白鬼
baihua 白話
baihuo 白禍
baizhong 白種
bang 棒
bao 報
baoguo 保國
baohuang 保皇
baojiao 保敎
Bao Shichen 包石臣
baozhong 保種
baozhongcunwen 保種存文
Beiping chenbao 北平晨報
benzi 笨子
Bi Gongchen 畢拱辰
Bixie jishi 辟邪紀實
biyanwuxu 碧眼烏鬚
biyan yinu 碧眼夷奴
Binchun 斌椿
bingzhan 兵戰
buzu 部族

Cai Yuanpei 蔡元培
cengqi 層期
Changyanbao 昌言報
Chen Changheng 陳長衡
Chen Da 陳達
Chen Darong 陳大榕
Chen Duxiu 陳獨秀
Chen Jianshan 陳兼善
Chen Lifu 陳立夫

Chen Liang 陳亮
Chen Lunjiong 陳倫炯
Chen Tianbiao 陳天表
Chen Tianhua 陳天華
Chen Xiang 陳相
Chen Yinghuang 陳映璜
chiyu 痴愚
chizi 痴子
chuanzhong 傳種
Chunqiu 春秋
chunxue 純血
chunyu 蠢愚
congshu 叢書
Cuibao 萃報

dahuang 大荒
da minzuzhuyi 大民族主義
Daqin 大秦
datong 大同
Datongshu 大同書
daizi 呆子
daoyi 島夷
Deng Mu 鄧牧
Deng Xiaoping 鄧小平
Di 狄
didu 帝都
difu 帝服
dineng 低能
diqi 地氣
dianfu 甸服
Dianshizhai huabao 點石齋畫報
dingwei 定位
Ding Wenjiang 丁文江
dōbun 同文

235

dōshu 同種
Dongfang zazhi 東方雜誌
Dong Xi yang kao 東西洋考
Du Yaquan 杜亞泉
Du You 杜佑
Duan Chengshi 段成式
duomin 墮民
duoyuan 多元

Ershi shiji 二十世紀

fagui 法鬼
fangui 番鬼
Fang Xiaoru 方孝孺
fei lishi de zhongzu 非歷史的種族
fei renlei 非人類
fei wo zulei qi xin bi yi
  非我族類其心必異
Fei Xiaotong 費孝通
fenlei xiedou 分類械鬥
Feng Guifen 馮桂芬
Funü zazhi 婦女雜誌
Furen xuezhi 輔仁學誌

Gaizao 改造
gerenzhuyi 個人主義
geyi 格義
Gezhi huibian 格致彙編
Gezhi xinbao 格致新報
gengzhan 耕戰
gong 公
gongminhua 公民化
Gongshang xuebao 工商學報
gongsuo 公所
Gong Tingzhang 宮廷璋
Gongyang 公羊
gouwei 狗尾
Gu Huan 顧歡
Gu Jiegang 顧頡剛
Gu Shoubai 顧壽白
Gu Yanwu 顧炎武

guanxi 關係
guinu 鬼奴
guizhong 貴種
guo 國
guocui 國粹
Guocui xuebao 國粹學報
guojiezhongjie 國界種界

Haidao yizhi 海島夷誌
Haiguo wenjian lu 海國聞見錄
Hailu 海錄
Hakka 客家
Han 漢
hanhua 漢化
Hanren 漢人
Han Yu 韓愈
Hao Qinming 郝欽銘
He Chengtian 何承天
Hekeer 赫克爾
Hekeerzhuyi 赫克爾主義
He Qi 何啓
hequn 合羣
He Xiu 何休
hezhong 合種
heigui 黑鬼
heinu 黑奴
heinu zhongzu 黑奴種族
heisi 黑廝
heizhong 黑種
Hirayama Shū 平山周
hongmaofan 紅毛番
hongyi 紅夷
houfu 候服
Houhanshu 後漢書
Hubei xueshengjie 湖北學生界
Hu Bingxiong 胡炳熊
Hu Buchan 胡步蟾
Hu Han 胡漢
Hu Huanyong 胡煥庸

Hunan tongsu yanshuobao
　湖南通俗演說報
huren 胡人
Hu Shi 胡適
Hu Zongyuan 胡宗瑗
huaxia zhi guo 華夏之國
huaze 化擇
huanchang 換腸
huangu 換骨
huangfu 荒服
huanghuo 黃禍
Huang Jie 黃節
huanglan 黃藍
huangse 黃色
Huangshu 黃書
Huang Wenshan 黃文山
Huang Zhenxia 黃震遐
huangzhong 黃種
huangzu 黃族
Huang Zunxian 黃遵憲
Huainanzi 淮南子
huibai 灰白
hundun 混沌
hunxue 混血
hunyin jieshaosuo 婚姻介紹所

jifu shenhei 肌膚甚黑
jile shijie 極樂世界
Jiaren qiyu 佳人奇遇
Jia Yi 賈誼
jiazuzhuyi 家族主義
jiancui 堅脆
jianmin 賤民
jianqi 間氣
jianse 間色
Jianzhen 鑑眞
jianzhong 賤種
Jiang Guanyun 蔣觀雲
Jiang Menglin 蔣夢麟
Jiangsu 江蘇

Jiang Xiangqing 蔣湘青
Jiang Zhiyou 蔣智由
jieji 階級
Jin 晉
Jin He 金和
jinhua 進化
jinhualun 進化論
jinshi 進士
Jinshu 晉書
jinzhong zhi xue 進種之學
Jin Zizhi 金子直
jing 精
jingqi 精氣
jingshi 經世
Jingshi wenchao 經世文潮
jiuxing yuhu 九姓漁戶
Juemin 覺民
juezhen 絕畛

Kang Youwei 康有爲
Kashiwabara Bantarō 柏原文太郎
kaozhengxue 考證學
Ke Xiangfeng 柯象峯
Kongzi gaizhi kao 孔子改制考
kuangdian 狂癲
kunlun 崑崙
kunlun cengqi 崑崙層期

laihua 來化
Lang 郎
lehu 樂戶
lei 類
li 鬲
Li 黎
Li Chunsheng 李春生
Li Dazhao 李大釗
Li Gui 李圭
Li Hongzhang 李鴻章
Liji 禮記
limin 黎民

Li Xuezeng 李學曾
Li Yu 李漁
Li Zhongkui 李仲揆
Li Zongwu 李宗武
Li Zubai 李祖白
lian 臉
lianhuan tuhua 連環圖畫
Liang Boqiang 梁伯强
liangmin 良民
Liang Qichao 梁啓超
Liangshu 梁書
Liang Souming 梁漱溟
liangzhong 良種
liedeng dongwu 劣等動物
liedeng zhongzu 劣等種族
Lienüzhuan 列女傳
lieshengxue 劣生學
liezhong 劣種
Lin Huixiang 林惠祥
Lin Yan 林炎
Lin Yaohua 林耀華
Lin Zexu 林則徐
Lin Zhen 林針
Lingwai daida 嶺外待答
Liu Huru 劉虎如
Liu Shipei 劉師培
Liu Xiong 劉雄
Liu Yazi 劉亞子
Lü Liuliang 呂留良
Lu Xinqiu 陸新球
Lu Xun 魯迅
Lu Zhengxiang 陸徵祥
Lu Zhiwei 陸志韋

Ma Duanlin 馬端臨
Ma Huan 馬歡
Ma Junwu 馬君武
maiban 買辦
Man 蠻
Mao Zedong 毛澤東

mihou 獼猴
Miao 苗
miezhong 滅種
miezu 滅族
Min 閩
min 民
Minbao 民報
Minduo 民鐸
Minduo zazhi 民鐸雜誌
minzu 民族
minzokushugi 民族主義
minzuzhuyi 民族主義
Mingshi 明史
Miyazaki Torazō 宮崎寅藏
mofanren 模範人

Nanren 南人
neiyi 內夷
nan gui nü jian 男貴女賤

Okamoto Kansuke 岡本監輔

Pan Gongzhan 潘公展
Pan Guangdan 潘光旦
Pei Fuheng 裴復恆
Pingzhou ketan 萍洲可談
Punti 本地

qi 氣
qishi 歧視
Qi Sihe 齊思和
Qianfeng yuekan 前鋒月刊
Qianhanshu 前漢書
Qianlong 乾隆
Qiantu 前途
Qiang 羌
Qiangxuebao 强學報
qinshou zhi guo 禽獸之國
Qing 清

qingbai 清白
qingjie 清潔
qinglei 清類
Qingloubao 青樓報
Qingyibao 清議報
Qiuwobao 求我報
qun 羣
quncequnli 羣策羣力
qunli 羣力
qunxue 羣學

Rangshu 讓書
ren 人
ren 仁
Renleixue jikan 人類學緝刊
renli 人鬲
Renmin ribao 人民日報
Renshenshuo 人身説
renyan 人言
Renxue 仁學
ren zhi rong jiehei 人之容皆黑
renzhong 人種
renzhongbu 人種部
renzhong gailiang 人種改良
renzhong gailiangsuo 人種改良所
renzhong gailiangxue 人種改良學
riyong baike quanshu
  日用百科全書
riyong leishu 日用類書
Rong 戎
Ru Chunpu 茹春浦

sanminzhuyi 三民主義
Sanpolun 三破論
Sanshouguo 三首國
semu 色目
Shanhaijing 山海經
Shang Yang 商鞅
shangzhan 商戰
shangzhi 上智

Shao Lizi 邵力子
Shehui xinli zazhi 社會心理雜誌
Shehui xuejie 社會學界
Shenbao 申報
shenjingbing 神經病
shenqi 神氣
shenqu 神區
shen ru heiqi 身如黑漆
shenshang 紳商
shenti xuruo 身體虛弱
shengfan 生番
shengfanzhong 生番種
Shengwuji 聖武記
shengyu geming 生育革命
Shijing 史經
Shishi xinbao 時事新報
Shiwubao 時務報
shiyong 實用
shizu 始祖
shou 獸
shufan 熟番
Shujing 書經
Shuoqun 説羣
Shuowen 説文
si 私
sihai 四海
siku quanshu 四庫全書
siyi 四夷
siyiguan 四夷館
Song Lian 宋濂
suifu 綏服
Suishu 隋書
Sun Benwen 孫本文
Sun Yatsen 孫逸仙

Tai Bai 太白
taijiao 胎教
taijiaoyuan 胎教院
Taiping guangji 太平廣記

Taixi renshen shuogai 泰西人身說概
Tan Sitong 覃嗣同
Tang Caichang 唐才常
Tao Menghe 陶孟和
taotairen 淘汰人
ti 體
tiyong 體用
tianming 天命
tianqi 天氣
tianran xuanze 天然選擇
tianxia 天下
Tianxia junguo libingshu 天下郡國利病書
tianze 天擇
tian zhi jiaozi 天之驕子
tong 銅
Tongdian 通典
Tong Runzhi 童潤之
tongwen tongzhong 同文同種
Tongxuebao 童學報
tongzhong 同種
Tufan 吐蕃
tuihua 退化

wai 外
waiyi 外夷
Wanguo gongbao 萬國公報
Wanguo shiji 萬國史記
Wang Dahai 王大海
Wang Fuzhi 王夫之
wangguomiezhong 亡國滅種
Wang Guan 王觀
Wang Hualong 王華隆
Wang Kaiyun 王闓運
Wang Mang 王莽
Wang Qingren 王清任
Wang Tao 王韜
Wang Yan 王衍
Wang Yunwu 王雲五

Wang Zhongyang 汪仲洋
Wei Juxian 衛聚賢
weisheng 衛生
Wei Yuan 魏源
wen 文
wenhua xuanze 文化選擇
wenti yu zhuyi 問題與主義
Wenxian tongkao 文獻通考
Wen Yiduo 聞一多
wonu 倭奴
wu 物
Wu Dingliang 吳定良
wujin 五金
wuguan 五管
Wu Tingfang 伍廷芳
wuwei 五味
wuxiang 五香
wuxing 五行
Wu Zelin 吳澤霖

xi 晰
xihua 西化
xiren 西人
Xixia 西夏
xiayu 下愚
Xia Yuzhong 夏宇眾
Xiandai pinglun 現代平論
Xiangbao leicuan 湘報類纂
Xiangxue xinbao 湘學新報
xiao heinu zhongzu 小黑奴種族
xiao minzuzhuyi 小民族主義
xiao shimin 小市民
xiedou 械鬥
xieqi 邪氣
Xie Qinggao 謝清高
Xinjiaoyu 新教育
Xinmin congbao 新民叢報
Xinminshuo 新民說
Xinshenghuo yu youshengxue 新生活與優生學

Xinshiji 新世紀
Xinwenbao 新聞報
Xinyijie 新譯界
xing 姓
xingchou 腥臭
xingfeng 腥風
Xiongnu 匈奴
Xu Jiyu 徐繼畬
Xu Shidong 徐時棟
Xu Shilian 許仕廉
xuebao 學報
Xue Deyu 薛德煜
Xuedeng 學燈
Xue Fucheng 薛富成
xuehui 學會
Xuesheng zazhi 學生雜誌
xuetong 血統
Xunzi 荀子

yacui 亞粹
Yamada Ryōsei 山田良政
Yan 炎
Yan Duhe 顏獨鶴
Yan Fu 顏復
Yan Shigu 顏師古
yang 洋
Yang Guangxian 楊光先
yanggui 洋鬼
yangguizi 洋鬼子
yaofen 妖氛
ye 野
Ye Dehui 葉德輝
Ye Lin 葉林
yeren 野人
Ye Shaochun 葉紹純
Ye Shi 葉適
Ye Xuesheng 葉血生
Yi 夷
yidi zhi guo 夷狄之國

Yi Jiayue 易家鉞
Yijing 易經
yimin 遺民
Yimuguo 一目國
Yi Nai 易鼐
yi se lie zu 以色列族
Yixialun 夷夏論
Yixue 醫學
yiyuan 一元
yizu 異族
yin 陰
Yin 殷
Yinghuan zhilüe 瀛環志略
Yingya shenglan 瀛涯勝覽
Yingzhao 英招
yong 用
Yongle 永樂
yongxiabianyi 用夏變夷
Yongzheng 雍正
You Jiade 游嘉德
you lishi de zhongzu
   有歷史的種族
youshengliebai 優勝劣敗
youshengxue 優生學
Yousheng yuekan 優生月刊
Youxibao 游戲報
You Xiong 幼雄
youxiu 優秀
Youxue yibian 游學譯編
Youyang zazu 酉陽雜俎
youyexue 優業學
youzhong 優種
yu 愚
Yugong 禹公
Yu Jingrang 于景讓
yunong 愚農
Yuqian 裕謙
Yu Zhengxie 俞正燮
yuan 鳶
Yuan Huang 袁黃

Yuan Shunda 袁舜達
Yunnan 雲南
Yung Wing 容閎

Zeng 曾
Zeng Guangquan 曾廣銓
Zeng Guofan 曾國蕃
Zhang Binglin 章炳麟
Zhang Deyi 張德彝
Zhang Junjun 張君俊
Zhang Junli 張君勵
Zhang Liyuan 張栗原
Zhang Xie 張燮
Zhang Xinglang 張星烺
Zhang Xueliang 張學良
Zhang Zhidong 張之洞
Zhang Ziping 張資平
Zhang Zuoren 張作人
Zhao Rugua 趙汝适
zhe 赭
Zhejiangchao 浙江潮
Zheng Chang 鄭昶
Zheng Chenggong 鄭成功
Zheng Guanying 鄭觀應
Zheng He 鄭和
zhengqi 正氣
Zheng Sixiao 鄭思肖
Zheng Xuan 鄭玄
Zhibao 直報
Zhigang 志剛
zhishifenzi 知識分子
zhishijieji 知識階級
zhong 種
Zhongguo 中國
Zhongguo baihuabao
  中國白話報

Zhongguo yousheng xuehui
  中國優生學會
zhonghuo 種禍
zhonglei 種類
zhongqu 中區
Zhong wei ti, Xi wei yong
  中爲體西爲用
zhongxing 種性
Zhongyang ribao 中央日報
zhongzhan 種戰
zhongzheng 種爭
zhongzu 種族
zhongzu jingzheng 種族競爭
zhongzu qishi 種族歧視
zhongzu sixiang 種族思想
zhongzu wu bie 種族無別
zhongzu zhian 種族治安
zhou 洲
Zhou Jianren 周建人
Zhou Qichang 周其昌
Zhou Qufei 周去非
Zhufanzhi 諸蕃誌
Zhu Weiji 朱維基
Zhu Xi 朱洗
zhuxia 諸夏
zhuyi 主義
Zhu Yu 朱彧
zhuzixue 諸子學
zhun heinu zhongzu 準黑奴種族
zise 紫色
zitangse 紫膛色
Zou Rong 鄒容
zu 族
zupu 族譜
Zuozhuan 左傳

INDEX